LEONARD BERNSTEIN

# Leonard Bernstein

## *An American Musician*

ALLEN SHAWN

Yale
UNIVERSITY
PRESS
New Haven and London

*Frontispiece:* Leonard Bernstein (left) and Aaron Copland, April 1981.
Photograph courtesy of Photofest.



Yale University Press books may be purchased in quantity for educational, business, or promotional use. For information, please e-mail sales.press@yale.edu (U.S. office) or sales@yaleup.co.uk (U.K. office).

Set in Janson type by Integrated Publishing Solutions.
Printed in the United States of America.

ISBN: 978-0-300-14428-4 (cloth)

Library of Congress Control Number: 2014941713

A catalogue record for this book is available from the British Library.

This paper meets the requirements of ANSI/NISO Z39.48–1992 (Permanence of Paper).

10 9 8 7 6 5 4 3 2 1

For Yoshiko

Books by Allen Shawn

*Arnold Schoenberg's Journey*
*Wish I Could Be There*
*Twin*

## CONTENTS

# *Introduction*

Shostakovich's First Symphony, written when he was nineteen, begins with a quiet, sarcastic-sounding little tune on muted trumpet, soon accompanied by a bassoon pecking out a droll counterpoint. Then two oboes join the bassoon for a short phrase in unison rhythm that peters out after seven beats. There is a pause, and a jocular clarinet breaks the silence with a brash upward run and a melody that is a mocking variant of the opening trumpet tune. Then the strings join in, and the movement is truly under way.

Leonard Bernstein is rehearsing an orchestra of young musicians at the Schleswig-Holstein Music Festival. It is summer 1988. In a month he will turn seventy. He is seated, chatting about the work. He is wearing dark glasses and a loose-fitting sky-blue shirt over a white T-shirt. Although he smiles frequently, there is a weariness in the set of his mouth and in the gravelly sound of his voice. The musicians themselves are not much older than Shostakovich was when he wrote this work, but it is Bernstein who is telling them about its wonders and paradoxes. He speaks about Shostakovich's antiauthoritarianism, about how quirky and unheroic the symphony's opening is, about its takeoffs on Wagner's *Tristan*, about how its first gestures end in sarcastic shrugs. He emphasizes that in the first and second movements the playing must be terse and witty so as not to anticipate that, in the Lento which follows, parody will give way to overflowing romantic feeling, unmasking the clipped diffidence of the opening of the work to reveal the intensity, the love of the very music it is rebelling against, behind it. He talks about an extraordinary place in the slow movement that is the most mysterious moment in the work. The sound in the strings must be as soft as humanly possible, yet also urgent. The only way to achieve this is to play with practically no bow at all, but with the fastest possible vibrato. It is as if, Bernstein seems to be saying, the music captures what Shostakovich was at that moment, what he was leaving behind, and what he would become—all in one work.

Bernstein speaks like an old scholar, immersed in a text, who suddenly looks up and starts to talk about it. Although he *is*, in fact, an old scholar, he doesn't look precisely "old." It is more as if he were young but tired, perhaps even tired of being himself. At the same time there is nothing resigned or routine in his bearing. He speaks of the score with the greatest immediacy, conveying excitement about every detail on the page.

He raises his hands to begin the symphony, and instantaneously there is discipline, a spring and economy in his gestures, an irresistible inner rhythm. The tinny trumpet tune sounds, the bassoon joins in; he brings down his arms in tiny increments, one for each beat, as the two oboes and bassoon make their unison diminuendo, then makes a brusque upbeat for the bawdy clarinet entrance. He soon stops the clarinetist, a young woman: "No, no—*forte*," he says. "Really." They start again, and again stop. "Surprise us. . . . Come." They start once more. "No, but on the right beat," he says with mild irritation, pausing. "Don't look so scared. Come on, just play the scale *forte.* One before 1." He calls out vigorously: "One, two, three! . . . Atta girl—good." But then he stops again. "It's not *forte.* Why aren't you playing *forte*?" Then he asks gently, "Why are you so frightened?" Although there is an audience watching the rehearsal and a film crew filming it, and there are a hundred musicians onstage, the moment feels private. He smiles, his hands come together. "*Forte.* Loud. Loud. Come on, and stay *forte* for four bars. Atta girl; good." Pausing again: "You see, in the last bar it comes down to *mezzo forte.* When the bassoon joins you, she has to join you *mezzo forte.* And she comes in sounding louder than you because you've already gotten to *piano.* I don't know why you are so shy. Is it just today?" (She shrugs.) "You're not a shy girl, right, by nature?" He sings out her clarinet line boisterously. "Do every note the same—*forte.*" Then in a slightly self-caricaturing tone he counts "One, two, three" and cues her. The passage sounds much better. He looks buoyant.

At the performance a week later, now dressed in his concert tuxedo and white bow tie, he is guiding the players through the score, giving signs little and big to remind them of everything they had worked on in rehearsal. In one sense the music is now in their hands. But he is controlling the journey, like a pilot steering an ocean liner, and there is enormous concentration and tension in his body. By the close of the last movement he is bathed in sweat, and he can hardly keep his eyes open for the rivulets of water streaming down his face. There is an ovation. He waits for several moments, seems to gasp for breath while a look of exhaustion passes over him, then nods to the players with satisfaction. Not yet turning to the audience, he hugs the concertmaster and first cellist. They suddenly look like boys, bashful, moved. He motions to the orchestra to rise, then finally turns and bows. On the way to the back of the stage he takes the hand of the clarinetist in passing, and she smiles. Returning toward the stage, he acknowledges the timpanist, then the first oboist, then motions for the clarinetist to rise and holds her hand up. She blushes. As he returns to the podium his face is gray with fatigue for a moment; he points with pride to the concertmaster and the first cellist, who stand. He bows; he receives flowers from a girl wearing a white dress with a red-and-green floral print on it and kisses her hand. He motions for the orchestra as a whole to rise again, bows and turns to them, throwing the flowers out one by one, and then as a bunch. For a moment Bernstein looks not seventy, but forty. He leaves the stage again and returns again, this time acknowledging the bassoonist and the pianist and reaching over one more time to congratulate the clarinetist. The pianist puts a flower in his lapel. As if suddenly seeing the moment as she will remember it years from now, the second oboist puts her head in her hands; a violinist looks down sadly, lost in thought, holding her violin and a flower together, her blond hair hanging over her face. Bernstein makes a gesture to the orchestra like a prizefighter at the end of a fight. The audience continues to applaud.

Another glimpse. This time it is from 1959, when *West Side Story* was still running on Broadway and he was in his second year as music director of the New York Philharmonic. "Everyone *thinks* they know what they mean by 'classical' music. But in fact we use that word because we can't think of a better one," he is telling the audience of ten-year-olds, who are dressed up in their best Sunday clothes and accompanied by their parents at a Young People's Concert. Bernstein is dynamic and improbably handsome, and seems like he is in his own living room. In fact he does not appear to be performing at all, but simply to be completely engrossed in his subject—the subject of what is meant by the term "classical music." He shows how inadequate the other terms besides "classical" are—"art music," "symphonic music," "highbrow music," "serious music," reserving particular scorn for the word "good": "Well, we all know that there is 'good' Beethoven, and there is 'good' Spike Jones, and they are both good in their way. So we're certainly not going to use that word 'good.'" He goes on to say that one aspect of so-called classical music is that it can't be changed—it is *exact* music—with tempo, dynamics, and phrasing carefully written down by the composer. Saying that it is fixed in all these ways that, say, the McHugh/Fields song "I Can't Give You Anything but Love" is not and isn't meant to be, he proceeds to sing the song in the style of Louis Armstrong and then Fred Waring, stirring delight in the audience and a ripple of amusement in the viola section behind him. (It is a throwback to his early teenage years, when he would entertain his father's friends by improvising in many styles.) Then he returns to his original subject that "classical" is the wrong word because "classical" properly refers to a specific period and place—eighteenth-century Europe—when the effort to create a perfection of form, modeled on that of the ancient Greeks, was paramount. He contrasts what was happening in America at the time—the struggle to create a new society in a savage land (there is an awkward reference to fighting "Indians" here)—with the bringing to perfection of an older culture happening concurrently in Europe.

Astonishingly, he then compares the construction of a fugue to building a Ferris wheel with an erector set, comparing the strands of counterpoint in the finale of Bach's Fourth Brandenburg Concerto to metal beams, and the way they sound when they are all playing together to the spinning wheel on top. When the cellos, violas, and violins have illustrated their parts and he then has them all play together, the children are leaning forward in their chairs. He moves on to the later eighteenth century with a heart-tugging melody from the slow movement of Mozart's C-Major Piano Concerto, K. 467, explaining that even though the aims of the generations immediately after Bach changed ("as different as milk is from orange juice"), the devotion to perfection of form was still a constant. He conducts the *Marriage of Figaro* overture and then, performing the last movement of Haydn's Symphony No. 102 in B-flat Major, he digresses to the subject of humor in Haydn ("in music you can only make jokes about music") and then doubles back to repeat part of the Mozart slow movement. The ineffable, indescribably tender music floats through the hall, deeply sad, yet weightless, luminous—not only nonverbal but without physical form, and gone as soon as he gives the musicians a cutoff. His voice gets quiet as he reminds the audience that the composers seeking perfection of form in this period are also full of emotion. All the great composers, regardless of idiom, "want to tell you something."

Nevertheless, he says, leaping forward to the next generation, in Beethoven the emotions are "bigger, and easier to see"; it is like "classical music under a magnifying glass." Instead of simply being "gay," it is "crazy with joy." Romanticism is about being free with your emotions, "not so proper and shy, but telling your deepest feelings right away, without even thinking about whether you should." He goes to the piano, plays part of a Chopin nocturne, then turns to conduct an intense passage from the slow movement of a Schumann symphony, his face furrowed with feeling. Some of the children in the hall are restive, but others are looking on with widened eyes, their heads propped on their hands. The Schumann is "burning, unashamed, real passion," he is saying, adding that this "Romanticism" wasn't a decision composers made, but rather a natural reflection of changes that were happening historically in the way people lived, thought, felt, and acted. And "it all started with that 'classicist' Beethoven. I guess you could say that he was a classicist who went too far. He was so full of feeling and emotion that he couldn't keep himself chained up in all of those rules and regulations of the eighteenth century, and so he just *broke* his chains and started a whole new kind of music." At the words "broke his chains," Bernstein looks out at his audience and mimes breaking the chains. "And that was the end of 'classical' music."

Professionally Leonard Bernstein was a conductor, pianist, composer, and teacher. But he was also a powerful cultural and political voice and symbol, transcending all categories. Because he had an extravagantly extroverted temperament and a burning need to create as copious and varied a record of his work as he could; and because he lived during the heyday of the recording industry, at the dawn of the television era and of video recording, and before the advent of the Internet and e-mail correspondence, he left behind him what may well be the most extensive documentation in recordings, films, and on paper of any musician in history. His archive at the Library of Congress already lists 400,000 items, upwards of 17,500 items in correspondence alone. Then there is the ever-expanding film record, including countless musical performances, the programs he made for *Omnibus*, *Ford Presents*, and *Lincoln Presents*, the fifty-three Young People's Concerts, the six Norton Lectures, and numerous assorted additional documentaries (some two hundred hours in all, not counting concerts filmed for one-time broadcast that may or may not have been subsequently taped over), as well as the recordings, the books, the articles. And then there are his musical works: the works for Broadway, the symphonies, the choral music, the two operas, the songs, the piano pieces, the early chamber works.

During the 1950s and 1960s Bernstein was not only the best known of all American classical musicians; he was almost as famous as Elvis Presley or Marilyn Monroe. The first American-born and -trained conductor to rise to prominence, he was young, gifted, and explosively vital at just the right moment in history to be recognized and eventually put at the helm of a major orchestra, and he paved the way for all the American-born conductors who followed him. He was also the first major American conductor to be recognized internationally. He had an immense following as a guest conductor, both before his assumption of the music directorship of the New York Philharmonic, where he presided for eleven years, and for the rest of his life, when his reputation only continued to rise. He conducted many thousands of concerts on every continent and in every major city in the world, over 1, 247 with the New York Philharmonic alone. He had special relationships with the Boston Symphony, the Israel Philharmonic, and, in the last two decades of his life, with the Vienna Philharmonic. He was also a superb pianist. He became a conduit to classical music to the millions who watched his Young People's Concerts and *Omnibus* programs on television, and who read his books. He composed for both the Broadway stage and the concert hall. *West Side Story* ranks among the best-known works of musical theater by an American. All this presents a dizzying record of activities in a bewildering number of fields. No single book could even touch on all the major events in such a life, let alone be comprehensive.

Like so many aspiring musicians who grew up in New York City in the 1950s, I went to Carnegie Hall and later to Lincoln Center to attend many of the early Young People's Concerts. I watched the rest of them at home, on my family's small black-and-white television screen, which was framed within a varnished wooden cabinet that had speakers on each side, little closing doors in front, and a rather rickety phonograph in a large, retractable lower drawer. When I sat at the piano making up my first musical ideas (one couldn't yet call them "compositions"), I had already encountered a great deal of music I would not otherwise have heard, had I not been a member of this "Bernstein generation." My childhood friend Hank Chapin was close to Bernstein because of his father, Schuyler, who worked at Columbia Records and later at Bernstein's Amberson Productions. On a few occasions in his family's company, I saw the conductor fleetingly at a restaurant, when he would appear, fresh from a performance at the Philharmonic, to have a late dinner, coffee, drink, and smoke at a distant table. At these moments, an electric current of excitement seemed to encircle his presence when he passed by and greeted us. Hank sang in the boys' choir of Mahler's Third Symphony and later narrated Benjamin Britten's *The Young Person's Guide to the Orchestra* at a Young People's Concert, during which I sat in the front row of the audience.

During my high school and college years, I returned to the Philharmonic to hear Bernstein conduct performances of Mahler, Beethoven, Ives, Stravinsky, and others. But my interests as a composer took a detour around Bernstein's own music. In this I might have been influenced, at least to a degree, by the fact that he was never mentioned in any composition class or course I took on twentieth-century music. The only time I remember his name coming up in discussions with a musical mentor occurred in a conversation I had when I was in my early twenties with the great composer Roger Sessions. Sessions spoke of being aggrieved at the degree to which Bernstein had wasted his remarkable compositional talent, after producing such a fine work as his *Jeremiah* Symphony at the age of twenty-five. He said that it was a shame that Bernstein had chosen "a life of fame and worldly success over one of achievement."

When I was close to fifty I came upon a letter from Hank's father in my parents' papers, asking them if they wanted to bring me over to play some of my music for Mr. Bernstein. Schuyler had told him about my teenage compositions, and the maestro had expressed an interest in hearing them. Somehow that letter was never mentioned to me. If I had met Bernstein I probably would have been awed but reticent. While I was precocious in my musical efforts, I knew that I was not yet a composer. I now regret not hearing what he might have had to say to me. I can't help wondering what advice he would have offered about musical study, about how to view a life in music, and about my sincere, if awkward, early compositions.

During his lifetime Bernstein was easy to criticize because he was so visible, so outspoken, so dramatic, so active. His mistakes, when he made them, became public knowledge. Some people saw him as divided and conflicted, or as a person pursuing too many goals to achieve all of them well; others saw him as a man of myriad gifts, excelling in many areas. But even now there don't seem to be many who have a tempered view of him. It remains hard to evaluate his work in an evenhanded way. Such a high degree of visibility has the paradoxical effect of being blinding.

Furthermore, Bernstein was by nature theatrical and did not fade into the woodwork as some of our favorite intellectual figures do. He was no Franz Kafka, tormented in his social relationships and asking that his works be burned after his death. He also wasn't Richard Rodgers, who, conventional-looking in a business suit, would not have stood out from a thousand other men on a subway platform waiting for a commuter train. He was more like a contemporary Franz Liszt, a personality on such a big scale that he would naturally manage to offend many people along the way. And his appetite for love was on a scale equal to Liszt's own, as is now evident from the voluminous archive of love letters to him, from both men and women, at the Library of Congress. Many of his relationships were of the flash-in-the-pan variety, but a surprising number turned into lifelong friendships. His self-regard and need for attention were also, to be sure, extreme. But if this was "narcissism," it was of an unusual kind, since it was also counterbalanced by passionate interest in others, extraordinary powers of observation and memory about people, and insight into them. One has the impression that, while Bernstein often took up all the oxygen in a room, he had an equal need to breathe oxygen back into it. Conductor Carl St. Clair described how Bernstein the teacher would enter a classroom at Tanglewood and hug, touch, and embrace everyone in sight. "He needs that energy from people," he wrote, "but whatever he takes from you, you get back with interest."[1]

Sometimes it is hard to remember that Leonard Bernstein is no longer alive. Today, when we see him conducting or teaching on film, his immediacy and communicative reach are such that he seems to leap out of the past into our present. It is sometimes difficult to remember that, despite the voluminous external record he left behind, he was also just a man living his life from the inside, and that his life was as temporary as anyone else's.

This book attempts to capture some of the shape and some of the details of his life, while placing an emphasis on the music and musical thinking at its heart. The general public long ago intuited that, like his ancestor at the New York Philharmonic, Gustav Mahler, and his successor there, Pierre Boulez, Bernstein conducted, played, taught, and talked about music from the perspective of his more hidden life as a composer.

In 1976 the peripatetic musician wrote, "Stillness is our most intense mode of action. . . . In stillness every human being is great; he is free from the experience of hostility; he is a poet, and most like an angel."[2]

# Part I

# 1

## *Dust*
## *1918–1927*

When he was four years old, Leonard brought some balls of dust he had gathered from under the bed into the bathroom sink to see whether he could construct a man. He was still an only child, living with his parents in Revere, Massachusetts, above a tailor shop. He must have heard his father, who was always quoting from the Talmud or the Old Testament, saying "Dust thou art, and unto dust shalt thou return"; or perhaps it was that "God formed man of the dust of the ground, and breathed into his nostrils the breath of life; and man became a living soul." Leonard put the dust into the bathroom sink, turned on the tap, and tried to mold the viscous blobs into lifelike forms. Then, as if in a bad dream, he couldn't turn the faucets off. Not only did the sink overflow and flood the bathroom floor, but the water then flowed through the ceiling into the tailor shop below, destroying some suits and dresses, and resulting in embarrassment and expense for his struggling parents. Years later, recalling this, he said, "There was hell to pay."

But for the most part Leonard brought his parents joy. His birth brightened their world, and for a brief time it almost seemed as if his existence had made sense of their marriage. Russian Jews transplanted to Massachusetts, they were both suffering, although in different ways. Almost from the day Sam and Jennie married, on Sunday, October 28, 1917, it had become apparent that their outlooks did not mesh, and that they lacked a romantic bond which could smooth over their differences. In the year Leonard was four, their fighting had even resulted in a two-week separation, and it was not the first one.

Sam (Shmuel) had been born in the town of Ozeryany, Ukraine, where his father, Yudel, was a scholar rabbi, the last in a long line of rabbis in the family tree.[1] The oldest of four children, Sam spent his childhood on a farm in nearby Berezdov (Ukrainian: Berezdiv). Here his father studied and prayed while his mother did the physical work on the farm and brought up the children. Although Sam was deeply religious and a born scholar himself, he bridled against the claustrophobic narrowness of an environment in which he could be beaten simply if he let his skullcap fall off during evening prayers. He entered yeshiva and even contemplated becoming a rabbi but, at the age of thirteen, shortly after his bar mitzvah, started dreaming of following his cousin Herschel to the "golden country." In 1903 Herschel had made the long journey from his hometown of Korets all the way to Hartford, Connecticut, where he changed his name to Harry Levy, married an American-born woman, Polly Kleiman, and became a barber. In 1908 Sam said goodbye to his two sisters and little brother and snuck out of the house at night, without saying goodbye to his parents, carrying only a few items of clothing and a blanket, with the sound of his siblings' crying still in his ears. He was sixteen years old.[2] The Atlantic crossing was a nightmare. A memory of the crowding, filth, vermin, bugs, excrement, and rotten food in the steerage hold stayed with him for the rest of his life.

Leonard's mother, Jennie, had been born Charna Resnick in the town of Shepetovka (Ukrainian: Shepetivka), only twenty-one miles from Samuel's home in Berezdov. She had been such a bright, lively, and imaginative child that her mother Perel had hired someone to tutor her in Russian and Hebrew, a rare privilege then for a girl. Family stories had her wandering off alone into the marketplace, and swimming where she wasn't supposed to. She particularly loved music, and once followed an itinerant band of musicians—klezmers—into the gentile part of town, where she fell asleep in a park and had to be returned home by a policeman. Jennie's ship crossing from Riga to New York in 1905 at the age of seven with her mother, younger brother, and younger sister was, like Sam's, a horrendous three-week ordeal of hunger, fear, and pain, during which she endured a broken wrist and lay famished, surrounded by the sick and dying on the heaving boat, while her mother repeatedly begged the ocean to spare them. Once in America, the family was reunited with her father, Simcha, who now worked in the textile mills of Lawrence, Massachusetts. She was placed in the Lawrence Elementary School's fourth grade at the age of only eight, and the next year she moved on to the Tarby School, where she did well enough to begin dreaming of someday becoming a teacher. But such aspirations were cut short when she was sent to work at the American Woolen Company to help support the family. There she experienced the appalling, often lethal conditions that precipitated the famous Lawrence Textile Strike, an uprising that eventually spread to the nine principal mills in the town and involved twenty-seven thousand workers.[3]

Jennie was an attractive and spirited young woman of eighteen when Samuel Bernstein first visited her.[4] Her parents had heard of his scholarly family even back in Ukraine. They admired his ambition and intelligence, and thought he had a future. In 1917, soon after buying Jennie an engagement ring, Sam was drafted into the army. Jennie had begun to appreciate his way with a joke and a story. She was touched seeing him in uniform marching down Essex Street, on his way to the train that would take him to Camp Devens. Not long after, when he was discharged due to poor eyesight and unexpectedly turned up in the Resnicks' kitchen, Jennie found herself, to her own surprise, embracing and kissing him in front of everyone. A wedding date was set.

At the time he married Jennie, Sam was working as an assistant manager at the Boston branch of Frankel and Smith, "suppliers of hair and beauty products." He had gone from a job helping out his uncle Harry in his Hartford barbershop to a stock boy position with Frankel and Smith, from which he had worked his way up.

Sam was devout, intense, rule-bound, sometimes harsh, like a "driven, diligent Horatio Alger hero," as Burton Bernstein puts it in his book *Family Matters*. His principal reading matter and point of reference for all things, worldly and unworldly, was the Talmud. By contrast, with her own education cut short, Jennie's "chief interests seemed to be food, the small available pleasure of life . . . movies and their celluloid celebrities, romantic novels . . . gossip with her coevals."[5] She dreamed of hobnobbing with elegant people and felt trapped by Sam's "consuming ambition and penny pinching." For his part, Sam had contempt for her family.

In August 1918, late in her pregnancy, Jennie moved temporarily from Sam's home in Chelsea to stay with her parents in Lawrence to await the birth. She went into labor at 3 a.m. on August 25 and was taken to Lawrenceville General Hospital, where, later in the morning, Leonard was born.[6] He was a colicky little fellow with a "weak chest," in Jennie's words, but he was also a great joy to his parents, even if his asthma attacks kept his mother up long into the night taking care of him.

By the time he was only a year and half, Leonard was already speaking so volubly that his parents dubbed him "the little old man." His neighbors in Revere had a piano, and he became hungry for the sound of it, banging on their door, shouting for "moynik" (music). Jennie claimed years later that when the Victrola played at home—novelty songs such as "Oh by Jingo" or Jewish cantorial music—the little boy would become calm and stare out the window, drumming with his fingers on the windowsills as if he were making the music himself.

Having a son who might someday inherit his business made Sam redouble his own efforts at work, if such a thing were possible, and within a year he was the manager at Frankel and Smith. By 1923 he would have his own beauty supply business, the Samuel J. Bernstein Hair Company, on 59 Temple Place in Boston. By seizing the chance to acquire the exclusive New England franchise for the Frederics permanent wave machine, Sam rode the quest of the 1920s craze for curly hair. Trucks painted with the slogan "In Boston, it's Bernstein—The Best in the Beauty Business" would travel throughout the metropolitan area, delivering his products to hairdressers, and a steady stream of merchants would line up at his store to buy wigs. Sam could be stern, judgmental, gloomy, and brooding, but he also had a playful side. He would dandle his son on his knee, singing "Ride away to Boston, / Ride away to Lynn, / You better be careful or you'll fall in," laughingly opening his legs as if to drop him. At a party, if Jewish music played, he would cut loose, dancing in the ecstatic Hasidic manner.

Through whatever combination of genetics, influence, and personal experience forms personality, all the characteristic traits of this mismatched couple can be discerned in the adult Leonard Bernstein and in his music: the religiousness, studiousness, traditionalism, strength, rebelliousness, and dark moods of his father; the sociability, warmth, gaiety, love of glamour, and attraction to show business of his mother. Along with these traits he inherited the intelligence and social liberalism the couple shared. Bernstein's childhood began on a footing that was unstable enough to account for his lifelong hunger for connection, particularly to his father, and his deep need for family. Even his tortured search for a lost faith could be traced to Sam's combination of reverence for the Talmud with flight from the constrictions of orthodoxy.

Leonard had started life as an only child. On October 23, 1923, Jennie gave birth to Leonard's younger sister, Shirley Anne. Brother Burton was born on January 31, 1932, when Leonard was thirteen. His parents made him, but it was with his two younger siblings that he formed the loving family he longed for.

# 2

## *A Piano*
## *1928–Spring 1935*

In 1923, the year Sam formed his own business and became the father of his second child, he also brought the family into the Mishkan Tefila Temple in Boston, which had built a "palatial synagogue" in a "monumental American Renaissance style" and was "the first synagogue in Boston to align itself with the new religious movement known as Conservative Judaism." The temple was a veritable symbol of what one Jewish newspaper called "the risen generation of the second migration," Eastern European Jews who had come to America with nothing and managed to build small fortunes. Philosophically, the temple was explicitly oriented toward "Liberalism, Zionism, and Social Service." By the time the Bernsteins became members, the temple boasted a magnificent organ and an exceptional cantor.[1] Eventually Sam became Mishkan Tefila's vice president.

Leonard began studying at the Hebrew school at age eight, and it was at temple that, at the age of ten, he was first thunderstruck by hearing live music. In 1928 the temple hired as music director a brilliant composer, organist, and conductor named Solomon Gregory Braslavsky (1887–1975), who had been a leading orchestral and choral conductor in Vienna and a professor at the Jewish Theological Seminary there before coming to Boston. Braslavsky performed repertoire from every era at the temple, assigning Hebrew texts to works by Mendelssohn, Verdi, and Schubert for choir and organ, and adding his own compositions, such as his contrapuntal Adon 'olam ("Lord of the World"), and the high holiday prayer Un'saneh tokef. When Leonard heard the cantor sing in his rich, sweet baritone, and the organ and choir join in, he became so overwhelmed with emotion that he would start to cry. He never forgot this music or Braslavsky, who became his first musical mentor.[2]

In the same year that Braslavsky arrived in Boston, Aunt Clara's piano arrived in the Bernstein household, an event that changed Leonard's life forever. Clara, Sam's sister, had come to America in 1911. She was an eccentric—a nutritionist, vegetarian, and nudist—with a commanding Wagnerian soprano voice, and when she married for the third time and moved to Brooklyn to run a bridal shop, she sent the Bernsteins a sofa and an old mahogany upright, with a middle "mandolin" pedal, that she no longer needed. From the moment he touched the piano, Leonard couldn't tear himself away from it. Caressing the keys and causing the sounds to issue forth from the strings made the world, and his place in it, suddenly come into focus: "I suddenly felt at the center of a universe I could control, or at least be at the center of, in that I felt it revolving stably around me, instead of [my] being tossed around in it, which I had felt up until then. . . . I was safe at the piano."[3] He began to play constantly, disturbing the peace of the household. He picked out "Goodnight, Sweetheart" by himself and quickly learned to read music notation under the guidance of a beautiful and exotic-looking girl in the neighborhood named Frieda Karp, who played well enough to give him lessons for a dollar each.

It soon became evident that he had an exceptional ear and an instinctive grasp of theory. Without knowing the proper names of chords, he made up his own system of harmony and could soon improvise plausibly on songs he heard on the radio, such as Irving Berlin's "Blue Skies." After only a year he was playing Bach preludes, Mendelssohn's "Spring Song," and other selections from a green-covered anthology called *100 Pieces the Whole World Loves*, which fifty years later he would still carry with him wherever he traveled. His father was willing to pay the dollar per lesson but was less than enthused about the piano playing itself, and he often shouted from his bedroom when it got too late at night. His mother was drawn to the music, as she had been attracted to the wandering klezmers as a child, and when Leonard played Chopin's Nocturne in E-flat Major, op. 9, no. 2, she would stand by the piano and weep.[4] When he started composing his own pieces at around the age of twelve, he would play them for her in different versions and ask her which she liked best.

His relationship with his father, however, was often fraught. Sam was subject to black moods and to bursts of temper. At least once Leonard interposed himself between Jennie and Sam during a heated argument, when Sam began to angrily chase after her, holding a raised bottle. Sometimes Leonard would hide under the dining room table when Sam came home.

By contrast, the happy marriage and healthy, laugh-filled atmosphere of family get-togethers at Uncle Harry Levy's home in Hartford left an indelibly positive impression on young Leonard. It was the one place where his parents seemed to relax and enjoy themselves. Moreover, there, on Harry's expensive Victrola, Leonard fell in love with Rosa Ponselle's rendition of the dramatic aria "Suicidio!" from Ponchielli's *La Gioconda*, Zez Confrey's piano solo "Kitten on the Keys," and W. C. Polla's

"Dancing Tambourine," which he analyzed as a "March made into a novelty piece," an early instance of his stylistic acumen.

Leonard's playing soon outstripped that of his teacher—he was "reading a Chopin ballade she could barely play herself," he recalled later—and she suggested that he seek instruction at the New England Conservatory. The teacher he found there, Susan Williams, started him on music that surpassed in complexity anything he had yet encountered, Liszt's Hungarian Rhapsodies. Fighting with Sam over the increased cost of the lessons forced him to earn money giving lessons to small children himself, as well as to start playing for weddings with two friends who played saxophone and drums. While Miss Williams ultimately proved an unreliable guide in terms of piano technique, she must have recognized the promise in his playing, since she placed the thirteen-year-old last in her student concert program of March 30, 1932, performing the Brahms Rhapsody in G Minor. No doubt the fiery music he was learning influenced his first unfinished attempt at composing, a Piano Concerto in C Minor he dubbed "The Russian–Gypsy War."

Siblings Leonard, Shirley, and Burton adored each other, forming a kind of independent minifamily of their own, with Leonard as the "father" in the constellation. By the time she was eight, Shirley was studying the piano under her brother's tutelage, and they were able to play through four-hand arrangements of Beethoven symphonies together. (They had volume 2: symphonies 6 through 9.) She was so talented that they were soon singing through entire operas together, she taking the female roles, he taking the male ones (in his enthusiastic but terrible voice), and both singing the choruses. He, rather than her parents, became the person she most wanted most to please. The two had an exceptional camaraderie and closeness that continued throughout their lives and ultimately eclipsed her other relationships with men. Despite many romances in later life, Shirley, who later worked in theater and television production and as a literary agent, never married and was candid about the fact that she hadn't found a man who interested her to the degree her brother had.

Leonard and a neighbor, Eddie Ryack, created an imaginary country, "Rybernia" (an amalgamation of their names), with leaders (themselves), a national anthem, and a language based on their parents' Yiddish and garbled English, and, with the heedless cruelty of youth, words based on the speech patterns of a local boy with a harelip. The language included a riotous collection of parental expressions such as "How you gonna did it?" and "smose snapas seven" ("almost half-past seven").[5] The three Bernstein children expressed their Americanness and independence from their immigrant parents by speaking "Rybernian" as a private code that they maintained throughout their lives.

Another citizen of Rybernia was Sid Ramin, an extraordinarily musical boy just a few months younger than Leonard who lived down the street. Leonard met Sid at age fifteen and taught him piano and his own version of "harmony." Ramin would remain a lifelong friend and became a masterful musician who co-orchestrated *West Side Story*, *A Quiet Place*, *1600 Pennsylvania Avenue*, and innumerable works by composers other than Bernstein. The two boys would take long walks almost every day, and Sid would mainly listen as Leonard expounded on everything under the sun. Ramin attended Leonard's bar mitzvah in 1931 at Temple Mishkan Tefila and was amazed, along with the congregation, by his friend's poise and eloquence. Instead of one of the standard prepared speeches, Leonard delivered "an articulate and personally crafted" one of his own that the headmaster of the Hebrew school, Solomon

Zuckrow, had helped him translate into Hebrew.[6] Samuel was so proud of his son that he bought him a baby grand piano as a present.

Leonard exuded confidence. One day he and Ramin were walking down Abbotsford Street in Roxbury when they heard a woman practicing the piano, repeatedly stumbling over the same passage. Leonard bounded onto her porch, climbed in her window (which was next to the piano), sat down next to her, and played the piece through for her, saying, "This is how it is supposed to go." She was so dumbfounded that she couldn't even catch her breath before he had bounded out again. Ramin also witnessed Leonard's bond with his sister. He remembers climbing upstairs with Leonard and tiptoeing into ten-year-old Shirley's room while she was sleeping. Awed by her mystery, Leonard held her finger, to see whether he could tell from that what she was dreaming.[7]

In 1929 Leonard finished sixth grade at the W. L. Garrison School and began studying at the prestigious Boston Latin School, where he was to stay six years. Boston Latin was the oldest public school in the United States, a kind of poor boy's Andover or Exeter, known for its rigorous classical training. It accepted students from all walks of life, but the workload was so arduous and the school's standards so high that only one in three students who entered it made it to graduation. In his years there Leonard received the "Modern Prize" for the highest combined grade average, the "Reading Prize," and the "Classics Prize" (he had to translate an average of forty lines of Latin a night), and he participated in the French Club, the Physics Club, and the Glee Club. At the weekly assemblies during his senior year, after the Old Testament reading by the headmaster, he would often play the piano. That year he received a prize for excellence in music and cowrote the class song, "All for One, and One for All." But his real musical development occurred outside of school, first in his piano studies with a new teacher and secondly in what must have seemed at the time a mere recreation, the informal theatrical productions he mounted with friends.

In October 1932 one of Leonard's first girlfriends, a talented pianist named Mildred Spiegel, whose family had a Baldwin grand on which he practiced, suggested that he audition for Heinrich Gebhard, one of the best-known piano teachers in Boston. Gebhard was encouraging but referred him to his assistant, Helen Coates. It was an important encounter. Coates was a tall, disciplined, rather prim woman eighteen years older than Leonard (just one year short of his mother's age). She was perhaps the first person who fully recognized how exceptional his musical abilities were. Leonard's playing was passionate but unruly. She would sit at the adjoining piano, teaching him, as he later put it, "how not to bang, [how] to use the pedal discreetly, how to discipline [his] crazed and raging fingers."[8] He was a superb sight-reader, learned music faster than any student she had ever had, and had an insightful responsiveness to everything she taught. In her chaste, protective, and maternal way, Coates was in love with him. She soon put his lessons at the end of the day so that they could stretch out as long as they needed to, including time for him to play his arrangements of Russian and Hebrew melodies, so that she could help him notate them. The lessons broadened his musical world and emboldened him as a composer. Over time, Helen Coates became Bernstein's lifelong secretary and "keeper of the flame." When he started to perform in recitals in 1933, she began to compile the first in a series of scrapbooks containing announcements, programs, articles, and reviews of her student's music and performances; these would eventually chronicle fifty-five years of his professional life.

It wasn't until the spring of 1932 that Leonard first heard a live orchestra. Surprisingly, he was seated next to his father. The event was a Boston Pops concert conducted by Arthur

Fiedler, held to benefit the Histadrut, the Zionist trade union movement in Palestine, for which Temple Mishkan Tefila had reserved a few tables. The concert left him crazed with excitement, particularly the performance of Ravel's *Bolero* that closed the program. After that, as often as Leonard could manage to squeeze ticket money out of his father, he started to attend Boston Symphony programs, either with Sid Ramin or with Mildred. He had a second musical epiphany when he heard Gershwin's *Rhapsody in Blue.* His father gave him the two dollars to purchase the sheet music, and he marked up his copy so that he and Ramin could play it as a four-hands piano piece.

While Sam shared Leonard's enthusiasm for *Bolero,* he was adamantly opposed to his thinking of music as a career. The only musicians in his experience had been the klezmers of the shtetl. It had taken every ounce of his strength to pull himself out of the poverty of shtetl life and up from the squalor of his first days in New York, when he had spent twelve hours a day cleaning fish in the Fulton Fish Market. He had seized on every opportunity that had come his way to move up the ladder of the beauty supply business and to establish a decent and stable life for his family. That his first-born son would scorn all his efforts and not continue to build on his achievements was unthinkable to him. When Leonard performed the first movement of the Grieg Piano Concerto with the Boston Public School Symphony at Roxbury High School on May 14, 1934, Sam did not attend.[9] Helen Coates wrote to Sam of her disappointment at not seeing him there, and on July 20, 1934, she received a reply typed on his business stationery, with "Samuel Bernstein Hair Company / 480 Washington Street" emblazoned at its top:

> Miss Helen G. Coates:
> While I am confident of his progress in his music education, I shall want him to continue to treasure his accomplishments in the connection solely from an idealistic viewpoint. Not-

> withstanding my respect for a professional career in the musical world, from a practical standpoint I prefer that he does not regard his music as a future means of maintenance.[10]

Sam's business was among those that, like the film industry, not only did not succumb to the Depression but actually flourished during it. The rise of his fortunes enabled him to build a small summer house on Lake Massapoag, in Sharon, Massachusetts. It was there, in the summer of 1934, that Leonard organized his first theatrical production, a drastically cut and rewritten, cross-dressing *Carmen* performed by neighborhood kids. Leonard was Carmen in a red wig and black mantilla, his friend Beatrice Gordon was Don Jose, and a Boston Latin schoolmate, Dana Schnittken, was Micaëla, wearing blond tresses supplied by Sam. Leonard spearheaded every aspect of the production, taught all the parts individually, and played the piano. Since much of the libretto included interpolations in Yiddish, or references to local events and people, he also wrote a helpful synopsis for ten-year-old Shirley to read as a prologue.

By the following summer, the entire neighborhood looked forward to the young musician's next venture, which turned out to be Gilbert and Sullivan's *The Mikado.* Leonard again took responsibility for every aspect of the production, from trimming the score, casting it, and getting props and scenery taken care of, to teaching everyone their parts in his "raw and unappealing voice," as one participant later described it, as well as playing the piano. He sang Nanki-Poo, and eleven-year-old Shirley was Yum-Yum. Seventy years later, members of the troupe in their late eighties remembered the Sharon productions with emotion as giving everyone a goal for the summer, and their leader as having extraordinary charm, energy, a joyful spirit, and seemingly endless patience. He had the gift of being able to galvanize them all with his enthusiasm and determination.

Leonard was physically attracted to both sexes. While he

had a series of girlfriends, among them the young pianist Mildred Spiegel; his "matador" Beatrice Gordon (whom he called "Tiger on Brocade," an anagram of her name); and petite, dark-haired Elaine Newman, who looked like Loretta Young and with whom he acted out scenes from Noel Coward's *Private Lives*, he could also be smitten with his male companions in a romantic way. When he was passionately drawn to someone—as he often was—his impulse was the same, regardless of gender. At sixteen, in his last year at Boston Grammar, he wrote a school essay titled "Friends and Freud" in which, under the guise of discussing what he had gleaned about Freud's views on homosexuality, he seemed to be trying to sort out his feelings:

> Most people have experienced, at some time during their adolescence, the psychological sublimation of consuming friendship . . . that companionship which has so exaggeratively [*sic*] theorized by the doctrinaire Freud as love between two members of one sex.
>
> . . . It seems to me that Freud has unnecessarily placed the subject in a decidedly unclear light which tends to affect destructively the relations of youth. . . . Why should beautiful relationships like these be smutted with talk of abnormality?[11]

Later in life, when he underwent psychoanalysis and came to admire Freud deeply, he surely came upon the psychoanalyst's 1915 observation that "by studying sexual excitations other than those that are manifestly displayed, it has [been] found that all human beings are capable of making a homosexual object-choice, and have in fact made one in their unconscious."[12]

In the spring of 1935 Leonard was accepted into Harvard University. Sid Ramin remembers standing with him on the street when he announced his plan to acquire a Harvard accent, which indeed he did.

# 3

## *Harvard*
## *Fall 1935–Spring 1939*

During the years that Leonard attended Harvard, he not only developed a "cultivated" accent but also encountered many of the ideas and met many of the people who would influence him for the rest of his life. Indeed, his trajectory through the school foreshadowed the meteoric rise, high accomplishments, and some of the difficulties of his future years. But when he arrived there he was only an aspiring pianist seeking a liberal arts education. Being a conductor couldn't have been further from his mind, and he had composed no music of his own other than the 1935 class song for the Boston Latin School, "All for One, and One for All," and a small psalm setting for voice and piano.

But, as his friend Mildred Spiegel put it with considerable understatement, Leonard "never hid his light under a bushel," and from the beginning he was a star at Harvard, bursting with energy and opinions, and becoming quickly known as a pianist. Friends from the time describe him as commandeering the piano at every party (not unlike George Gershwin, who was likewise magnetized by the presence of the instrument). He would often walk in the front door and go directly to the piano, simply moving aside whoever might have gotten there first. He had a seemingly endless repertoire of popular songs and lighter pieces in his memory and fingertips. He would play boogie-woogie, Chopin, and light classics such as Ernesto Lecuona's "Malagueña." Often he could be found there hours later, still wearing his overcoat, playing passionately, with a cigarette dangling from his mouth. (He had started smoking at the age of fourteen.) Throughout his life he never required much sleep. If he was not at a party, he would spend long hours drinking beer into the night with friends at the dorm, discussing God, art, politics, and sex.

According to Spiegel, he "became bored if made to have a regimented existence," and he always seemed to need to have many projects going at once, not necessarily including homework.[1] He was irregular in his attendance of classes and an inveterate procrastinator, yet he tended to do brilliantly. Friends from the time later remembered his habit of waiting until the last day to write an assigned essay, tearing his hair out, deciding to address another topic entirely rather than the assigned one, writing feverishly through the night, and ending up getting an A. While classmates struggled on the four-part harmony exercises assigned in A. Tillman Merritt's counterpoint and harmony course, he completed them swiftly, with an ease and skill that far outstripped theirs. He loved to be the center of attention, even if it meant being obnoxious. He once derailed an entire session of Merritt's class with his stubborn insistence that Bach should have notated a G-sharp as an A-flat. Toward the end of term, having been an intermittent participant in the course at best, he suddenly showed up to play a dissonant, dancelike piano piece he had composed, rather than the study in sixteenth-century counterpoint that was due. When Merritt said, "Well, Leonard, this is not exactly what we are doing in this class," Leonard "banged his fist loudly on the piano and said, 'Well, I like it!'"[2]

As of freshman year, Leonard was now studying piano regularly with Heinrich Gebhard, and he continued to do so until graduation. Among Leonard's many performances as an undergraduate were the Ravel Concerto in G Major, Gershwin's *Rhapsody in Blue*, and the Grieg Concerto, with the Massachusetts State Symphony, all sponsored by the Federal Works Progress Administration, and solo music by Bach, Chopin, Liszt, Brahms, Debussy, Ravel, and Hindemith. He was praised in the press for "authority, ease and clarity" in the Ravel and "virtuosic brilliance and profound interpretation" in the Grieg. Response to the Gershwin was more muted, with one critic calling it "adequate" and another as "hardly up to those we are in the habit of hearing."

Leonard was headstrong and on his own schedule, but he was also a born student, and one with charm, depth, and a hunger for fatherly understanding and guidance. In the space of only a few years, many father figures did appear in his life who sought not only to guide him but also saw him as a friend. One of his mentors at Harvard was a philosophy teacher named David Prall, who taught courses in aesthetics. Leonard attended Prall's classes more consistently than he did the music courses, and also became a regular at the informal discussion groups Prall held at his home, which were sometimes also attended by the young painter Robert Motherwell and future literary scholar Harry Levin. In his lectures Prall was able to draw the kinds of connections between the arts, and to express a view of the way the arts combined the intellectual and the sensual, that must have confirmed Leonard in his own creative outlook. One can see the traces of Prall's thinking in Bernstein's scripts for the Young People's Concerts of many years later, and in the worldview behind the Norton Lectures given when he returned to Harvard in 1973.

Deeply knowledgeable about music (his sister was a music professor at Mills College in California), Prall had a great gift for explicating its surface. But he also abhorred the idea of making art into an abstraction that could be separated from lived experience. He was an intellectual who, in a manner surprising for an academic, included the body and the senses in his consideration and valuation of art: "Written music . . . offers to the technically trained musician the very structure of the beauties he silently hears. . . . [But when the music is actually played] the most gifted composer has a new experience of his music, in which it takes on its proper sensuous proportions and achieves its full volume and richness and the precise specific quality that is given to the outer ear, and never its absolutely full, intricate, subtle tonal quality to the inner ear, the 'ear of the mind.'" He discussed the elements of an art form's language in physical terms, emphasizing, for example, that the swiftness or slowness of a rhythm cannot be measured in absolute terms but only in "relation to the time-rates of human processes, breathing, pulse, and other organic functions which are beyond our conscious control."[3] Prall further stimulated an interest in the world of the ancient Greeks, which Leonard had first developed at Boston Latin and which would bear fruit in his incidental music for Aristophanes's *The Birds* and *The Peace*, as well as in his 1954 *Serenade*.[4]

As Leonard frequently reminded his own students in later life, the words to "learn" and to "teach" are one and the same in many languages. Burton Bernstein was on the receiving end of Leonard's compulsion to teach almost from the moment he learned to talk, and he received his own "Harvard education" by proxy when he was only four or five, during his brother's weekend visits. As bedtime stories he learned about intervals, the modes, and the circle of fifths, and then he went to sleep to the sounds of Leonard practicing the Ravel Concerto or some other difficult work in the living room below. (He eventually became a staff writer at the *New Yorker* and the author of nine books.)

In the summer of his freshman year, Leonard again mounted a production in Sharon, this time of Gilbert and Sullivan's *HMS Pinafore*, with Mildred Spiegel as Buttercup and interpolated music from *Aida*, to which Shirley and two neighborhood girls performed "Egyptian dances" choreographed by Leonard. When not playing *Pinafore* on the piano, Leonard would sit on the porch listening rapturously to Indian music on a small phonograph, exclaiming, "Isn't this wonderful? I could have an orgasm!"[5]

In his junior year Leonard met another talented young composer, Harold Shapero, who was a freshman. The two young men discovered that their families lived just a few houses from each other in Newton, and soon they were spending long hours at the library listening to music together.[6] During vacation, in one of their conversations after playing catch in Leonard's backyard, they discussed their ambitions. Harold said that he wanted to win the hearts of as many girls as he could. Leonard said that he wanted everyone in the world to love him. Leonard borrowed all the four-hand music the library owned, and soon they were playing through arrangements of Beethoven, Mozart, and Schubert symphonies together. Leonard would get them jobs playing concerts and entertaining at suburban parties as a four-hand and two-piano team. They eventually played more than twenty concerts together, performing Hindemith's Sonata for Piano, Four Hands; Stravinsky's Concerto for Two Pianos; Mozart's complex Sonata for Keyboard Four-Hands in F Major, K. 497; and a work considered a classic today, Shapero's own Sonata for Piano, Four Hands, which was dedicated to Leonard. They would also sometimes play musical pranks at the expense of their listeners. One involved flatting all the dominants in a Mozart four-hand sonata, so that the music came out sounding "like Grieg." On another occasion they improvised compositions on the spot that were listed in the program as works by Prokofiev and Shostakovich.

Shapero found Leonard to be endlessly fascinated with matrimony and attracted to couples as a pair, and he later recounted an incident hinging on this that scarred their friendship. After their most prestigious concert, at the Boston Institute of Modern Art, at which Shapero's marvelous sonata had received its premiere, they were treated to a fancy dinner. When Leonard started to flirt and "smooch" with the wife of a guest, the more prudish Shapero whispered words of disapproval to him, at which point Leonard slapped him. The slap—hard enough to startle, but not to hurt—was utterly uncharacteristic of him.

Leonard listened to as much modern music as he could, and he had a remarkable ability not only to remember it but also to penetrate its inner workings and grasp its technical means. To earn extra money he played for silent films. An audience of a thousand Harvard students gave him a standing ovation at the end of his accompaniment for Sergei Eisenstein's *Battleship Potemkin,* in which he improvised for over an hour, riffing on Stravinsky's *Petrushka,* jumping from one Russian folk song to another, and managing to hold his on-the-spot soundtrack together with aplomb.

Leonard already adored Prokofiev's *Classical* Symphony and Stravinsky's *Le Sacre du Printemps* when an older Harvard friend, Arthur Berger—who was later to become a distinguished composer, professor at Brandeis, and a founder of the journal *Perspectives of New Music*—took him to the Cambridge music store Briggs and Briggs to listen to a recording of Aaron Copland playing his Piano Variations. Leonard was bowled over by this oracular, stark, and dissonant work and was determined to learn it. Since he couldn't afford the sheet music himself, David Prall bought it for him, encouraging him to write a paper about the work for class. Leonard soon had the piece memorized, and it was added to his "party pieces," albeit one that, as he frequently joked, would "clear the room." He had a vision of Copland as a bearded patriarch.

Leonard couldn't afford a full subscription to the Boston Symphony, but by sharing one he attended concerts every other week. As luck would have it, in January, during midterm week, he attended the American conducting debut of the inspiring Greek conductor Dimitri Mitropoulos. On the program was Mitropoulos's string orchestra arrangement of Beethoven's String Quartet No. 14 in C-sharp Minor, op. 131.[7] There are several competing accounts of Bernstein's meeting with the charismatic conductor, but however they met, their connection, as so many connections seemed to be for the younger musician, was personal, resulting in an invitation for Leonard to watch him rehearse with the Boston Symphony. This was the first time Leonard grasped how a conductor worked with musicians, and what his role entailed. The older man listened to Leonard play some of his first compositions and thought him destined for greatness. (Mitropoulos was himself a composer as well as a conductor.) The two subsequently exchanged intense, confessional letters and at one point spent two weeks together in Minneapolis, but it appears doubtful that the two became lovers, despite the implications of a mutual attraction in a fictional account Leonard wrote about their meeting, called "The Occult."

In spring term of his sophomore year Leonard completed a work for a piano trio that Mildred Spiegel had formed with two friends, Dorothy Rosenberg and Sarah Kruskall. Despite its polyglot mix of influences and some compositional loose ends, the work makes a confident impression. The first movement begins strikingly, with a passionate, Hebraic lyricism reminiscent of Ernest Bloch. Its angular and almost atonal ideas are then taken on a somewhat discursive journey, through harmonic territories suggestive of Scriabin and Ravel, with quite a bit of imitative counterpoint along the way. (In fact, some of the music appears to have been drawn from exercises written for counterpoint class.) A few climaxes hearken back to Brahms and Tchaikovsky. By contrast, the witty and ebullient middle movement, a marchlike scherzo, has both moment-to-moment appeal and consistency. Apart from a few Gershwinesque turns of phrase, it sounds Russian in character, and its piquant modern tonality—not too far from that of Prokofiev—is handled with deftness. The finale returns to themes from both movements but suggests that the composer has grown since writing the first one, managing a reconciliation between its transparent French textures and the Russian/Hebraic materials. The final cadence is ingenious. With its directness, concision, and clarity of expression, the work was an early sign that, for all his bravado and distractibility, writing music drew a kind of purity and even restraint out of the nineteen-year-old composer. He may have been an inveterate show-off at a party, but on paper he was precise and serious.[8]

In the summer of 1937 Leonard had his first summer job, as music counselor at the all-Jewish Camp Onota, in Pittsfield, Massachusetts, where he taught the campers rounds and campfire songs, led a small band, and music directed the summer show. On July 11, during parents' weekend, he was asked to play the piano during lunch. At first he declined. But when the news came over the radio of George Gershwin's sudden death of a brain tumor at age thirty-nine, he went to the piano in the noisy mess hall, played a loud chord, silenced the campers and their parents, and announced that "America's greatest Jewish composer" had died. He then played Gershwin's Prelude No. 2, experiencing an almost eerie sense of identification with the composer. A month later he made an ingenious arrangement of *Rhapsody in Blue* for a motley collection of camp musicians playing clarinet, recorder, accordion, two ukuleles, percussion, and piano solo, with an additional part for three male singers.

Later that summer a brilliant, eccentric, theater-loving young man from the Bronx named Adolph Green, who could do imitations of Al Jolson, recite Kipling's "Gunga Din" and endless numbers of other poems by heart, and was reputed to have a photographic memory for music, came up to the camp from New York to play the role of the Pirate King in *Pirates of Penzance*. Leonard greeted Adolph by dragging him instantly into the mess hall, where, on an old upright piano, he played the old Harold Shapero prank of performing a brilliant five-minute "prelude by Shostakovich," asking him whether he had heard it. When Green replied that, surprisingly, he didn't find it familiar, Leonard threw his arms around him, saying that he was the first person who had admitted not knowing it. (The music was, of course, Bernstein's own.) Their friendship was immediate and always remained a central one for both of them.[9]

Fortuitous meetings seemed to proliferate throughout his undergraduate years. November 14, 1937, became a banner day in Leonard's life when he found himself seated next to Aaron Copland himself in the balcony of a dance debut by Anna Sokolow at the Guild Theatre in New York. Since it was Copland's thirty-seventh birthday, he invited everyone in the row over to his loft for a party afterward, whereupon Leonard sat down at the piano and performed the Piano Variations for him by heart. The composer was astonished by Leonard's playing, by his lively personality, and by the "sheer amount of information about music new and old, and not only about music" that the eighteen-year-old knew. For his part, Leonard thought that the man he already considered America's greatest composer was "about the most sensational human being I'd ever come across."[10]

When he heard Copland's new, exuberant *El salón México* in 1938, he was as bowled over as he had been by the Variations, this time by the snazzy orchestration, gemlike construction, and joyful inventiveness, which made the work what he called in a letter to Copland "a perfect roller-coaster ride." "It's a secure feeling to know we have a master in America," he wrote, railing against those who couldn't see that "a composer is just as *serious* when he writes a work, even if the piece is not defeatist . . . and weltschmerzy and misanthropic and long."[11] He was so taken with *El salón México* that he made himself a solo piano version to play.

Leonard absorbed lessons and techniques from both sides of Copland's music. The spare four-note opening of the Piano Variations, as stern as the beginning of Beethoven's Fifth, yet somehow so "American," was an object lesson in leanness, in the power of just the right notes at the right time. Copland managed to derive every bit of this work from its opening eleven measures. This was *multum in parvum*, as they would have said at Boston Latin, "much from little." This quality of stark, surprising specificity was the finding of what Nadia Boulanger, Copland's teacher, used to call "la note choisie" (the chosen note). Like the uncluttered prose of E. B. White, Thornton Wilder, or Robert Frost, or the plain frankness of an Edward Hopper or Georgia O'Keeffe painting, Copland's music was suggestive of the relative newness of the nation, of its geographical openness, its rawness and lack of pretense, and of a kind of barrenness—an American loneliness. For all his apparent unruliness, Bernstein had a fastidious mind. His first compositions were already notable for their transparency of texture. Looking at Copland and showing him his first music solidified his own tendency to an uncluttered kind of writing and allied him more with the Francophile neoclassical Boulanger school of composition (which included, along with Copland, Virgil Thomson, Roy Harris, Elliott Carter, and dozens more young Americans), than with the denser, thornier, more chromatic and introspective Austro-German school. Without knowing it, he was like a Boulanger student, at one remove.

Bernstein was also fascinated by Copland's rhythms, by the way idiomatic folk and popular tunes could be woven into the fabric of a complex work such as *El salón México*, generating such vibrancy and immediacy with their syncopations, irregular meters, asymmetrical phrase structures, and those moments when two competing beat patterns were superimposed. Copland was able to distill his folk sources and modify them, and to invent his own ideas modeled upon them, so that they could be extended into symphonic structures. Leonard also thought that the elements that seemed so distinctively American in Copland's work all bore some relationship, however distant, to the elements of jazz. Ideas of this kind would eventually generate the premise behind his undergraduate thesis.

Around this time, Leonard started writing about music for the *Harvard Advocate*, where he was music editor, and for the important New York music journal *Modern Music*. In his article "Boston Carries On," in *Modern Music* on May 6, 1938, he wrote cockily that Prokofiev's first piano concerto "shows up wretchedly" compared with that composer's ballet *Chout*, adding, "Truly it is not a good piece . . . its one real tune is worked to death." But he also shrewdly noted that, due paradoxically to Prokofiev's very inability "to write profoundly tragic music," his rendering of Romeo's grief at Juliet's grave in *Romeo and Juliet* has its own "very strange beauty." About his teacher Walter Piston's first symphony, given its premiere at the same concert, he wrote that, despite its fine lyrical sense, expert orchestration, and masterly construction, "adverse criticisms were profuse and diverse: some thought the Largo unduly long and uninteresting; others found the work lacking emotional appeal."

At some point in his junior year, Leonard started working on a Piano Sonata dedicated to his piano teacher, Heinrich

Gebhard. A kind of improvisatory fantasy in two movements, the darkly introspective sonata shows surprising authority and craft, if not yet a unified style. The work derives all its ideas from those stated at the outset: a spiky, fleet-fingered passage reminiscent of Copland; a hortatory chordal statement in a minor key that sounds like Scriabin; a tone row; and some angular, jazzy figurations in the spirit of Gershwin. (It is worth noting that the three musical role models evoked by these materials shared Leonard's Russian ancestry.) In the lyrical slow movement, the shape of the long, continuous melody and the way in which the asymmetrical rhythms of the chords in the accompaniment break up 4/4 time into unequal eighth-note groups inaugurate a dancelike lilt characteristic of so many passages in Leonard's future music—whether slow or fast. Unlike the Piano Trio, the sonata maintains its unsettled, brooding tone throughout; after fifteen minutes it slows to a bleak standstill, ending with the tone row in isolated pitches in the upper register.

Leonard's senior year was a time of burgeoning interests and startling accomplishments. To begin with there was his thesis, which took as its central proposition the bold (and un-Harvardian) notion that jazz was the first truly American music to have penetrated into the soul of the people to the degree that it could constitute the foundation of a national idiom. His position was argued with considerable specificity. Beginning with comments on musical "nationalism" generally, he distinguished between a superficial kind, in which folk music is cited or quoted without affecting the overall language of the music, and a more "spiritual" one, in which the smallest elements and the very cut of the form are permeated with the folk traditions of a given culture. He argued that, unlike hymnody, American Indian music, or other folk music, specific elements derived from jazz, such as the blues scale and the syncopated rhythms originally associated with an explicit beat (but not dependent on one), had seeped into the metaphorical soil in which the first uniquely American concert music was growing. (In a letter, Copland approved of his musical examples but—characteristically—advised him not to "try to prove too much.") In making this case, Leonard dismissed many nineteenth- and early twentieth-century American composers in such general terms that one exasperated faculty reader scrawled on the manuscript: "What sweeping criticism! I wonder what critics in 1975 will have to say on young American composers of 1938!"[12]

He was still hard at work on his thesis when he was asked to serve as composer, music director, and conductor for an undergraduate production of Aristophanes's comedy *The Birds*, to be given by the Harvard Classical Club at Sanders Theatre in April. The musical score for *The Birds* built on the fun of the "Yiddish *Carmen*" from his Sharon summers, and presaged much that was to come from its composer. The eclectic score made references to everything from Debussy, to "La donna è mobile," to Louis Armstrong, to the Indian music Leonard had recently heard in a performance by the dancer Uday Shankar (brother of Ravi Shankar). In keeping with the tone of Aristophanes's wildly imaginative satirical allegory, the music was full of "energy and jagged rhythms, with occasional moments of lyricism." Turning Aristophanes's "ragged poet" into a "jazz poet," Leonard taught the student playing the role how to "sing the blues in Greek," writing the words out for him phonetically. The instrumental ensemble consisted of winds, strings, percussion, and harp. Passages from the score later made their way into *Fancy Free* and *On the Town.* Nearly ten years later, a duet for muted violin and cello from *The Birds*, transcribed for two clarinets, became the lonely opening of Symphony No. 2 (*The Age of Anxiety*).[13]

Both Helen Coates and Aaron Copland attended the performance of *The Birds.*[14] It was the first time that Leonard had conducted in public, and Copland was immediately struck by his natural conducting ability and the appropriateness of the role to his personality. He had the energy, intelligence, conviction, and personal skills needed to pull together an elaborate production—he had, after all, been organizing musical events and music directing ever since his teenage years—and he also had the musical knowledge, score-reading skills, leadership abilities, and physical coordination conducting requires.

All these qualities helped him to carry off an even more impressive theatrical undertaking just one month later, on May 5, 1939, when he organized, music directed, and played the piano for a production of Marc Blitzstein's musical *The Cradle Will Rock*, modeled on the already fabled New York production, in which Blitzstein himself had been the onstage pianist. Bernstein cast his fifteen-year-old sister Shirley (under the pseudonym Shirley Mann) as Moll, the prostitute. Blitzstein came up from New York to attend the dress rehearsal and opening night, and spent the afternoon walking and talking with Leonard along the Charles River. He thought the performance "packed a thrilling wallop" and that Bernstein was like a reincarnation of himself.[15] Their bond was instantaneous, intense, and lasting. Perhaps no living composer other than Copland was a greater influence on the young musician than Blitzstein turned out to be. The mastery of text setting in his vocal music left an indelible imprint on Bernstein, his clear life choices less of one. A fine pianist, Blitzstein declared himself a composer first. While he had written some superior concert music, his deeper allegiance was to music theater with a social message. Although briefly married, he was unapologetically homosexual.

Blitzstein was also a communist (until 1949, the year of his operatic masterpiece *Regina*, based on Lillian Hellman's *The Little Foxes*), and *Cradle* was an incendiary, pro-union work dedicated to Bertolt Brecht. Unbeknownst to all at the time, Leonard's production, favorably reviewed in the Boston press, first gave rise to notes on the young musician and his "left-wing associations" in a folder at the Federal Bureau of Investigation.

After graduation Leonard spent the summer in New York, where he lived with Adolph Green at 61 East Ninth Street. He looked unsuccessfully for work, composing at night while Green was off performing at the Village Vanguard with his five-member comedy group, the Revuers, which also included Betty Comden and Judy Holliday. Comden never forgot the night Green brought Leonard to the club and how much he loved their show. After the act he went to the piano and proceeded to play for them all until six in the morning, everything from Bach and Buxtehude to the "Honky Tonk Train Blues." He seemed to know every song ever written, lyrics included, and it wasn't long before he had memorized the Revuers' entire repertoire too. In 1938 he played the piano in their musical satire of Hollywood, "The Girl with Two Left Feet," and in June 1940 he performed with them on NBC television, with Aaron Copland (unbilled) turning pages. Years later, as Comden wrote, if they forgot an old lyric, they would call Leonard and he would immediately sing the entire song for them.

By August 29 he had completed a setting, in Hebrew, of words from the Lamentations of Jeremiah for mezzo-soprano and orchestra, and had also written out his expert solo piano transcription of *El salón México*, a labor of love that Copland thought Boosey & Hawkes might be interested in publishing. The publishers took the arrangement, paying Bernstein $25 for it. It was his first publication. Copland considered the Hebrew lament to be Leonard's best work so far, particularly the outer sections. He found the middle "less spontaneous and stiff in the joints." He cautioned his young friend on the "romanticism" of his idiom: "somehow, someday," Copland admonished him, "that richness of feeling which I call romantic will have to be metamorphosed so that it comes out more new-sounding, more fresh." Copland identified a Hebraic strain in Bernstein's music but may not have recognized that this very quality distinguished Bernstein's gift from his own. It was the same ardent intensity that he later brought to his conducting. In an interview with Vivian Perlis forty years later, Copland admitted that in the beginning he perhaps "didn't take [Bernstein] very seriously as a composer, because he could do everything, and that was just one more thing Lenny could do."[16]

In late July, with Copland and others now recommending that he seriously pursue conducting, Leonard auditioned for Fritz Reiner at the Curtis Institute of Music in Philadelphia, armed with endorsements from Copland and Mitropoulos but suffering from an acute case of hay fever.[17] When quizzed by the renowned Hungarian maestro (who was conductor of the Pittsburgh Symphony Orchestra at the time), he fortunately recognized that the score he was asked to sight-read was the Brahms *Academic Festival Overture*—not because he knew the entire work, but because an old school song he'd learned had made use of one of its melodies. Dimitri Mitropoulos sent Leonard the extra financial support he needed—$75 a month for living expenses—to take advantage of the scholarship he received from Curtis, and in the fall Leonard moved to Philadelphia.

# 4

## *Curtis, Tanglewood, Boston, and New York*
## *Fall 1939–1942*

At Curtis, Leonard was plunged into a professional musical world that was in stark contrast to the broadly intellectual environment he was accustomed to at Harvard. He took orchestration with Randall Thompson and conducting with Fritz Reiner. Turned down for piano studies with Rudolf Serkin, he was assigned instead to the redoubtable Isabelle Vengerova.

Bernstein was extraordinarily fortunate to encounter three utterly different conducting styles as a student. Where his principal future mentor Serge Koussevitzky, soon to be encountered at Tanglewood, would be inspirational and expansive, a conductor of warmth, flexibility, and large gestures, who emphasized what he called music's "internal rhythm," Reiner, a far sterner personality, was the epitome of discipline and control, managing to convey all the musical power he needed to with a tiny beat pattern and an impassive facial expression. From Reiner Leonard learned once and for all, if he needed to, that one could not stand in front of an orchestra unless, at the very least, one had internalized every last detail of the score one was conducting. Leonard was also deeply marked by his encounter with the saintly, lonely Mitropoulos, a man who emanated humility in person but was extraordinarily impassioned on the podium, even more extravagant in his conducting style than Koussevitzky, and an early advocate for Gustav Mahler, who would become such a central figure in Bernstein's world.[1]

Isabelle Vengerova had a similarly transformative effect on Leonard's pianism. She was born in Minsk and, like Heinrich Gebhard, had studied in Vienna with Theodor Leschetizky, who had himself studied with Beethoven's celebrated pupil Carl Czerny. Her piano lineage was thus impeccable.[2] Bernstein dubbed Vengerova "Tyranna," and the name stuck, because she was indeed a terrifying figure, as much for the relentless psychological torture that could characterize her lessons as for her uncompromising attention to detail and devotion to the composer's markings. She believed that one had to be "200 percent prepared" for a performance, since one was destined to lose 100 percent of it onstage. Certainly no one dreamed of being unprepared for a Vengerova lesson, since she seemed able to tell from only a few notes not only how many hours you had practiced, but even, it was rumored, on which days of the week. While she sometimes taught through "intimidation, fear, and personality destruction," in the words of one student, she was a great pedagogue of the piano and was fiercely devoted to her students.[3] She had an ability to inculcate a beautiful legato; she paid a rare degree of attention to the physical distinction between playing on black keys and white keys ("One plays on two levels") and to matters of pedaling, balance, and dynamics.[4] She taught Leonard how to hear himself.[5]

Renée Longy-Miquelle was his teacher in score reading, a task at which he was a spectacular natural. The two also had a brief romantic liaison, despite the age gap. (She was forty-four, and he was twenty-two.) He studied orchestration with Randall Thompson, whose Second Symphony would later figure in his repertoire, and counterpoint with Richard Stöhr. Stöhr was a middle-aged refugee from Vienna, who had known Mahler and Korngold and had once had a flourishing career.[6] Having previously studied counterpoint with Walter Piston, Leonard gave him a hard time at first but ended up as his friend and later co-taught the class with him. (Stöhr lost his job when the theory department was downsized years later, and Bernstein sent him $500 a month for the rest of his life.)

Bernstein's talent and brash self-confidence incurred enmity from some of his classmates, to the extent that another conducting student reputedly purchased a gun and told Thompson that he was going to shoot Bernstein, Reiner, and Thompson, too. After this rival was escorted away, tensions apparently eased between Leonard and his fellow students.

Before the year was out, Leonard had conducted both the *Tannhäuser* overture and Brahms Third Symphony. But for a few months, his plans for the following year were thrown into disarray when Dimitri Mitropoulos proposed that Leonard join him the following year in Minneapolis as pianist for the orchestra and apprentice assistant conductor. By mid-April an apologetic Mitropoulos had written Leonard that the plan had turned out to be impractical, and that he should return to Curtis for his final year after all. Meanwhile, in March, Copland wrote Koussevitzky's secretary urging the conductor to admit Leonard as a summer conducting student at the newly formed Berkshire Music Center: "I have seldom met his equal for sheer musicianship. His musical memory is remarkable, and so is his ability to sight-read both scores and piano music. He is besides a first-rate pianist. . . . Randall Thompson told me that Mr. Reiner considered Bernstein one of the best students he had ever had."[7] Later that month, Leonard met with Koussevitzky in Boston and was instantly accepted into his summer class.

In the spring of 1940, thanks to Thompson, Leonard's Four Studies for Two Clarinets, Two Bassoons, and Piano were included, almost apologetically, on a League of Composers broadcast from Philadelphia, alongside works by Samuel Barber, Vincent Persichetti, Oscar Levant, and others. (Bernstein was, of course, not a composition student.) Writing in *Modern Music*, composer Conlon Nancarrow singled it out as the most interesting of the works played.[8]

The summer of 1940 was the fulfillment of a dream Serge Koussevitzky had cherished even while still in Russia: the establishment of a music academy of international standing, with renowned musicians and composers on the faculty. Situated on the idyllic Tanglewood estate (named for the *Tanglewood Tales* Nathaniel Hawthorne had written while staying there), with its serene great lawn and giant oak and spruce trees, what had been a short summer festival of Boston Symphony Orchestra performances was now expanded to include a school, in which 312 students, many on scholarship, would study with a faculty that included Aaron Copland, Paul Hindemith, and Gregor Piatigorsky. As Koussevitzky's student at the Berkshire Music Center, Leonard once again found a champion and father figure who had much to teach him. For the older conductor it was the discovery of a surrogate son and potential successor at the very moment when his lifetime dream was finally being realized. In the first summer, Leonard was already conducting the Institute Orchestra of the Berkshire Music Center in works by Haydn, Brahms, Copland, and Gardner Read. He roomed with several friends: Harold Shapero, violinist (later violist) Raphael Hillyer from Harvard, and Lukas Foss from Curtis.[9] Copland and Hindemith were teaching composition, and it is noteworthy that Leonard never enrolled in either of their classes, as he similarly had avoided formal composition study at Harvard and Curtis. (Walter Piston once remarked that, as far as composition went, Bernstein seemed to just "have it" and didn't need to study.) Fortunately, during this period he had many opportunities to show Copland his music. Copland's focus was on Leonard's recognizing his own voice and discarding outmoded influences. "That's all warmed over Brahms or Scriabin," he would say, "but these two bars are you. Go back home and work on these two bars."[10] Such meetings, looking his music over with Copland during the first years of their friendship, constituted the only real lessons in composition he ever had, and they taught him about "taste, style, and consistency," as he later put it.

When the summer was over, Leonard nostalgically recalled the time he and Copland had spent together: "Not seeing you is something of a shock. . . . I've never felt about anyone before as I do about you, completely at ease, and always comforted by you. This is not a love letter, but I'm quite mad about you."[11] For his part, Copland's letters to Leonard convey a degree of warmth, abandon, and joy matched nowhere else in his correspondence, even while being tempered frequently, as the years went on, by practical, paternal advice and sometimes stern admonitions. The exchanges between the two show that they had briefly been lovers, but their enduring connection was on a far more essential level. Copland was among the sanest, shrewdest, most level-headed and generous of artists, and he would remain a lifelong source of common sense in Leonard's peripatetic life. He always took the long view. Even in his composing, he made it a habit to give compositions a "cooling-off period" before making final critical refinements in them. In one letter written right after news of the *Anschluss* had reached America in March 1938, he cautioned Leonard, "As for your general 'disappointment' in Art, Man, and Life I can only advise perspective, perspective and yet more perspective. This is only 1938. Man has a long time to go. Art is quite young. Life has its own dialectic. Aren't you always curious to see what tomorrow will bring?"[12] Over the years there were several shifts in their relationship, as Bernstein's fame grew and "mentorship" was left behind. But they remained close and profoundly affected the course of each other's lives.

The presence of Copland and Hindemith in the same environment, combined with Leonard's friendship with the young violinist Raphael Hillyer, who would later help found the Juilliard String Quartet and remain with it as violist for twenty-three years, apparently stimulated Leonard to compose his first fully integrated work. The Sonata for Violin and Piano, begun in 1939 and dedicated to Hillyer, fulfills the promise of the earlier Trio and Piano Sonata and leaves behind the youthful disjunctions of idiom the earlier pieces contained. The work owes at least as much to Hindemith's quartal harmonies, long lyrical lines, and lucid counterpoint as to Copland's bold Americanism, but it has its own voice: serious, lonely, honest, on the pastoral side.

The two-movement structure of the Violin Sonata capitalized on a faculty of Leonard's musical mind that was to mark many of his works: a penchant for variations, for musical forms that evolve forward in a straight line through continuity and change, rather than through development and return. Perhaps this associative thinking related to his gift for word games—anagrams, crossword puzzles, acrostics. It is noteworthy that two of the first pieces that had a galvanizing effect on him were Ravel's *Bolero* and Copland's Piano Variations, two obsessive works that mine a succinct musical idea in a succession of transformations.[13]

The Violin Sonata employs variation principles in a highly original way, concealed behind what seems like an unaffected stream of plaintive, lyrical invention, much of it in three-part counterpoint. The first movement could be described as a modified sonata form, with a compressed recapitulation in which the second theme returns before the first, making it a kind of palindrome.[14] The second movement is a long footnote to the first: four variations on its second theme, followed by two variations on its first theme. Variation four is arguably one of the most beautiful passages in all of Bernstein. He later used it, with some modifications, as the third variation in the "Seven Ages" movement of his *Age of Anxiety* Symphony.

The poignant Violin Sonata became overshadowed by the more outgoing Clarinet Sonata of 1942, and remained virtually unknown and unpublished until after the composer's death. One could argue that it was an equally strong work, and that young Leonard seriously underestimated it.

Back in Philadelphia, Leonard lived in a second-floor apartment above a grocery store, just down the street from the Delancey Pharmacy on South Twenty-Second and Pine Streets, which was a central gathering place for students at Curtis. Shirley Gabis, a sixteen-year-old pianist, used to see him there, and in the fall of 1940 he sat next to her at a concert and they soon began spending a great deal of time together. He was her first boyfriend, and they remained close for the next fifty years. (Gabis eventually married composer George Perle.) The young pair played the Hindemith Four-Hand Sonata together, and she found him "an incredible teacher, the way he sat there and labored with me over those pages. And I remember once when he sat down with my mother and analyzed a Beethoven Sonata for her . . . you knew he was a born teacher. He had an extraordinarily electrifying communicative gift. . . . He was a gorgeous young man, warm, charming, all embracing of the world. His extroversion was extreme. . . . I found myself always backing away slightly from that aspect of him. No one at Curtis had ever seen anyone like him. There were camps—there were people who were for Lenny and there were people who couldn't stand Lenny. The ones who loved him were in love with him, and the ones who didn't, hated him." Yet Leonard's detractors often ended up on his side. For all his air of knowing more than everyone else—and of being a literate Harvard student and not just a "pianimal"—he was not someone Gabis saw as being self-centered. On the contrary, he had an unmatched ability to take in other people and to understand them. "When you were with Lenny, it was as if he saw right into you" she said. "He would listen, and he knew what you were—he was very smart that way, very intuitive. He almost understood you better than you understood yourself in some way that was quite uncanny." He may have had passionate impulses toward anyone of either sex that he was drawn to, but his homosexual side tormented him. According to Gabis, "he was still torn," not yet the openly "omnisexual" person of later years. He told Gabis: "I have a canker in my soul."

Gabis's mother, Rae, ran a beauty salon. One day Samuel Bernstein visited her and ended up discussing his son's life. He said to her, "What does he have to go and be a musician for? If he worked for me, I could pay him $100 a week."[15]

In his final year at Curtis, Leonard was an active pianist and conductor. Among other things, he performed the Scriabin Fifth Sonata and the Stravinsky Concerto for Two Pianos (with Annette Elkanova, to whom he may also have proposed), and conducted the Brahms Serenade No. 2 in A Major. He received his diploma in the spring, with As in orchestration and form, an A+ in piano from Vengerova, and the only A that Fritz Reiner ever accorded a student in conducting.

Before returning to the Berkshires, he appeared in Boston's Jordan Hall on May 26 as soloist with the Women's Symphony Orchestra conducted by Alexander Thiede, performing both Joseph Wagner's *Fugal Triptych* and Beethoven's Piano Concerto No. 1, op. 15. On June 11 he had the unexpected opportunity to conduct the Boston Pops in Wagner's *Die Meistersinger* overture in front of twenty-two thousand people at the Esplanade on the Charles River, where he acquitted himself very well.[16]

In his second summer at the Berkshire Music Festival, he

and Harold Shapero both went out with Kiki Speyer, a beautiful young woman who was the daughter of the English horn player at the Boston Symphony. Kiki was in love with Leonard, and the two even talked of marrying. But in the end he disappointed her, confessing his attraction to both women and men and saying that he didn't think he would ever marry. (He confided to some of his friends at the time that he found men even more beautiful than women.)

That summer he performed the piano in Copland's *Vitebsk* trio and conducted young William Schuman's *American Festival Overture* and Randall Thompson's Second Symphony. In the *Berkshire Eagle* he was described as talented and inspiring, "although unable to obtain complete hold on his players."

Before facing his unknown future, he took a train to Key West, Florida, where he was able to escape from his romantic entanglement with Kiki and, inspired by hearing Cuban bands over Radio Havana, wrote sketches in a Latin American style for a ballet he called *Conch Town*.[17] These sketches would later be put to use in *Fancy Free* and *West Side Story*. He also began working on a Sonata for Clarinet and Piano for his friend David Oppenheim.

Samuel was becoming grudgingly reconciled to his son's choice of career. He helped find him a studio in Boston at 295 Huntington Avenue, printing up business cards advertising lessons in piano and musical analysis. Unfortunately, Leonard set up shop on December 5, 1941, just two days before Pearl Harbor. (Leonard was of draft age but had received a deferment as a result of his asthma.) Few students materialized, and the following year was a frustrating one, although it included the premiere of his Sonata for Clarinet and Piano with clarinetist David Glazer at Boston's Institute of Modern Art. (Dedicatee Oppenheim played the New York premiere with Bernstein and recorded the work in 1943.)

The Clarinet Sonata is a luminous little piece that crystallizes Leonard's early forays into composition into ten minutes. It is outgoing compared with the Violin Sonata, due to the sonorousness and precision of the piano writing, the prioritizing of the melodic line in the clarinet, the relegation of counterpoint to a more textural and accompanimental function, the danceable, often motoric rhythms in the fast sections, and the gemlike clarity of the form. The first movement is probably the purest and most audible sonata form in Bernstein's output, with first and second themes that are instantly distinguishable (they could be described as "Hindemithian" and "Bernsteinian," respectively).[18] The pensive, heartfelt second-movement Andantino in 3/8 time introduces lively, deftly accompanied dance music in 5/8 that anticipates the Broadway Bernstein with its jaunty, songlike melody, to which words could easily be set.

The sonata is a model of balance that Nadia Boulanger would surely have admired. Copland found too much Hindemith in it. He jokingly warned his young friend that he wouldn't talk to him until he had written something that had "no Copland, no Hindemith, no Strav[insky], no Bloch, no Milhaud and no Bartok in it."[19]

After only a few compositional efforts, Leonard had developed the ability to settle on an idiom and vocabulary for a given work. While the Violin Sonata and the Clarinet Sonata are both refined and classically restrained works, the Violin Sonata speaks in an internalized, psychologically exploratory voice, and the Clarinet Sonata in a more sociable and genial one.[20]

Koussevitzky hoped that Leonard would eventually succeed him as conductor of the Boston Symphony, but he worried about the effect of his homosexual tendencies (which he called "pederastical"), and of his Jewish name, on his chances.[21] When, in his third summer at Tanglewood, Koussevitzky suggested to his protégé (now also his official assistant) that he change his name to "Leonard S. Burns," the young conductor told him he wouldn't do that, apparently saying, "I'll do it as Bernstein or not at all."[22]

With prospects for work in Boston grim, Leonard moved to New York in the fall of 1942, where he worked at the Harms-Wittmark publishing company and played the piano for dance classes. He expressed his frustrations to Harold Shapero in anguished postcards. At Harms his job was to transcribe tricky improvised solos from jazz recordings and to make piano versions (including four-hand and two-piano versions) of popular songs. These appeared under the pseudonym "Lenny Amber." (The word "Bernstein" means "amber" in German.) With his phenomenal ear he was ideally suited for the first task, and with his pianistic and compositional skills he was well-prepared for the second. Drudgery though it often was, the work drilled into him the structures, idioms, and notational norms of the American popular song tradition, preparing his imagination and technical skills for the many works he was to write that included popular songs or in which he evoked improvisation and jazz.

Koussevitzky had told him about a contest the New England Conservatory of Music was holding for American composers, which would award the first-prize winner the opportunity to conduct his or her work with the Boston Symphony. Koussevitzky himself was to be one of the judges. Leonard decided to orchestrate the Hebrew *Lamentation* he had written more than two years earlier and precede it with two movements for orchestra alone also inspired by the Book of Jeremiah, the first intensely dramatic and songful, evoking Jeremiah's "pleas to his People," and the second a kind of pagan dance, suggesting "the destruction and chaos brought about by . . . corruption within the priesthood and the people." The spread of the war and the news about the fate of Jews in Europe had given the text from Lamentations and indeed Jeremiah's entire prophecy a new relevance. This was the first of countless times that

Bernstein would build a major work by using materials drawn from his own earlier music. He decided that the three movements would be played together without pause, and that the pagan dance would lead directly into the last movement, with its mezzo-soprano soloist.

He was still in the middle of orchestrating the music for the third movement as the December 31 deadline for the score's submission neared. It took an entire team of musician friends plus his sister, Shirley—who came down from Mount Holyoke College—to help notate his pencil score into ink in the final three days of 1942, while he finished the orchestration. He had an asthma attack while rushing to complete the work.[23] With no time to mail it, he took it with him by train to Boston on the 31st and, completely exhausted, submitted it in person. After all this effort, it still lost the competition to Gardner Read's Second Symphony. Yet it was an enormous artistic leap forward, and it was one major work he never felt the need to revise, even when both his father and Fritz Reiner urged him to add an optimistic fourth movement after the poignant Lamentation.

The language of the *Jeremiah* Symphony brings to fruition a kind of full-throated lyricism hinted at in the opening of the youthful Piano Trio and in passages in both the Violin Sonata and the Clarinet Sonata. (In fact there are already fragments of the melody that opens the Symphony's first movement, in the first page of the Violin Sonata.) As much as the pagan dance, with its restless shifting meters, hemiolas, woodblock claps, and bass drum thwacks, builds on the kinetic side of Copland's *Appalachian Spring* and *Billy the Kid* (which in turn have their roots in Stravinsky's *Firebird* and *Petrushka*), the dance also has its own distinctly Hebraic tone. In the lyrical movements of *Jeremiah*, the melodic lines are longer and more vocal in character than Copland's are (closer in spirit to those of Leonard's friend and contemporary William Schuman) and are sometimes drawn directly from music sung in temple. As there are in later Bernstein works, there are abrupt stylistic shifts in the work that can be disconcerting. Listening now, there is no mistaking the future composer of *On the Town* and *Wonderful Town* in the infectiously lilting middle section of the Profanation movement, which also seems to derive from the earlier Clarinet Sonata. Here, in the midst of a symphony, as in the later *Age of Anxiety*, the idea of "profanation" seems to have led Bernstein as if by instinct to music evoking show business. And when the "Broadway" music is then joined by the French horn declaiming the prophecy from the first movement, one hears ancient Jerusalem in collision with 1940s New York. But the composer *was* living in 1940s New York, and if the music suggests a composer in collision with the prophets in his life, and divided within himself, this only adds to its heartfelt authenticity.

The vocal lament reflects Bernstein's own most direct, clear-cut musical self. It draws on his distinctive gift for both melody and harmony and, most important, like the limpid, plaintive counterpoint that begins his Violin Sonata, shows that he has the ability to be alone and to write what he hears when he is alone. It is beautiful and unaffected music. The notes are the right ones (Boulanger's "la note choisie"), and the final chord—like the last chord in *West Side Story* of fifteen years later—combines the main notes of the theme into the right harmony to rest on. Although it was certainly unusual to have a vocal soloist in a symphony, there were of course precedents for that in Beethoven's Ninth and in Mahler. What was more uncommon in concert music was the use of Hebrew for the text. Leonard, grandson of a rabbi, who had proudly kept his own family name, was here affirming his allegiance with grandfather Yudel Bernstein of Ukraine and his imperiled kin across Europe. He no doubt also hoped that the work would be meaningful to his father, and he dedicated it to him.

In the spring of 1943, Sam Bernstein sat behind Harold Shapero when Leonard performed the 1941 Copland Piano

Sonata, at that time his favorite of all of Copland's works, at an all-Copland concert presented by New York's Town Hall Music Forum. After the score's near mystical closing moments, the audience erupted in cheers. Sam tapped Shapero on the shoulder and said, "Fine, but where's the money?"

The year 1943 would change Bernstein's life and would change his father's perception of him too. In 1940 Samuel Bernstein had sat in Rae Gabis's parlor in Philadelphia, worrying about his son's future. Three years later he would famously defend his previous apprehensions to a reporter with the exclamation, "How could I know my son would grow up to be Leonard Bernstein?"

# Part II

# 5

## *Wonderful Times*
## *1943–1948*

In the summer of 1943 Bernstein was introduced by Koussevitzky to Jennie Tourel, a beautiful Russian-born mezzo-soprano of passionate temperament, who had become known for her performances of Carmen at the Paris Opéra-Comique and was scheduled to join the Metropolitan Opera in the fall.[1] Tourel was at least eight years older than he was (her year of birth is variously given as 1900 or 1910); she could sing in six languages, including Hebrew. The two became fast friends and gave a recital together in the Lenox, Massachusetts, Public Library on August 24, 1943, the eve of Bernstein's twenty-fifth birthday, adding as an encore a song cycle he had composed for her entitled *I Hate Music.* Apparently Koussevitzky disapproved of the songs, probably because he considered them too lightweight for Tourel. Tourel's manager also thought them unworthy of her, saying that they were "not art songs." Bernstein's original texts for the cycle's five songs express his identification with children, capturing their longing to understand life:

> I have lots of thoughts;
> like what's behind the sky; and what's behind what's behind
>     the sky:
> But everyone says,
> "Isn't she sweet? She wants to know everything!"

The lyrics for the title song imagine a child's mystified impression of classical music concerts:

> I hate music! . . .
> Music is a lot of men in a lot of tails,
> making lots of noise like a lot of females;
> Music is a lot of folks in a big dark hall,
> Where they really don't want to be at all . . .

The music for this unpretentious song cycle shows a gift for finding just the right intervals and harmonies to convey emotions, and an aptitude for making the flexible rhythms of American English sing. Bernstein exhibited the same wit, concision, and dramatic flair in a later cycle for Tourel, *La bonne cuisine*, settings of his own translations of recipes from a French cookbook, which are as light and enjoyable as a soufflé.

A touching succinctness informed a group of *Seven Anniversaries* he finished in 1943, the first in an ongoing series of twenty-nine such *Anniversaries* completed over the next forty-five years. Named for important people in his life, these short character pieces often served Bernstein as sketchbooks, furnishing the thematic materials for larger works. There is virtually no touch of Broadway in any of the twenty-nine pieces. They test a quiet, personal voice, shorn of pretense. Once tested, the ideas then surfaced in works as diverse as the *Serenade*, *Mass*, *Dybbuk*, and *A Quiet Place*, where they infused the music with a personal, confessional resonance. It was appropriate that they were portraits of family members, friends, and mentors, and not still lifes or pictures of clouds or hillsides. Bernstein may have been manifestly "full of himself," but he would have found no meaning in that fullness without constant interaction with others. He wasn't dissembling when he began his one-minute contribution to the radio series *This I Believe* with the words, "I believe in People. I feel, love, need, and respect people above all else." Conductor Marin Alsop, who studied with Bernstein in the late 1980s, once said of him that "he didn't look at people as a means to an end. He looked at people *as* the end."[2]

Of all the sets of *Anniversaries*, the first set may be the most significant from a personal point of view, in that it forms a portrait of the composer's world at the age of writing. There are his two crucial musical father figures, Copland and Koussevitzky, exemplifying his two principal musical pursuits—composing and conducting; his family, represented by his sister Shirley, female confidant and emotional anchor; his male peer group, represented by a piece written in memory of his Eliot House roommate Alfred Eisner, sadly dead of a brain tumor at twenty-two years old, and by another for his friend the optimistic and gifted young composer William Schuman; and his literary, theatrical, and, perhaps, sexual side represented by the multifaceted composer-writer Paul Bowles, a friend since their first encounter at Copland's loft.[3]

From these and other early works, one can see that a preoccupation with the details of performance was a lifelong compositional trait. For example, in Anniversary No. 6, a short adagio in mostly quarter-note motion dedicated to Koussevitzky, Bernstein carefully differentiates between four types of articulation. In seventeen measures there are fifteen different dynamic markings. There are three *sforzandos*, and two double *sforzandos*. At one point he gives a different increasing dynamic marking on each of five successive quarter notes, to distinguish it from a less precise, gradual crescendo. Such notations convey the future conductor's knowledge of the practical means needed to achieve a desired musical result.

A letter to David Diamond from 1940 illustrates Bernstein's frequently blunt way of expressing his opinions about details in the work of friends, which they didn't always appreciate. He had agreed to record Diamond's Prelude and Fugue No. 4 in C-sharp Minor for Henry Cowell's New Music Recordings (this was to be his first recording), but he had reservations about some of the fugue ("there are 'stains'; your second stretto, for instance") and also about the notation: "From my point of view there must be a dynamic growth—involving especially a drop to piano in the 17th measure, & a rise to the first climactic stretto, and possibly the same thing again (modified) before the second stretto." Miffed at first, Diamond ultimately made the suggested changes and later acknowledged that they had made the work "perfect."[4]

At the end of the summer, Bernstein was rescued from the prospect of another season of professional drift when he was invited to meet with the great conductor Artur Rodzinski at his farmhouse in Stockbridge, Massachusetts, and was offered a job as assistant conductor of the Philharmonic Society of New York (later the New York Philharmonic). Rodzinski may indeed have told him that "God said 'Take Bernstein,'" as has been frequently repeated, but in view of the earlier correspondence back and forth between the two men, the process was evidently not purely supernatural. In any event, by September, Bernstein was living in a studio room at Carnegie Hall, fulfilling his duties as assistant conductor, composing, and often getting a bite to eat at the Russian Tea Room on the same block.

One afternoon he had a visit from a young choreographer who was a soloist with Ballet Theatre, a company that performed at the Metropolitan Opera House and was known both for its Russian repertoire and its new works by Fokine, Tudor,

Massine, Bronislava Nijinska, and Agnes de Mille, all of whom worked directly with it. Jerome Robbins was only a month and a half younger than Bernstein. Like him, he was a first-generation American, born to Russian Polish immigrants. (His family name, Rabinowitz, means "son of a rabbi.") Although there were several ballroom dancers, acrobats, and vaudevillians in the family tree, his father, who ran a corset business in Weehawken, New Jersey, had been deeply antagonistic to his son's interest in being a dancer. Like Bernstein, Robbins had a sister, Sonia, to whom he was closer than he was to his parents. A child star at the age of four, she had been his first role model as a dancer.[5] Robbins had likewise followed her example in becoming a member of the (then legal) Communist Party in 1943, attracted to its promotion of minority rights and unemployment benefits and its opposition to Jim Crow and poll taxes. Robbins had been an extraordinarily artistic child—he played the piano and violin and composed; he painted pictures, wrote poetry, and played with a toy puppet theater. As a child, he later said, "art seemed like a tunnel to me. At the end of the tunnel, I could see light where the world opened up, waiting for me."[6] He had come to ballet late, after dropping out of New York University at nineteen, and started out under the wing of Gluck Sandor, the charismatic modern dance choreographer. In his early twenties he choreographed a number of small works, many on political themes, some for musicals. Like Bernstein he was driven by creative ambitions and also by the need to prove to his father that he could make a career out of his art.

When he knocked on Bernstein's door he was still living with his parents in Weehawken but had finally broken out of the chorus and had excelled in several solo roles, notably in Tudor's *Pillar of Fire* and *Romeo and Juliet* and in Fokine's *Bluebeard* and, apparently unforgettably, in the role of Petrushka.[7] The ballet project for which he needed a composer, his first opportunity to create a major work, had an entertaining premise: three sailors on shore leave for a day in New York who compete for the attentions of two girls and finally run off after a third. The scenario had been inspired by a Paul Cadmus painting, *The Fleet's In,* which had an implied homosexual subtext that Robbins would ignore. Like Bernstein, he was wrestling with a divided sexuality (he had had affairs with both women and men), about which he was deeply ashamed. (It needs to be remembered that in this era, while homosexuality was often accepted among artists, it was otherwise almost universally regarded as a mental illness and as a "problem" to be "solved.")

The composer and conductor practically started to work right then and there. Only that afternoon Bernstein had jotted down a lively theme on a paper napkin at the Russian Tea Room. When he played it for Robbins, the young choreographer shouted, "That's it, that's what I had in mind!" So began *Fancy Free* and perhaps Bernstein's most crucial creative partnership.

While work on the ballet proceeded, with Bernstein and Copland sometimes making four-hand recordings of the music to send to Robbins while he was on tour, Leonard continued to study all the scores that the principal and guest conductors at the Philharmonic were scheduled to conduct, to attend all rehearsals, and to theoretically be ready to step onstage to take over at a moment's notice, should the conductor of a program become indisposed. As far back as anyone at the Philharmonic could recall, however, no conductors had ever been sick. That fall he recorded his Sonata for Clarinet and Piano with clarinetist David Oppenheim, and otherwise things were quiet.[8] The main excitement was hearing the New York premiere of his song cycle *I Hate Music* at Jennie Tourel's New York recital debut at Town Hall on November 13. Leonard's parents and younger brother journeyed down from Boston for the occasion, and the audience response to the cycle was enthusiastic. Leonard returned home from the postconcert party for Tourel at four in the morning on Sunday, November 14, 1943. It was the date of Copland's birthday (and the date the two had first met at Anna Sokolow's concert).

Leonard was suddenly awakened, at 9 a.m., hung over, by a telephone call from the gruff-voiced Bruno Zirato, manager of the New York Philharmonic, saying, "Well, this is it; you are on for this afternoon." Guest conductor Bruno Walter had come down with influenza, and Rodzinski was out of town and unable to return to New York. Years later Bernstein remembered the rest of the day as segments with blank spaces between them. He remembered rushing over to the ailing Walter in his hotel room to look at Schumann's *Manfred* overture (named for Byron's dramatic poem), the contemporary work, Miklós Rózsa's *Theme, Variations and Finale*, Strauss's thirty-five-minute tone poem *Don Quixote*, which would open the second half, and Wagner's prelude from *Die Meistersinger*, which was to conclude the program. He had never rehearsed these works with the orchestra, and there wouldn't be time for a minute with them before the performance. Fortunately, he had been fascinated by the complex Strauss score and had painstakingly studied its intricacies and how they mirrored events in the Cervantes novel. Walter, dressed in his robe, coughing in between each point, helpfully went over beat patterns, tempo changes, tricky spots, and urgent cues.

After this Bernstein remembered wandering around in his one good suit (there was no way to get to his tuxedo hanging in the Carnegie Hall closet) and stopping at his local pharmacy, where he sat at the counter having several cups of coffee, telling the pharmacist that millions of people would soon be hearing his concert in a coast-to-coast broadcast. The pharmacist thought he looked anxious and drained, and gave him two pills that he should take five minutes before walking out onstage, saying, "One pill will quiet you, and the other will give you energy." Leonard remembered waiting in the wings backstage while the orchestra was tuning up, feeling the tension in the air as the gigantic Bruno Zirato came out to tell the audience that Bruno Walter was ill, and hearing a collective groan from the audience. He remembered taking the pills out of his suit pocket and flinging them across the Carnegie Hall backstage, walking out to the podium, and raising his arms for the three strong opening chords of the *Manfred* overture. He remembered how the sound of the chords had steadied his nerves and focused his mind on the music. He remembered that during intermission the principal violist and cellist had hurried into his dressing room to go over how he was going to handle certain passages in the Strauss.[9] But he didn't remember anything else of the concert until the end, when the entire audience and even the orchestra were on their feet, cheering.

In *Family Matters*, Burton later recalled what it was like to sit in the box seats that had been hastily arranged for the visiting family; how Jennie had clutched his knee and Samuel had sighed when their son walked onstage; how he had recognized *Die Meistersinger* from hearing his brother pound out its themes on the family piano; how in the intermission Leonard had a smile "so broad that it covered his whole face," and how at the end of the concert "the house roared like one giant animal in a zoo. It was the loudest human sound I had ever heard—thrilling and eerie."[10] Violinist Jacques Margolies later recalled the Schumann as "the most exciting *Manfred* overture I ever played in my life. . . . The idea was he'd follow us, but it didn't work out that way. You couldn't believe a young man could create that kind of music. . . ."[11]

The front page of the *New York Times* of November 15, 1943, carried the story, and there was even an editorial about it the next day ("The warm friendly triumph of it filled Carnegie Hall and spread far over the air waves"). There were also instant rumors that Sam Bernstein had bribed Bruno Walter to pretend to be sick so that his son could have a chance on the podium, a hint of the double-edged nature of fame that Bernstein would experience often in later years. Within the next two weeks, the young conductor was interviewed by *Life*, *Time*, *Newsweek*, *Pic*, *Look*, *Vogue*, *PM*, *Pix*, *Harper's Bazaar*, the *Times*, the *Herald Tribune*, the *Jewish Forward*, the *Jewish Telegraphic Agency*, *Jewish Day*, the *News*, the *Post*, and the *New Yorker*. He basked in the attention and talked so unguardedly to reporters —at one point referring to a newspaper chain as being run by "fascists"—that both of his parents cautioned him to be more circumspect. Jennie wrote him, "Lenny, dear, please don't tell reporters of your personal views. . . . It may have bad repercussions."[12]

As if unhinged by the presence of such a talented understudy waiting in the wings, a second Philharmonic conductor, Howard Barlow, fell ill on December 16, bringing Bernstein back to the podium to lead the orchestra in works by Brahms, Delius, and Beethoven. Virgil Thomson's review of this concert offered the opinion that "Bernstein's striking quality as a conductor is largely due to his rhythmic understanding. His enlightenment in this respect is superior to the contemporary great, save only Beecham."[13] Rodzinski himself became indisposed later in the season, and there were signs of his jealousy, culminating in a moment of anger when he turned on Bernstein and "grabbed him fiercely by the collar."

All the excitement surrounding the young musician did not guarantee a career, of course, and would have dissipated in a month had he not continued to prove himself. But in fact his conducting debut was only the beginning of an astonishing series of successes over the next year. He was invited by Fritz Reiner to conduct the premiere of his *Jeremiah* Symphony with the Pittsburgh Symphony Orchestra on January 28, 1944, and this was followed by his conducting the work with the Boston Symphony in February. The symphony so moved and excited audiences and critics that Rodzinski compensated for his flare-up in the fall and generously invited him to conduct another entire program with the Philharmonic in the spring, as long as it included the *Jeremiah*. In May it received the New York Critics Circle Award for best new work of the season.

Thomson's review of the *Jeremiah* held that "Bernstein orchestrates like a master but does not compose with either originality or much skill. His pieces lack contrapuntal coherence, melodic distinction, contrapuntal progress, harmonic logic, and concentration of thought."[14] Paul Bowles differed, thinking it outranked "every other symphonic product by an American composer . . . of the younger generation" and particularly drew attention to the last movement, with its "definite personal tenderness expressed in the simplest and most direct terms," as "the most moving of the three."[15]

In March Bernstein directed his first concerts outside the United States at Les concerts symphoniques de Montréal. That same spring, work on the ballet with Robbins went into high gear. Robbins was constantly observing how people walked and moved and chewed gum and gestured, and he folded these real-life details into the elegance of ballet steps.[16] Choreographically, he drew from the world he saw around him: the sailors on the street in Times Square, social dances such as the Lindy hop, shorty George, and boogie-woogie. He was also able to articulate exactly what he needed from the composer, from "mood and tempo" to the exact number of beats. Like Bernstein, he had traveled to Mexico and been drawn to the people and music he had encountered there. The composer was able to make wonderful use of material from his abandoned Cuban-inspired *Conch Town* ballet sketch for the "Mexican" solo Robbins wanted for his own character, a *danzón* that culminates in a blazing tutti orchestration redolent of the climax of Ravel's *Bolero*.[17]

The high-spirited score of *Fancy Free* is in nine sections linked by a few memorable recurring ideas: the joyfully swinging sailors' motive that starts the work; the lyrically descending melody after it, first played by the French horn; the sashaying, sexy music heard when the girls enter; the syncopated jazz figurations on the piano that echo it; and the hornpipe motive that follows. As he would in *On the Town*, Bernstein introduced the piece with a quiet musical prologue, the bluesy song "Big Stuff," heard on an onstage jukebox in the bar before the sailors enter. Written with Billie Holiday's voice in mind, and later recorded by her, "Big Stuff" was sung in its first performances by Shirley Bernstein.

The work's craft and satisfying structure (which hints at sonata form) are disguised behind a manner of carefree spontaneity. Within the first twenty measures of the orchestral opening, Bernstein creates an infectious rhythmic variety using only the opening sailors' idea, setting the pace for the inventiveness to follow. The tranquil Coplandesque music in the bar cunningly anticipates the theme of the *danzón*. The fourth section, a sensuous, stirring pas de deux, is a variation on "Big Stuff." The "competition scene," coming at the work's midpoint, is a development section in which the motives associated with both sexes are finally combined. This is followed by three character pieces for the sailors: a manic, Satie-esque "Galop"; a blues-tinged waltz in unevenly shifting meters of 3/4, 3/8, and 4/4; and the Latin *danzón*. Bernstein manages to insert variations on the lyrically descending horn theme in all three of them.

The premiere of *Fancy Free* was given on April 18, 1944, at the old Metropolitan Opera House at Thirty-Ninth Street and Broadway, with the composer conducting. There were twenty-four curtain calls. Robbins was so stunned by the response that Agnes de Mille had to cradle him in her arms backstage. The ballet received a rapturous reception in the press and was such a success that it was in demand wherever the company toured and became a kind of signature work for it.

Robbins proved to be the catalyst Bernstein needed to

move from the realm he had occupied in his early chamber works and his first symphony into the world of theater for which he had such an aptitude. One of the parallels between the two young artists was their shared immersion in both the popular and classical realms, and their ability to bring equal seriousness to both. And it was their collaboration on *Fancy Free* that was, in the words of Bernstein's daughter, Jamie, the "bridge" that allowed him "to go from Symphony to Broadway stage." That the score came to epitomize New York for many people is confirmed by its use as the music heard issuing from the window of the young ballet dancer, "Miss Torso," working on her routine in Hitchcock's film *Rear Window*.

Set designer Oliver Smith, who was also a producer, suggested that a Broadway musical could be developed out of the concept behind the ballet. Both Bernstein and Robbins were at first reluctant but then agreed to do it. Bernstein suggested that Betty Comden and Adolph Green could draft the book and lyrics. Hitherto completely untested in such capacities, the duo were currently performing at the Blue Angel on Fifty-Fifth Street, having unsuccessfully taken their nightclub act to Hollywood. As it turned out, the assignment transformed their lives.[18] Robbins and Bernstein were twenty-six years old; Comden was twenty-five; Green was turning thirty. The electricity generated between Robbins and Bernstein now went four ways, helping to carry Bernstein across what might have otherwise been an intimidating aesthetic divide.

Comden later described their work process as "spontaneous combustion." As she put it, it was "as if some bomb planted in a marble quarry had exploded and, as we all closed our eyes and plugged our ears, a million pieces had miraculously fallen together to form Michelangelo's 'David.'" None of them had previous experience working on Broadway, and therefore defying musical theater conventions came naturally. Yet they were also courageous—creatively and socially. *On the Town* was the first racially integrated musical on Broadway, and it even starred a Japanese American, Sono Osato, during the very period when the United States was at war with Japan, as the "all-American girl," Miss Turnstiles. The show also celebrated the modern American woman. The three sailors in *Fancy Free* had had to fight over two available women, but in *On the Town* there are three female leads, all of them confident, employed, and sexually bold. Comden and Green wrote central parts for themselves: Green was the debonair sailor Ozzie; Comden played the anthropologist Claire de Loone. And Bernstein's sister, Shirley, having made her professional debut as the voice on the radio at the start of *Fancy Free*, was in the chorus. She stayed with the musical until 1946, eventually with a speaking role.

Other than the three sailors on leave, there is no overlap between *Fancy Free* and *On the Town*, either in story or in the music. There were long ballet sequences—thirty minutes of dance in all. In rehearsals, choreographer Robbins alternated between being lovably fun and being a tyrant who was sadistically critical of particular cast members. Facing problems during the Boston previews, he panicked and disappeared for two days. It was Oliver Smith who convinced director George Abbott to wait before finding another choreographer.

The breakthrough Bernstein made in composing *Fancy Free*—in which he had let loose the balletic potential of his rhythms and achieved a superbly successful overall form out of episodic sections—continued in *On the Town*, which moved seamlessly between musical comedy songs and elaborate ballet numbers that bring bitonality, polyrhythms out of Stravinsky, and canonic imitations at different speeds into a Broadway context. As he did later in *West Side Story*, Bernstein found a way to speak in his own accent, building on precedents in Gershwin, Copland, and Stravinsky's *Petrushka*, *Le Sacre du Print-*

*emps*, and *L'Histoire du soldat*, which he had been studying since his undergraduate years. The score has a huge range of musical reference points: from ballet and symphonic music (the eleven-minute overture, the dance interludes "Times Square" and "The Imaginary Coney Island"); to the musical cubism of Satie, Milhaud, and Les Six; to nightclub rhythms (the rumba "Ya Got Me"), vaudeville (the topical review song "I Can Cook Too"), and big-band jazz.[19]

The show gave Bernstein a chance to contribute to the "American songbook" he knew so well. In his hands, upbeat comic numbers such as "I Can Cook Too" are no less sophisticated than serious ballads such as "Lonely Town," which, with its uneven phrase lengths, harmonic ambiguity, and soaring melodic shape, has the emotional depth of an aria. As Sir Arthur Sullivan had done in *Pirates of Penzance*, Bernstein could also create parodies of opera ("Carried Away" in this show) that were all the funnier for being excellent, genuinely operatic music. He could bring an unparalleled harmonic variety to songs that still sound plausible as sung by the show's "everyday" characters (as in the modulations that give "New York, New York" its air of excitement). He could write a hilarious blues parody ("I'm Blue"), in the middle of the nightclub sequence, that is both wonderfully funny and strikingly original.[20]

In some cases, as with "Come Up to My Place," Comden and Green handed Bernstein a complete lyric and he set it to music.[21] Sometimes they created lyrics alongside him. At still other times, they looked through music he had already composed, found songs they particularly liked, looked for places where these could be fit into the show, and then wrote lyrics for them. This happened with "Lucky to Be Me" and the poignant "Lonely Town," where their collaborative alchemy achieved perfection.[22] In the latter instances, Comden recalled later, "We tentatively, nervously showed him these, and he was sort of taken aback." Then, after a pause, "he would say, 'Gee, that's really good.'"[23]

The extended dance episodes allowed Bernstein's penchant for variations free rein (for example, there are seven character variations on the waltz-like "Miss Turnstiles" song in the ballet that follows it, corresponding to the series of male types Miss Turnstiles courts); he also used them to develop motives from the songs, giving the score an almost symphonic unity.[24] He also didn't hesitate to draw from his old chamber music. The scherzo from his undergraduate Piano Trio for Mildred Spiegel makes an appearance in the brief interlude between "Lonely Town" and the pas de deux based on it.[25]

Fifty-seven-year-old director George Abbott, whose previous productions had included, among others, *On Your Toes* in 1936, choreographed by George Balanchine, and *Pal Joey* in 1940, choreographed by Gene Kelly, both of which had scores by Richard Rodgers, left Bernstein's complex dance music alone. He just kidded him about it, calling it "that Prokaaaafieff stuff."[26]

The combination of the show's youthful energy, the refinement and range of its music, and the harsh reality it gracefully incorporated made for something original and affecting. In December 1944 the war was at its height, and although the Allies were winning, a positive outcome was not assured. Sailors on shore leave for one day faced trauma, maiming, or death when they returned to the front. Betty Comden's own husband was in combat at the time. The underlying poignancy of the work surfaces especially in the tenderly understated song at the day's end, "Some Other Time."

*On the Town* opened December 28, 1944, at the little Adelphi Theatre and was such a hit that it was moved to the 44th Street Theatre and then the Martin Beck, running for a total of 463 performances. Robbins, now a success in ballet and on Broadway, was soon writing in the *New York Times Maga-*

*zine* about his vision of a form of musical theater that would combine all the arts into a completely integrated, thoroughly American work.

In the wake of Bernstein's spectacular conducting triumph with the Philharmonic, he was now in demand as a guest conductor all over the country. Gunther Schuller, soon to be a famed composer, conductor, and music scholar himself, was in the first horn chair at the Cincinnati Symphony when Bernstein filled in for Eugene Goossens, in November 1944, conducting a program that included Stravinsky's *Firebird.* He noted Bernstein's physical gifts and musical dynamism: "We were all bowled over by Bernstein's conductorial talent, especially the lightninglike almost explosive physical energy, his ability to abandon himself totally to the music and yet not lose technical control. . . . What I noticed particularly was the suppleness of Bernstein's hands; it was as if he had ball bearings in his wrists that enabled him to bend, flex, rotate them at will—a remarkable gift, that I believe . . . was unique to him."[27]

In March 1945 Bernstein wrote Helen Coates a humorous poem about his struggle to find ideas for a choral setting commissioned by the cantor of the Park Avenue Synagogue in Manhattan.[28] *Hashkiveinu,* a five-minute work for tenor, choir, and organ, performed two months later, was the result, the composer's only work written for use in synagogues. The Hebrew Sabbath prayer expresses a hope for peace in the outer sections and speaks of warding off threats in the middle one. Bernstein scholar Jack Gottlieb has written of the music's perfectly symmetrical arch form, and of the tranquility generated by organ pedal points occurring in the outer sections. At the arch's center, the mode and tempo shift and the music becomes more animated, evoking the terrors of the world with folk fragments reminiscent of Stravinsky's *Les Noces.* As peace is restored, and the cantor's slow tenor line enters over the mellifluous Phrygian canons in the choral parts, the listener can imagine what the young Bernstein must have felt, hearing the devotional singing in Roxbury's Temple Mishkan Tefila.

In May Bernstein made extensive sketches for a setting of words from W. H. Auden's poem *For the Time Being*, a sixty-page "Christmas oratorio" in verse written during the war, that with its choruses of angels, recitatives, wise men, and shepherds, was tailor-made for music. He wrote the title "Songs of Fear" on the cover page but soon abandoned the effort. He would return to Auden for inspiration a few years later.

Bernstein led fourteen different American orchestras in 1945. Everywhere he went he chatted with members of the press in the green room, playing the piano (everything from Haydn to the "Weeping Willow Blues"), and in almost every respect behaving with an informality and expansiveness that was the polar opposite of what people had come to expect a classical music conductor to be like. Feeling pressured by his mentor Koussevitzky's disapproval of his excursion onto Broadway, he swore off further involvements in show business. "I've done that now," he said in St. Louis. "I like to do everything once, just to see what it feels like."[29]

He was ready to direct an entire concert season of his own and to develop a relationship with one ensemble, and an opportunity to do so came at the end of the 1945 season, when Leopold Stokowski resigned his position as director of the New York City Symphony to become conductor at the Hollywood Bowl. Koussevitzky wrote Mayor La Guardia suggesting that his protégé would be the perfect person for the job, and Bernstein received the offer on his twenty-seventh birthday. The orchestra played its concerts in the City Center (formerly the Shriners' Mecca Temple), also home to George Balanchine's New York City Ballet.

Posters for the first season of the New York City Symphony featured a striking photo of a casual-looking Bernstein and promised "Vital Music old and new—superbly performed under a stimulating young conductor." Programs included many premieres and unusual works, including Blitzstein's *Airborne Symphony* (narrated by Orson Welles), Carlos Chávez's *Sinfonía india*, Stravinsky's *Symphony of Psalms*, Hindemith's *Concert Music for Strings and Brass*, and Bartók's Violin Concerto No. 1. Bernstein also led Mitropoulos's string orchestra version of Beethoven's String Quartet No. 14 in C-sharp Minor, op. 131. In the *New York Herald Tribune*, Virgil Thomson had high praise for Bernstein's innovative programming, while offering cautionary words about his extravagant podium manner.

After a performance of the Brahms Piano Concerto No. 1 in D Minor on February 5, 1946, in which Chilean pianist Claudio Arrau was soloist, the conductor attended a party at Arrau's house in Queens. There he met an elegant, intelligent, and beautiful young actress, Felicia Montealegre, who had grown up in Chile and was currently studying piano with Arrau. Although deeply interested in music and literature, she considered acting her true vocation and, unbeknownst to her parents, was honing her skills at the Herbert Berghof Studio at the New School. The previous summer she had appeared in Federico García Lorca's play *If Five Years Pass* at the Provincetown Playhouse in Greenwich Village.

Born Felicia Montealegre Cohn in Costa Rica, to an American Jewish father and Chilean Catholic mother, she was four years younger than Bernstein. She had grown up Catholic in a privileged environment (her father, the grandson of a rabbi, was the president of the American Smelting and Refining Company in Chile). Bilingual and with dual citizenship, she had made the choice at twenty-one to become an American citizen. With her finely shaped nose, delicate features, and dignified but animated personality, she could perhaps almost have passed for a Bernstein sibling, were it not for her Spanish accent. Yet she also had an aristocratic reserve that was not a characteristic Bernstein trait.

According to those who attended the party, Leonard and Felicia were instantly smitten and sat together on a sofa talking animatedly. It was rumored that Felicia had already fallen for Bernstein while watching him conduct and had determined to marry him. All indications are that they went home together that night and were together the next morning, February 6, which was Felicia's twenty-fourth birthday. But then Bernstein was off to San Francisco, then Vancouver, and on to Czechoslovakia and England, where he played the Ravel Piano Concerto in G Major, tabling the romance for the time being. In letters to Helen Coates, Leonard's attentions appear to have instantly turned to someone named Seymour.

In the summer of 1946 at Tanglewood, Bernstein finally got to meet composer Benjamin Britten, whom he greatly admired, in the context of conducting the American premiere of his opera *Peter Grimes*. Although the performance suffered from being performed by students, it left a deep impression on Koussevitzky, on Bernstein himself, and on many in the audience. In his very last concert, forty-five years later, Bernstein would conduct the Four Sea Interludes from the work. But at this time, in spite of being on good enough terms to have dinner together twice a week, the older and younger composer were somewhat cool to each other. Bernstein was apparently disturbed when Britten invited Leonard's younger brother, Burton, then fourteen, to sit on his knee backstage. While Britten was in a monogamous relationship with tenor Peter Pears, he plainly enjoyed the proximity of all the young men at the festival. Perhaps the connection between the two musicians had not gotten off to the best start. When he was still at Curtis, Bernstein, then just twenty-three, had written Britten a letter praising his new *Sinfonia da Requiem*, describing the work as Britten's "best so far." To this the English composer had answered "maybe there is something in what you say," but that in terms of perceived flaws in previous works, "maybe those particular vices are less vicious than some others I can think of—such as inhibitions, sterility, self-conscious ideas of originality."[30] At the cast party after *Peter Grimes*, where he played boogie-woogie, Bernstein got to speak with the living poet whose work he most revered: W. H. Auden. Auden was in fact in the midst of writing the poem *The Age of Anxiety*, which Bernstein would later use as the basis for his Second Symphony.

On the heels of the production of *Peter Grimes*, Jerome Robbins arrived at Tanglewood to sketch out a scenario with Bernstein for a new ballet that would need to be completed within a month. The collaborators developed their scenario in five days, and Bernstein then spent the next three weeks, during which time he turned twenty-eight, composing the score. By September he had made a piano recording of the ballet for Robbins to work with in New York. *Facsimile* opened at the Ballet Theatre on October 24. The theme of the ballet was one that, as much as the search for faith, could be applied to many of Bernstein's large-scale works: the search for meaningful connection with others. The triangular relationship between two men and one woman was also one Bernstein could relate to from firsthand experience.[31] In a program note Bernstein described the dancers as "unintegrated personalities," "three lonely people —a woman and two men—who are desperately and vainly searching for real interpersonal relationships." He called the music "neurotic," "mirroring the neuroses of the characters involved." (Both Bernstein and Robbins were in psychoanalysis by this time.) The scenario resembles that of Vaslav Nijinsky's 1918 ballet *Jeux*, which had a luminous one-movement score by Claude Debussy.[32] The three young people who romantically tussle with each other on the beach in the Robbins/Bernstein work find, in Jack Gottlieb's words, "only a facsimile of companionship" and are left with a sense of emptiness; hence, the title. The work is full of interesting music but leaves a tenuous impression. Even though it is economical and rigorous in the way it develops a small cluster of musical ideas, it seems to lack a thematic and stylistic center. This is partly because its reference points in music other than Bernstein's own do not feel digested and internalized, as they do in most of his other works. (In *On the Town*'s "Lonely Town" pas de deux and "Imaginary Coney Island" pas de deux, for example, we may hear Gershwin, but it is still Bernstein's Gershwin.) The best passages in *Facsimile* are the slow sections derived from the first theme of the Violin Sonata of 1940. Otherwise, the eighteen-minute work echoes Copland and Stravinsky in short episodes that seem to skate on thin musical ice, lacking sufficient conviction to override a sense of impersonation.

*Facsimile* was also at the heart of a strained moment between Bernstein and his mentor Koussevitzky, sparked by a discussion between them about Bernstein's planned guest appearances with the Boston Symphony, in which the protégé had voiced his intention to program his new work. Koussevitzky's stern letter of December 26, 1946, echoes in a paternal way Rodzinski's discomfort with the young conductor's ambitiousness:

> Dec. 23, 1946
> Dear Leonard,
> My last talk over the telephone with you left a very disturbing impression. . . . Speaking of your programs you stubbornly insist on the performance of your own composition, even for broadcast. Do you realize that you are invited as a guest conductor, to show your capacities as interpreter of great musical works? May I ask you: do you think that your composition is worthy of the Boston Symphony Orchestra and the Boston Organization? Can it be placed on the same level as Beethoven, Schubert, Brahms, Stravinsky, Prokofieff, Bartok, or Copland? . . .

Bernstein quickly penned a contrite reply:

> Dear Serge Alexandrovich,
> I have been deeply grieved all day on account of your last letter. . . . And you know I am happy to play only what you suggest and approve in my Boston concerts. . . . Certainly I believe in my music, or else I would not have written it—not on a level with Beethoven and Bartok, naturally, but in its own smaller terms. . . . I have had a very difficult year trying to adjust myself to the conventions of my profession. The réclame means absolutely nothing to me . . . the whole desperate race with time would be worth nothing were it not for the magical joy of music itself.
> Forgive me . . .[33]

In September Bernstein had caught Felicia's final performance in Ben Hecht and Charles MacArthur's *Swan Song* on Broadway, and their romance had been rekindled. Late in December they announced engagement plans, to which his parents had very different responses. Jennie, alone in Brookline with Burton while Sam vacationed in Florida, questioned his choice: "I tell you dear that I'm not too happy about this affair of yours. Aside from the religious angle I still don't think she is the girl for you. You deserve someone better. Don't let that accent fool you."[34] Meanwhile Sam, writing from Florida, was overjoyed: "My dear Son, Your letter this morning came to me like a sunrise after a dark night. . . . It was the most wonderful news I dreamed of for a long time."[35] But over the course of the next several months, during which Felicia briefly pursued her prospects in Hollywood, while Leonard conducted in Boston, New York, Belgium, and Palestine, the momentum behind their plans dissipated, and by the end of 1947 they were called off.

Meanwhile, during his rise to prominence as a conductor and composer, Bernstein's FBI file had filled with references to his left-leaning affiliations. Such things as his support for organizations in opposition to Franco's Spain (which was now receiving the American support it had been denied in the Roosevelt era); his appearances at rallies and functions with Paul Robeson, Dashiell Hammett, Billie Holliday, Rockwell Kent, and Lena Horne; his membership in the Council on African Affairs, the National Negro Congress, and the National Council of American-Soviet Friendship—all put him at risk of scrutiny by the powerful House Un-American Activities Committee (HUAC) and to attacks by the anticommunist crusader Senator Joseph McCarthy. He had begun to feel the pressure. For example, in February 1946, when he was about to give a speech and performance at a Joint Anti-Fascist Refugee Committee dinner in San Francisco, he received a telegram from his manager Arthur Judson forbidding it and threatening him with breach of contract. Unbeknownst to him, his file was further augmented in December 1946 by a Musicians' Union informant's declaration that he was "a Communist." (He had not, in fact, ever joined the Communist Party.) Bernstein meanwhile lent his support to left-wing composer Hanns Eisler when he was threatened with deportation, and he conducted a concert of Eisler's music. He participated in a trip to Washington by delegates from the film and Broadway communities in support of the "Hollywood Ten" screenwriters who had opposed testifying before the House Un-American Activities Committee. Reassured by studio heads that they too planned to protest the intimidation and totalitarian tactics of HUAC and to call for its dissolution, he was aghast when Eric Johnston, president of the Motion Picture Association of America, reversed position and announced complete support for the committee's investigations into communism in Hollywood. (The members of the Hollywood Ten were subsequently cited for contempt of Congress and fired by the studios, and the Hollywood blacklist became official.)[36]

In April 1947 Bernstein, accompanied by his father and sister Shirley, had an emotional first visit to Palestine and his initial encounter with the Palestine Symphony Orchestra. At that time, Palestine was still a British protectorate with a population that was one-third Jewish. He arrived there in the middle of a tense conflict between rival Jewish groups, some pacific, others violent, seeking the formation of the independent Jewish state mandated by the 1917 Balfour Declaration. Bernstein had broadly humanitarian and pacifist inclinations but was also staunchly pro-Zionist. He bonded with the members of the orchestra, many of them survivors of the Nazi scourge, who had once been prominent instrumentalists in Germany, Poland, Austria, and Russia. His concert at the Edison Cinema in Tel Aviv consisted of his *Jeremiah* Symphony (dedicated to his father), the Ravel Piano Concerto, and Schumann's Second Symphony (also a favorite work of Sam Bernstein's). As they would later in Haifa, Jerusalem, and on a kibbutz in the Jezreel Valley, the audience responded with an overwhelming ovation and tears. With his ability to speak Hebrew, his affinity for the place and its people, and the passionate bond he had created with the members of the orchestra, Bernstein felt himself deeply at home.[37]

In May he was in Prague, conducting the first European performance of Copland's expansive Third Symphony. In a letter to his friend extolling the symphony's virtues, he wrote, "Sweetie, the end is a sin. You've got to change." Later he unilaterally inserted a cut in the finale, which he pronounced very effective. Though briefly offended by this unauthorized editing, Copland eventually did cut eight measures from the finale.

The 1947–48 season with the New York City Symphony was Bernstein's third and last with the orchestra. It was bookended by two memorable performances, the Mahler "Resurrection" Symphony, Bernstein's first performance of Mahler, and the premiere of the orchestral version of Marc Blitzstein's *The Cradle Will Rock.* The season also included all-Mozart and all-Stravinsky evenings.

In March 1948, when Bernstein received word that Charles Munch had been named music director of the Boston Symphony, he decided that he would accept the position of music director of the Palestine Symphony, beginning with a residency there in the fall of 1948. But it wasn't long before he questioned the wisdom of such a move and adjusted his role down to that of musical adviser. Nevertheless, an almost familial connection with the orchestra remained. He would conduct it frequently, without fee, for the rest of his life.

In the spring he toured Europe, appearing in Budapest, Milan, Vienna, and Munich. Having declined to conduct in Vienna the previous year, he now followed Yehudi Menuhin's lead in considering it an opportunity to perform as a Jewish musician in formerly Nazi territory. He was shocked by the destruction, starvation, and misery he saw on the ruined streets of Munich, and by the physical frailty and undernourishment of the orchestra members. His May 9 concert with the Bavarian State Orchestra elicited a frenzied response from his German and American audience, after which he was carried through the streets as a hero. The German papers called him a "Paganini of the Symphony" and praised his "astounding, demonic gifts." At a refugee camp he gave two concerts, conducting an orchestra of survivors of Dachau, now homeless, in which he accompanied Jewish soloists, and played *Rhapsody in Blue.* Five thousand refugees attended each concert.

He continued his European tour in Budapest, where the excitement generated by the first part of the broadcast orchestral concert made people rush to the hall from their radios to hear the final works live. Once again he was carried by happy crowds through the streets. In Paris his fingers "went dead," as they sometimes did, playing Beethoven's First Concerto on the air. In Vienna he was received with enormous audience enthusiasm but with open hostility from the Vienna Symphony (Wiener Symphoniker). In the middle of this Vienna trip, on

May 14, came news that the state of Israel was now an official reality. Yet this was immediately followed by a summer in which the new state came under siege from all sides. Bernstein made plans to return there in the fall, and in the meantime he organized a benefit for the Palestine Resistance Fund. Yet here his idealism collided with the complexities of Israel's internal political realities. The violent extremist group Irgun, led by Menachem Begin, was engaged in its own struggle with the moderate government of David Ben-Gurion. Unsure which Israel faction would benefit from the concert, several prominent participants, including his friend Jennie Tourel, withdrew from it.

In the summer of 1948, with the Boston Symphony awaiting a new composition for performance the following year, and a commission from Woody Herman's band also due, he was at Tanglewood teaching fifty-seven conducting students, performing the Mahler Second Symphony, and celebrating Koussevitzky's seventy-fourth birthday. After the season ended, he and his brother, Burton, accompanied Stephen Spender on a road trip to the D. H. Lawrence Ranch near Taos, New Mexico, where he worked on an out-of-tune piano on his new symphony, inspired by Auden's *Age of Anxiety.* From there they continued on to Sheridan, Wyoming, where they stayed at a cattle ranch run by a Tanglewood student's family, rode horses, and worked as ranch hands.

In September Bernstein arrived in war-torn Israel accompanied by Helen Coates, performing forty concerts in sixty days under terrifying conditions. Artillery explosions accompanied Beethoven's *Leonore* Overture No. 3 in his October 14 Jerusalem concert with the orchestra, now renamed the Israel Philharmonic. He played the piano at kibbutzim and for wounded soldiers at hospitals. He conducted Copland's Third Symphony. At Rehovot he was called offstage after the first movement of Beethoven's First Piano Concerto, to be alerted to the threat of an imminent air raid, and played the ensuing Adagio as if it were the last music he would ever hear. He took thirty-five volunteers from the orchestra with him from Jerusalem through the Negev Desert to the contested city of Beersheba, an active war zone, to play for troops and settlers in an amphitheater there. Thousands gathered to hear him play three piano concertos—Mozart's Concerto No. 15 in B-flat Major, K. 450, Beethoven's First, and Gershwin's *Rhapsody*—in such numbers that Egyptians viewing it from the air thought that it was a military maneuver. His last concert in Jerusalem consisted of Mahler's transcendent "Resurrection" Symphony.

While in Israel (where he was briefly in love with an Israeli army officer) he also composed the Dirge movement of his new symphony, orchestrated it, and presented it at a benefit in Tel Aviv. It wasn't until the following winter, at a time when he was already writing music for what would eventually become *West Side Story*, that he completed it. At that time he told Louis Biancolli of the *New York World-Telegram* that in a way he contained two personalities: "The composer, besides being independent, is an introspective person, with a strong inner life; his primary mode of activity is to stay at home and compose whenever he feels the impulse. The conductor . . . is an extrovert. He is dealing constantly with audiences, orchestras, critics . . . great numbers of people. . . . When you find yourself being both people, being . . . a born performer and a born creator, you discover that you are supporting two lives, psychologically speaking." He added, "I'm always just barely keeping up with myself."[38]

Those who had recognized his gifts early on—Helen Coates, David Prall, Dimitri Mitropoulos, Aaron Copland, Marc Blitzstein, and Serge Koussevitzky—would surely have agreed with this self-portrait.

# 6

## *Age of Anxiety*

W. H. AUDEN started writing his "Baroque eclogue," *The Age of Anxiety*, in July 1944, near the end of the war, when he was living in the United States. He was reading through the first six volumes of Arnold Toynbee's *A Study of History* at the time, along with Joyce's *Finnegans Wake*, both of which left their marks on the poem. In the summer of 1945, after a year on the faculty at Swarthmore, Auden visited Germany for three months under the auspices of the Morale Division of the U.S. Strategic Bombing Survey, with the mission to assess the physical and psychological impact of the allied bombing campaign against Germany. (Auden was fluent in German.) He was stunned by the wreckage of German cities he witnessed, and he also began to comprehend the unimaginable scale of the horror that had been visited upon European Jewry.

Upon his return from Europe, Auden became immersed in the study of Judaism, reading even such obscure kabbalistic mystical texts as the thirteenth-century *Book of Splendors* (the Zohar), with its listings of the ten "sefirot"—attributes of God associated with parts of the human body. He even pondered converting to Judaism.

In the spring of 1946, during a term when he was teaching at Bennington College, Auden, a lifelong homosexual, had his one serious romance with a woman. His experimental affair with Rhoda Jaffe, a Jewish woman who had worked for him as a secretary in New York and whose marriage had fallen apart, lasted a year and half. The relationship resolved something in Auden's understanding of his own sexuality: he no longer viewed his homosexuality as "a curse," as he had once deemed it, but as a voluntary choice. He also added Rhoda's name to the private list he kept of the crucial romantic relationships in his life.[1]

*The Age of Anxiety* also belongs to a period when Auden was influenced by Carl Jung, particularly by his 1921 book *Psychological Types* with its presentation of binary human categories (intuition/sensation; thinking/feeling). In the poem, four lonely "solitaries" (three men and one woman) meet during wartime in a Third Avenue bar. They appear to represent Jung's four human faculties: Malin is "thought"; Quant, "intuition": Emble, "sensation"; and Rosetta, "feeling." Rosetta is also a combined portrait of Auden and Rhoda Jaffe. She is Jewish, like Rhoda has worked as a buyer for a department store, and has, like Auden, a deep nostalgia for the English countryside. The four strangers spend a long night in conversation. Their quest for meaning and community leads them into a dream space of parallel meditations on the course of life ("The Seven Ages"), and into an even more abstract quest, in poetic form, for a lost Eden ("The Seven Stages"), which Auden based on the sefirot, transforming the ten attributes to seven and associating them with seven areas of the body. These reveries are interrupted by disembodied accounts of war from the radio.

The protagonists then take a taxi back to Rosetta's apartment in "a mood of discouragement," reflecting that neither nature nor humankind could have survived long without "some semi-divine stranger" coming to their aid from time to time as rescuer. In the taxi, mourning the death of this mythical hero, "Our lost dad, / Our colossal father," they chant a dirge in one voice ("Sob, heavy world, / Sob as you spin").

Once at Rosetta's apartment, they are determined to "banish such gloomy reflections." At this "masque," they again drink, sing off-color songs, dance, and continue their philosophical musings. Dancing together, Emble and Rosetta kindle romantic feelings; a kind of mock wedding ceremony is enacted. Malin and Quant tactfully depart. But the romance is not consummated: Rosetta finds Emble passed out on her bed. In the end the four go their separate ways, seemingly as alone as before. Yet after failing to recover the mythical Eden they felt they had lost, realizing that no semi-divine hero will come to their rescue, and that romance is transitory, the Christian Malin and the Jewish Rosetta discover, beneath the emptiness, something like faith. Overcoming the anxiety of their disconnectedness, they feel the presence of God's watchfulness, in an Epilogue that echoes Psalm 139:

> In our anguish we struggle
> To elude Him, to lie to Him, yet His love observes
> His appalling promise . . .
> Minding our meanings, our least matter dear to Him
> (Malin)

> Though I fly to Wall Street
> Or Publisher's Row, or pass out, or
> Submerge in music, or marry well,
> Marooned on riches, He'll be right there
> With His eye upon me
> (Rosetta)

Auden scholars believe that Rosetta's speech immediately preceding this Epilogue is the first explicit poetic reference in English to the Holocaust:

> . . . for we are His Chosen,  
> His ragged remnant with our ripe flesh  
> And our hats on, sent out of the room  
> . . . time-tormented  
> But His People still.

Her words culminate in the traditional Hebrew:

> Sh'ma' Yisra'el.  
> Adonai eloheinu, Adonai echad.
>
> [Hear O Israel,  
> The Lord our God, the Lord is One!]

Despite its length and daunting complexity, *The Age of Anxiety* became celebrated almost immediately upon its publication. Auden was featured in *Time* magazine, and the poem won the Pulitzer Prize for poetry in 1948. The title itself seemed to capture the postwar mood. Auden's "anxiety" was not primarily psychological but rather existential. He was concerned with modern humanity's loss of faith and the quickness with which the horrors of war could be forgotten.

As a devotee of poetry and of language, Bernstein was surely drawn to the alliterations, metrical ingenuity, and lyrical beauty of Auden's text, could identify with those eclectic sections that employed vernacular verse forms and suggestions of popular songs, and must have been moved by its reflections on war and its allusions to the Jewish faith. But he could hardly evoke such a complex text in detail.[2] Instead he theatricalized Auden's work and remade it in his own image.

Yet Bernstein's work is also emotionally and structurally modeled on Auden's to a remarkable degree. Whether or not

Bernstein knew of Auden's interest in Jung, he seems to have intuited that the characters could be seen as four aspects of one self. The solo piano part (the symphony is a piano concerto in all but name) could be seen as representing a melding of the four protagonists. Surely he also intended the symphony as a sequel to his first, in which the loss of faith was a central concern. Looked at this way, his Masque could be viewed as a kind of jazzy version of the Profanation movement in the *Jeremiah* Symphony, and the Dirge as its instrumental Lamentation.[3]

Having broken off his engagement to Felicia, Bernstein was also still seeking to understand his conflicted sexuality. While his homosexual side may not have been public knowledge, his confessional temperament was surely at odds with concealing it. His works had always expressed the full range of his nature, sometimes in code. For example, in his *Four Anniversaries* of 1948 he placed portraits of Felicia Montealegre and Johnny Mehegan, two lovers from different sides of his romantic life, next to each other. In choosing Auden as a literary source, and later by choosing Plato's *Symposium* as a basis for his *Serenade*, he could express his own bisexuality artistically. In his program note for the work's Boston Symphony premiere, he explicitly related Auden to Plato by describing the protagonists' discussion in Auden's poem as "a symposium."

Another aspect of Bernstein's nature is suggested by the use of jazz materials in the Masque movement. Just as he incorporated techniques from the concert hall in *On the Town*, he now brought techniques from jam sessions and nightclubs into a symphonic work. But here he viewed them from the other side, deliberately using them as a foil, representations of frivolity, transience, and vanity. The Auden poem is full of references to mirrors. One of the most telling moments in Bernstein's work is the moment when a distant pianino echoes—mirrors—the jazz stylings of the solo pianist. (The pianino is a small upright piano with a tinny, barroom sound.) It is perhaps particularly relevant in this connection that the symphony was commissioned by Koussevitzky, who disapproved of Bernstein's work on Broadway.[4]

Bernstein's symphonic structure, like Auden's poetic one, takes the form of two large, symmetrical halves; Prologue–Seven Ages–Seven Stages; Dirge–Masque–Epilogue. For the Prologue Bernstein used a duet for muted violin and cello from his music for *The Birds*, now performed by two clarinets, to evoke the loneliness of the protagonists as they encounter each other in the bar. He had given this same music, transcribed as a piano piece, to Koussevitzky for his seventieth birthday. He then added an unusual descending scale in the flute, against ascending fourth chords in the low strings. After composing this section on the upright piano at the Lawrence Ranch in Taos, he had considered removing the scale, but his brother Burton particularly liked it. Burton wrote the word "KEEP" in capitals over the flute scale in the pencil sketch, and his older brother kept it.

After the Prologue, Auden's Seven Ages become seven variations in the symphony. But rather than being variations on the Prologue theme, they follow a "chain reaction" principle first noted by Bernstein's assistant (also a composer in his own right) Jack Gottlieb: each variation elaborates on an idea that was subsidiary in the previous one.[5]

The method evokes the characters' stream-of-consciousness monologues, while each variation individually could be seen to correlate to an "age" in the Auden. For example, the first variation introduces the piano solo in a reflective meditation on the clarinet duet, whose purity could suggest infancy. The descending scale figure that closed the original theme is now heard in the harp, and it is this which becomes the subject of a more propulsive second variation (childhood?). A secondary idea introduced here becomes the warmly melodic "third age" (adolescence?), which is a nearly exact replica of the fourth variation from the Violin Sonata, now orchestrated for strings and horns.[6] The "ages" continue through a seventh variation that closes with a gigantic version of the descending scale in the harp, starting in its upper reaches and reaching down to the lowest C, as winds ascend harmonically to a bright but hollow-sounding C-major triad, surely a depiction of death itself. At the corresponding point in the poem, Auden's words are:

> . . . there's a white silence
> Of antiseptics and instruments
> At both ends, but a babble between
> And a shame surely.[7]

The variations of the Seven Stages follow without pause. The first variation introduces a melody that becomes the explicit theme of the set. Here the variations evoke Auden's metaphorical travel through mental landscapes.[8] The tumultuous fourteenth variation suggests Rosetta and Emble's climactic lines:

> . . . Storm invades
> The Euclidean calm. The clouds explode.
> . . . Violent winds
> Tear us apart.
> Terror scatters us . . .

and ends on a powerful cadence, in which piano and orchestra pound out five minor triads in unison rhythm, ending once again in C major.

The beginning of the second half, Bernstein's eloquent Dirge, is the symphony's focal point, the vortex where many of its themes coalesce and merge, just as Auden's Dirge merges the four speakers into one poetic voice in the taxi. The Dirge alludes to twelve-tone music without using a twelve-tone row systematically, beginning with a series of rising pitches in the piano solo that are sustained into a twelve-note chord.[9] This is followed by static, ritualistic music in the woodwinds, above which the piano and piccolo outline a ten-note melody derived from the opening chord. The brooding music eventually leads to a terrifying orchestral tutti consisting of the opening twelve-note chord, now played *fortissimo*, in the unison rhythm of the ritualistic music, in dialogue with powerful offbeat timpani strokes.[10]

The Masque that mirrors Auden's party scene affords Bernstein a chance to exult in his dancelike vernacular mode, and the result is a spectacular set piece of rhythmic, melodic, and pianistic virtuosity that can stand alone as a kind of jazz scherzo, and has sometimes been performed independently. It is ironic that the Masque, meant as a study in frivolity and insincerity, has sometimes been viewed as the most convincing moment in the symphony.

Although mainly in 2/4 time, the Masque's rhythmic wit makes us confuse strong beats and syncopations. The piano's initial riff consists of a melody in duple meter over a "stride" accompaniment in 3/8 and in a different key. This is followed by an insistent syncopated figure that, as if improvised, completely defies rhythmic regularity. A kind of tickling motive in the right hand of the piano, doubled by the celesta, acts as a bridge passage to the Masque's most memorable tune, a bluesy melody in F major, based on a song eliminated from *On the Town* called "Ain't Got No Tears Left," which is the most traditionally tonal music in the symphony.[11] The two basic sections of the Masque alternate twice, each time glitteringly varied by the piano soloist. The orchestration has a bubbly champagne lightness: as the fleet-fingered piano part ripples through its jazz licks, it is accompanied by harp, celesta, glockenspiel, xylophone, double bass, timpani, and light percussion, with high-low wood blocks suggesting, with their "ticking clock" motive, the evanescence of the party's high spirits. (Bernstein observed that the four reiterated E-flats in the celesta could suggest a clock chiming 4 a.m.)

The Masque's coda evokes the evaporation of the festivities, as the offstage pianino sparkles with a distant mirror image of the gaiety, and a muted trumpet intones the solemn motto associated with the Epilogue. Nothing in the symphony projects the image of the brash, public Bernstein more vividly than the Masque movement. Consequently the end of the party communicates a very personal sense of solitude. The sound of the jazzy music vanishing into the distance suggests words from Quant's opening speech, as he regards himself in the mirror:

> My deuce, my double, my dear image,
> Is it lively there, that land of glass
> Where song is a grimace, sound logic
> A suite of gestures?

The Epilogue links the work with the *Jeremiah* Symphony. The descending four-note motive (A-flat–E-flat–D-flat–A-flat) that sounds distantly in the trumpet over the dying echoes of the Masque is a relative of the theme that opened the earlier work. (It is also the retrograde of the "New York, New York" tune.)[12] It is intended to represent, in Bernstein's words, "what is left beneath the emptiness," the acceptance of faith by Malin and Rosetta (Malin: "It is where we are wounded that is when He speaks / Our creaturely cry"). This "something pure" then combines with the theme of the Prologue, played by strings (and, in Bernstein's revised version, by the piano) along with the descending scale motive, now transformed into an ascending one. Jack Gottlieb sees this melody as a musical representation of the Hebrew tetragrammaton, which is translated as "Jehovah." He believes that the one-beat rest before the final unison chord refers to Rosetta's parting declaration "Adonai echad" (The Lord is One).[13]

But the "Jehovah" motive could also be connected to the theme of the third variation, and therefore all the way back to the Violin Sonata. It shares a key center (C-sharp) with the earlier theme, and three of its four initial pitches (G-sharp–D-sharp–C-sharp). One could make a case that the rejected Violin Sonata, as much as monotheism, was that "something pure."[14]

The symphony's finale struck some critics as bombastic (Virgil Thomson compared it to something "out of Strauss's *Death and Transfiguration*"), and others as uncomfortably close to kitsch. It is remote in tone from the quiet concluding pages of Auden's poem. Gottlieb calls it is "a kind of Hollywood hope, more hollow than holy." Yet it conveys an inborn optimism that was true to its composer's personality.

The premiere of *The Age of Anxiety* on April 8, 1949, with Koussevitzky conducting the Boston Symphony and Bernstein himself at the piano, was a high point in the relationship between the two men. Koussevitzky had warmed to the work, even accepting the Masque movement as a "refined sort of jazz." But by this time Bernstein knew that he would not be Koussevitzky's successor with the orchestra. On March 15 the board had finally selected Charles Munch for the position, despite the fact that Koussevitzky had argued strongly in Leonard's favor. Whether politics was a factor in the decision—or which kind of politics—is an unknown. Just days after the premiere, Bernstein was depicted in a *Life* magazine photo spread of what looked like a rogues' gallery, next to photos of Dorothy Parker, Arthur Miller, Alfred Einstein, Thomas Mann, Lillian Hellman, Charlie Chaplin, Clifford Odets, Norman Mailer, Copland, and forty others at a Cultural Conference for World Peace. The headline read "Dupes and Fellow Travellers Dress Up Communist Fronts." Behind the scenes, in the same month, investigators for the Truman administration had determined that the president should not appear with Bernstein at an event honoring the Israeli president, Chaim Weizmann, due to the conductor's leftist activities.

Critical response to *The Age of Anxiety* was decidedly mixed. Louis Biancolli predicted in the *New York World-Telegram* that "it will some day rank as a landmark in American Music." Cyrus Durgin in the *Boston Globe* called the Masque "the finest single movement in the American idiom and feeling I have ever heard." But when the symphony was given its New York premiere in February 1950 by the Philharmonic, with Lukas Foss at the piano and the composer conducting, Olin Downes averred that it was "wholly exterior in style, ingeniously constructed, effectively orchestrated, and a triumph of superficiality." As usual, Virgil Thomson found the orchestration admirable but its form "improvisatory, its melodic content casual, its harmony stiff, its counterpuntal [*sic*] tension weak."[15]

The opinion that the work lacked originality and substance was reiterated in many reviews. As late as 1968, Harold Schonberg described it as "a tepid rehash of Copland, dated jazz and mild dissonance. Even when it was composed it looked backward rather than forward, and time has not been kind to it."[16] It is not clear how Auden regarded the symphony, but it is known that he did not care for the ballet Jerome Robbins fashioned from its score. Hearing the work in Venice in 1959, Stravinsky, probably the living musician Bernstein most revered, walked out on it. (He hadn't cared for the *Jeremiah* Symphony either.)

One wonders whether Bernstein, who seemed fearless in most respects, did not in fact "hide his light under a bushel" when he presented this piano concerto as a symphony, with a title derived from a monumental poem and implicitly bearing the weight of an entire age. To be sure, the work's connection to Auden was, if anything, even deeper than the composer let on, but this remarkable work might have been more likely to have been evaluated on its own merits had he titled it a piano concerto.

Something about Bernstein caused even his friends to question the quality of his compositions. Aaron Copland contributed an article titled "The New School of American Composers" to the *New York Times* on March 14, 1948, while Bernstein was finishing *The Age of Anxiety*. Copland wrote about seven American composers coming of age in an era when distinguished European role models, uprooted by the war, had come here to teach, and when an established older generation (Copland's own) could now, for the first time, be looked to for inspiration and guidance. The article gave particularly unguarded praise to the least known of the group, a young composer of serious bent, Robert Palmer, while also touting the virtues of Bernstein's old friends Harold Shapero and Lukas Foss. Copland's words regarding Bernstein were guarded. He began by saying that his compositional gifts were overshadowed by his "brilliance as a conductor and pianist" and that it would almost be "strange if he could not compose." He described him as "equally at home in the world of jazz and in the world of serious music" and as a composer of a particularly communicative kind, whose music melodically and harmonically "has a spontaneity and warmth that speak directly to an audience." Then he offered a mixed assessment: "At its worst Bernstein's music is conductor's music—eclectic in style and facile in inspiration. But at its best it is music of vibrant rhythmic invention, of irresistible élan, often carrying with it a terrific dramatic punch."

# 7

## *Serenade*
## *1949–Fall 1954*

After completing his Second Symphony, Bernstein plunged into work on the commission for the Woody Herman band, completing it on November 4, 1949. Clarinetist Herman had put together a new group (the "Second Herd") in 1947. Having commissioned Stravinsky's *Ebony Concerto* for his first band in 1946 and performed it in Carnegie Hall, he was hoping to continue to add to his repertoire of commissioned works by "classical" composers for jazz ensemble. Unfortunately, the new band had dissolved by the time that Bernstein turned in his contribution, and Herman apparently never even acknowledged receiving it.

*Prelude, Fugue and Riffs* remained unperformed until 1955. It is one of Bernstein's most viscerally exciting compositions, seeming to come from a different impulse than did either the symphonies or the musicals. It is sophisticated, intricate, concise, yet wild. In contrast to the *Ebony Concerto*, which does not attempt to actually swing or truly embrace a jazz idiom and is more of a Brandenburg Concerto for jazz ensemble, Bernstein's music is an insider's take on jazz, which does swing.[1] Bernstein told his assistant Gottlieb that he had a particularly "difficult time writing this piece." One can perhaps see traces of the difficulty, while also attributing the work's power to the challenge he set himself. Along with 1940s big-band music, the clarinet styles of Goodman and Herman, the piano playing of Fats Waller, Art Tatum, and others, and some early bebop influences, at least three classical works stand behind the piece: Gershwin's *Rhapsody in Blue* (Paul Whiteman's commissions having served as a model for Herman's own commission series), Stravinsky's *Ebony Concerto*, and Darius Milhaud's *La création du monde*, with its joyful, bluesy fugue. The ensemble itself would have been a daunting one for many classical composers: solo clarinet plus five saxophones, five trumpets, four trombones, piano, percussion (two players playing traps, tom-toms, xylophone, vibraphone, wood block, two timpani), and bass.

The work consists of three linked movements played straight through as a continuous sequence. The Prelude for brass and percussion pits cool, neat, and understated Harmon-muted brass figures in asymmetrical groupings, against a middle section that is a full-throated outburst in a slower, steady, swinging-triplet 4/4 rhythm. The outer sections are rather Stravinskian and also suggest Copland's wry early takes on jazz; the middle section comes from inside jazz. A humorously galumphing trombone transition, later used in *Wonderful Town*, moves the music from this middle section back to the drier, faster, less symmetrical opening material.

The tiny Fugue, for saxophones alone, is similarly tripartite. In the first part there are fugal saxophone entrances on a perky theme and an altered inversion of it. The middle section drops this fugal premise and presents canonic imitations of a contrasting lyrical tune. This is the closest the work ever comes to the songfulness Bernstein is known for. The last section blends the two previous ideas.

Longer than the previous two movements put together, Riffs continues the momentum with the first entrance of the piano, playing a fast stride accompaniment that looks like Stravinsky on the page but sounds like Fats Waller's left hand. Over this the solo clarinet enters for the first time with a lick at a dangerous metrical tangent to the piano. Bernstein maintains the risky, offbeat dialogue for thirty-five measures before bringing in the winds, playing their fugue theme in canon between choirs of three, accompanied by bass, drums, and a Lionel Hamptonesque vibraphone. An ingeniously pointillistic passage in four-part counterpoint follows, after which two brass trios perform their own canon on the fugue subject. Then there is a buildup to a reprise of the big-band outburst from the first movement, after which both themes from the fugue movement (the subject and the lyrical contrasting theme) are combined with the clarinet solo theme over the fast-walking bass.[2] Then the clarinet riff catches fire with the whole ensemble, which simulates an improvised free-for-all that turns into a repeated tutti loop, a blowout that brings to mind the composer's description of *El salón México* as a "roller-coaster."

Two characteristics set this piece apart from other Bernstein works: an emphasis on motive over melody, and the uninterrupted fast tempo. The title suggests a light, jazzy diversion that pokes fun at classical forms (like Alec Wilder's "Pop, What's a Passacaglia?"). In fact the music is an intense attempt on the part of a nonimprovising jazz enthusiast to notate music that has the fervor of the real thing. Sidelining his lyrical side, Bernstein has poured all his skill and love of jazz into the work, without irony of any kind.[3]

On December 2 and 3, 1949, Bernstein conducted the premiere of Olivier Messiaen's incandescent, ecstatic *Turangalîla-*

*symphonie* with the Boston Symphony, first in Boston and then at Carnegie Hall. Yvonne Loriod (who later became Messiaen's second wife) was the piano soloist, and Ginette Martenot played the electronic keyboard instrument her brother, Maurice Martenot, had invented, the ondes martenot.[4] One of the great musical masters of the second half of the twentieth century, Messiaen was also the teacher of the man who would one day succeed Bernstein at the Philharmonic, Pierre Boulez. *Turangalîla* had been commissioned in 1945 by Koussevitzky.[5] Messiaen entrusted *Turangalîla* to Bernstein in a charming letter expressing confidence in the young conductor's understanding, calling him "a man of genius."[6]

On December 8, 1949, the film version of *On the Town* opened, minus the bulk of Bernstein's music. With many new songs provided by Roger Edens (with words by Comden and Green), and even Bernstein's few contributions reorchestrated and altered, the film version of the show, delightful as it was, left little intact of what had made the original music innovative. Successful as it had been, the show had not produced any hit tunes. Gone from the film are "Lonely Town," "I Can Cook Too," "Some Other Time," "Carried Away," and "Lucky to Be Me," among other songs. Much of Bernstein's contribution to the Miss Turnstiles ballet was also jettisoned, along with the polytonality and unexpected metric shifts in the score. Bernstein remains in only two songs, "New York, New York" and "Come Up to My Place," although even these suffer from cuts, beefed-up instrumentation, and the removal of subtleties such as the vocal canon in "New York, New York."[7] The ballet music for "A Day in New York" appears to be pure Bernstein, but it is a recombination of passages that were in different places in the original show ("Opening: New York, New York," "Dance: Times Square," and "The Imaginary Coney Island"). Bernstein, who was paid a "consultation fee," was brought in for two weeks to rework this ballet. Privately, he was disheartened by the whole experience and even by Comden and Green's participation in it, but he didn't dwell on it or hold it against them.

In Florida that December he completed eight songs with lyrics, as well as a copious amount of incidental music, for a theatrical production of *Peter Pan* that would eventually open on April 24, 1950, and run for a full year. Although the music would be widely praised in the press, much of what was most interesting in the score had in fact been cut before the opening. Gone was the incidental music, replaced by instrumental segments by Alec Wilder.[8] While the original and beautiful "Dream with Me" was gone, five Bernstein songs remained in the production. Of these, Wendy's "Who Am I?" and "Peter, Peter" are particularly inventive and touching. The "Plank Round" for pirate chorus contains a vigorous instrumental interlude modeled after Bach's Brandenburg Concerto No. 3. Largely unused at the time and then superseded by the music for the Disney film of 1953 and Jules Styne's 1954 score for the famous Mary Martin production of *Peter Pan*, Bernstein's complete score remained forgotten until it was reconstructed and recorded in 2005.

With his three-year position at the helm of the New York City Symphony over, Bernstein began once again to be invited to guest conduct the New York Philharmonic at Carnegie Hall. When he appeared there in February 1950 to perform his *Age of Anxiety* Symphony, it was his first time back since January 1945. During his two-week stint with the orchestra, he also conducted Schumann's Fourth Symphony, William Walton's 1939 Violin Concerto with Jascha Heifetz as soloist, Harold Shapero's *Symphony for Classical Orchestra* (a work praised by Stravinsky, and which Bernstein considered a masterpiece), Beethoven's Piano Concerto No. 1 in C Major, op. 15, conducting from his position as its piano soloist, and Beethoven's Eighth Symphony. He returned the following February to perform two concerts featuring the phenomenal young pianist

William Kapell performing Prokofiev's Piano Concerto No. 3 in C Major, op. 26, and Rachmaninov's Concerto No. 2 in C Minor, op. 18. On Washington's Birthday, February 21, 1951, he led the premiere of Charles Ives's Symphony No. 2. By way of situating it (and American music) within Western music history, the Ives was preceded by an all-Mozart first half.[9]

At seventy-seven years old, Ives was still an unfamiliar name to most in the audience. To Bernstein, as to many of his fellow composers, he was the true father of an unapologetically American music.[10] The 1910 Second Symphony had remained unplayed for forty years. Much of it is structurally and orchestrally in the vein of a late nineteenth-century symphony, yet it is willfully eccentric, containing jarring discontinuities and several passages that boldly anticipate the rhythmic and tonal inventions of Ives's later music. Juxtaposed with phrases that would not be out of place in Dvořák, the symphony's final boisterous pages create a controlled pandemonium of a peculiarly American kind. Its layered orchestral brouhaha could stir patriotic feelings in a stone, yet it also conveys, as Ives's music often does, dark and disturbing undercurrents. The final chord is a wake-up call to the present: a dissonant eleven-note cluster that amounts to a Bronx cheer directed at the audience. One can thank the prospect of a Philharmonic debut for this touch; Ives added it in 1950, while he, Henry Cowell, and Lou Harrison were preparing the score for Bernstein's performance.[11] With its colorful quotations of dozens of familiar American folk songs, hymns, marches, and ditties, including "Reveille," "Columbia, the Gem of the Ocean," "Bringing in the Sheaves," "Turkey in the Straw," and many others, the symphony might have come across as a mere novelty. Bernstein's respect for the work's structural integrity and his understanding of its language led to a performance that was meticulous, humorous, noble, and moving.

Deeply shy and, in any case, too ill to travel, Ives listened to the national broadcast on a neighbor's radio.[12] He expressed his appreciation through his wife, Harmony, who wrote to Bernstein that it "was a wonderful and thrilling experience to hear Mr. Ives 2nd Symphony as you conducted it on February 22nd. . . . People did like it, didn't they? . . . Mr. Ives . . . wants me to say to you that 'the enthusiasm with which it was received was due so much to your devoted interpretation and wonderful conducting.' . . . Mr. Ives heard the broadcast . . . and it took him back so to his father and his youth that he had tears in his eyes. You will be interested to know that his comment on the allegro movements was 'too slow'—otherwise he was satisfied."[13]

Bernstein's championing of Ives continued throughout his time at the Philharmonic and was a crucial element in the advancement of Ives's music in the concert hall.[14] It is tempting to think that Bernstein was emboldened by getting inside the mind of an American original outside the musical mainstream, who revered Beethoven but scorned musical academicism and could respect a simple carol as much as a rigorous exploration of quarter-tones.[15]

Had it been scheduled for the following year, it is unlikely that this historic broadcast would have taken place. Although it was not publicly known until recently, Bernstein had in fact been put on a blacklist by CBS radio and television in 1950, the year he was listed as a subversive in the witch-hunting periodical *Counterattack* and in its book *Red Channels: The Report of Communist Influence in Radio and Television.* In June he had also been "banned from official State Department functions overseas" as a "loyalty and security risk."[16] Jerome Robbins had already been subject to virulent harassment in print by *New York Daily News* columnist Ed Sullivan, who pointedly referred to Robbins's contacts among "conductors and arrangers in concert music," and reportedly privately threatened him with exposure of his homosexual affairs if he didn't testify against his friends. Bernstein didn't know it but, in accordance with the

Internal Securities Act of April 1951, his name had also been placed on a list of those prominent persons to be placed in detention facilities in the event of a "national emergency." In January 1951 Hollywood producer Boris Morros told him to his face that he would never hire him because he was "a Red." By the end of 1951 two of his actor friends, J. Edward Bromberg and John Garfield, would both be dead of heart attacks in early middle age, after being interrogated by HUAC and blacklisted. On May 16, 1951, just a few days before Lillian Hellman spoke her unforgettable words of defiance in front of her interlocutors in Congress, Bernstein wrote to his sister, "It can also happen to all of us, so we had better start preparing our blazing orations now," and then added, "I hope I am as brave as I sound . . . when it catches up to me." Bernstein had good reason to suspect that, if he wasn't careful, his entire conducting career and all that went with it would be in jeopardy. And indeed he did not appear on any regular Philharmonic subscription programs between February 1951 and December 1956.

In the hiatus after Felicia and Leonard broke off their first engagement in 1947, she had become involved with a married actor named Richard Hart, who had three children. She shared an apartment with him on the West Side and was apparently very much in love, hoping that he would leave his wife. He was a heavy drinker, however, and apparently physically abusive when under the influence. She had also been having considerable success as an actress, appearing in such television dramas as *Of Human Bondage* on November 21, 1949; Studio One's *Flowers for a Stranger* on February 23, 1950; and, perhaps most impressively, as Nora in Ibsen's *A Doll's House*, which aired on April 5, 1950, and was seen by millions of viewers. In *Flowers for a Stranger*, she played a half-Chilean pianist traumatized by the childhood memory of her mother's death. The character is married to a psychiatrist who unknowingly introduces her to her mother's murderer, Dr. Nestri, played by Yul Brynner. Felicia brought a touching credibility to her role. With her lovely, delicate, and expressive face, and an almost birdlike animation and lightness of manner, she moved fluidly between moods, showing a remarkable aptitude for inhabiting her character and making the viewer forget the artificialities of the plot. In her role she also played several Chopin excerpts at the piano: from the Etude in E Major, op. 10, no. 3, and the second theme from the Ballade No. 1 in G Minor, op. 23.

From Israel, Leonard confided to his sister Shirley that he finally understood what Felicia meant to him. After two pages on other things, he started to pour his heart out to her for six more tightly written pages: "Ever since I left America she has occupied my thoughts uninterruptedly, and I have come to a fabulously clear realization of what she means—and has always meant to me. I have loved her, despite all the blocks that have consistently impaired my loving-mechanism, truly and deeply from the first. Lonely on the sea, my thoughts were only of her. Other girls and/or boys meant nothing." He wrote that he now understood it would have been wrong for them to marry in 1947, in the midst of the complex tensions of their lives at that time, but that now he would marry her in an instant. Having sent her a letter declaring this, he had not heard back and was fearful. At the end of this long letter to Shirley, he wrote, "Last night I dreamed at length that I had found her and solved our problems together. It was a hard dream, but full of richness. And, on awakening, I was desolate at the thousand of miles that still lay between us, and the grayness of doubt and not-knowing."[17]

He also wrote of being ready to curb the distracting impulses of his homosexual side and of being ready to live his life, as opposed to only being "on the circumference of it." He expressed the hope that his world would change from one of "abstractions and public-hungry performances to one of reality." He hoped to be "through with the conductor-performance life (except where it really matters)" and instead to opt for "inner living, which means composing and Felicia."[18]

Many of Bernstein's friends seemed to doubt that he was ready to make a commitment. Copland famously remarked that he was not yet "housebroken." His mother and some of his friends thought that Felicia was "wrong for him."[19] But Leonard and Felicia did love each other passionately. Leonard's chemistry with men may possibly have been more exciting (it did, ultimately, prevail over his heterosexuality), but it was also more fleeting and did not lead to a stable bond. His passionate connections to women, beginning with his mother, sister, and his first girlfriends, grounded him. He had called young Shirley Gabis a "steadying hand." Helen Coates was another stabilizing influence. (She too thought Felicia was wrong for him.) He longed to have a steady home life and had dreamed of having his own family at least as far back as his days at Curtis.[20] He needed to share his life with someone, and there is ample evidence that he could not share his life with a man, at least not during that period of his life.

In the summer of 1950 he visited Felicia, hoping to win her back, but found her tied to Hart. At the same time he also summarily fired his devoted assistant Helen Coates, who had been keeping his life together—more than any spouse could—for six years. Her disapproval of Felicia may have been a factor in the decision, since Coates's aggrieved letter to him mentions his complaint that she was "overly involved" in his personal life. It is as clear that her involvement could verge on overprotectiveness as it is that his reliance on her was completely his own doing. In any event, he hired her back within days.

In January 1951 Richard Hart collapsed in a Third Avenue bar and died later in the day, with Felicia at his side. He was only thirty-five years old. A devastated Felicia could not even attend the funeral or be properly consoled.

In 1951 Leonard took the Israel Philharmonic on an American tour, at the end of which he decided, not for the first or last time, to devote the next two years or more to composing. "I have never felt so happy and strong about a decision," he wrote to Copland. "It will be so good to get in contact with myself again, live a little more innerly."[21] In the past year he had conducted twelve different orchestras in 100 concerts.

Settling in Cuernavaca near his friend the journalist Martha Gellhorn in May 1951, he drafted the libretto and sketched most of the music for his one-act opera *Trouble in Tahiti.* But this creative interlude was interrupted by the news that Koussevitzky was now gravely ill. Bernstein rushed back to Boston, and on June 3, 1951, he was at Koussevitzky's bedside. They talked at length "about music, life, and love." Koussevitzky died the next day, and it would now be Bernstein's responsibility to lead the orchestra and teach conducting at the Berkshire Music Festival. Meanwhile, Felicia had been traveling by herself in Europe. When she heard about Koussevitzky's death, she wrote Bernstein a long letter from Cannes that began with condolences and concluded with the news that she would be back in the States in July.

Having danced around each other and their uncertainties for more than five years, Leonard and Felicia finally embraced the prospect of marriage after they were reunited at Tanglewood that summer. On September 9, 1951, with the groom wearing a white suit and shoes bequeathed to him by Koussevitzky, the couple married at the Temple Mishkan Tefila in the presence of Leonard's brother and sister, his parents (both now reconciled to their son's choice), David Oppenheim and other friends, Dinah, Leonard's paternal grandmother, Felicia's mother, Clemencia, and a number of Chilean relatives. While Felicia and Leonard were relatively calm, the bride's Catholic mother, who had sent her three daughters to convent school to be educated, was trembling and "white as a sheet" throughout the ceremony in the imposing temple. The two best men, Burton Bernstein and David Oppenheim, stood on either side of her holding her up.

Marc Blitzstein wrote to his friend Mina Curtiss that he was "relieved" that the marriage, which had been "simmering" for so long, was finally a reality and would take whatever course it would now take.[22] Although the marriage began in a state of uncertainty, it was an uncertainty that both partners fully acknowledged. The tone of Bernstein's letters to family members during the course of the honeymoon expresses a caution worthy of the composer-librettist of *Trouble in Tahiti.* From Cheyenne, Wyoming, on route to Cuernavaca, on September 18, 1951, he expressed admiration for the fortitude his parents had shown in remaining together:

> . . . Sometimes I wonder how you two ever survived a marriage; it's a very hard thing to do, you know, and there's a million adjustments that have to be made. . . . How must it have been for you, who barely knew each other, and were so limited in your worlds? I think it is wonderful that you have come through it. It must have taken the strength of Hercules.
>
> As for us, we are so grateful for each other; and we treasure our marriage as something very precious.

On the same day he wrote to his brother about a meltdown that had occurred a few days before: "Every day marriage gets better. It may take a lot of days, but I think the big crisis is over."

Leonard and Felicia Bernstein were clearly deeply attracted to each other, and on the outside they were a well-matched, elegant couple. Yet from the beginning Bernstein's homosexual side was a built-in fault line in their relationship. There was also the danger that Felicia's acting career would be crushed under the weight of her husband's headlong musical celebrity.

Felicia was a risk taker who had traveled to America to seek an acting career under the guise of continuing her music studies. Before the wedding she converted to Judaism without telling her parents. In some sense she may have been drawn to the very duality in Bernstein's nature that was a built-in threat to their stability as a pair. Looking at photographs and films of the couple, one senses deep romanticism and companionability; this is not a marriage of opposites but of discovered kinship, of two people who love and understand each other, and in some ways mirror each other. The rumor of Felicia's first sighting of her husband was correct: a year after her arrival in New York, a friend who had met the conductor had written to tell her that he was the right man for her. She was sufficiently curious to go to see him perform. As she put it to a journalist in 1961, "The minute I saw him conduct, I knew it was true. That moment was the coming into focus of my whole being, the completing of myself."[23]

Bernstein's need for her was equally fundamental. As Martha Gellhorn put it, he was "impulsive, and rambunctious and a force of nature." Felicia was accomplished and beautiful, a warm, refined, emotionally available person, who had the "steadiness, judgment, and sense of proportion" to give him a home and an emotional home base.[24] There is a poignant note in Bernstein's hand written on the day of their marriage: "Feli Sweetest— . . . I want to say that I love and respect you and that I know we are beginning a beautiful life—more beautiful in that we understand each other's tough moments well enough to share them and turn them into good ones. Every blessing on you today and every day—and the warmest kiss—L"[25]

There were doubtless very few people in whom the couple could confide about the sexual tensions that complicated their relationship. Although these tensions erupted publicly twenty-five years into the marriage, they were present from its outset. An undated letter from Felicia to her husband written early in their married life summarizes her efforts at the time to put the "mess" of their "connubial life" in perspective:

> I've done a lot of thinking and have decided that it's not such a mess after all.
>
> *First:* we are not committed to a life sentence—nothing is really irreversible, not even marriage (though I used to think so).
>
> *Second:* You are a homosexual and may never change—you don't admit to the possibility of a double life, but if your peace of mind, your health, your whole nervous system depend on a certain sexual pattern what can you do?
>
> *Third:* I am willing to accept you as you are, without being a martyr or sacrificing myself to the L. B. altar. I happen to love you very much—this may be a disease, and if it is—what better cure? It may be difficult but no more so than the "status quo" which exists now—at the moment you are not yourself and this produces painful barriers and tensions for both of us—let's try to see what happens if you are free to do as you like, but without guilt and confession, please![26]

If this letter constituted the beginning of a pact between the two, it surely can't be construed as the last word on a marriage that continued for another twenty-five years, produced three flourishing children, and a rich family life. Bernstein clearly fought a losing battle to remain monogamous as a husband, but he seemed to mostly succeed in compartmentalizing the other side of his love life until 1976.

During the honeymoon, he found it difficult to resume work on the one-act opera that had been interrupted at the time of Koussevitzky's death. His creative concentration suffered further when, after only two months, the newlyweds were visited by not just one but both sets of parents. Then the world beckoned them back. Felicia was asked to appear in two television plays, *Crown of Shadows* and *The Wings of the Dove*, in February, while Leonard was summoned to conduct the Boston Symphony in place of Charles Munch, who was ill. Most important, Felicia was pregnant.

Leonard had already agreed to be visiting music professor at Brandeis University in June 1952 and to direct a Festival of the Creative Arts there. Now convinced by composer and fellow Brandeis professor Irving Fine that his opera should have its premiere at the festival, Leonard went into seclusion at the Saratoga Springs artists' colony Yaddo, leaving his pregnant wife alone for five weeks, to complete the work in the same studio in which Marc Blitzstein had recently written some of his opera *Reuben Reuben*. In the *New York Herald Tribune* Bernstein was quoted as calling the work a "lightweight piece for which I wrote the libretto and it lasts only thirty minutes or so. The whole thing is popular-song inspired," with "roots in musical comedy, or even better the American Musical Theater."[27]

But whatever comedy *Trouble in Tahiti* contains has a cruel edge, and not only because the character Sam has the same name as the author's father. (Bernstein changed the wife's name from that of his mother, Jennie, to his grandmother's name, Dinah.) In chipper scat singing, the work's Greek chorus, a trio of two men and a woman, extol the virtues of suburban paradise, oblivious to the pain of the opera's protagonists. Their saccharine, close harmonies cut like a knife, suggesting a toxic conformity. The scenes in the psychiatrist's office, where Dinah recounts dreaming of a garden, the "quiet place" which would later became the core idea behind Bernstein's 1983 opera, and on the street, where the unhappily married husband and wife unexpectedly meet and exchange awkward greetings, are heartbreaking. Meanwhile, one can't help associating Junior, the neglected child of this dysfunctional couple, with the composer. Bernstein's America is one in which the human soul is suspended in emptiness and yearns for connection, finding depth only in solitary dreams and fantasy. A letter from the composer to Felicia written May 6, 1955, offers an accurate description of the work and also says much about their relationship: "Why won't people realize that it is the touching parts that the opera is really about? . . . The rest is only either comment or diversion. I'd love to see you direct it one day."[28]

The work certainly is serious in terms of the rigor of its construction and the expertise of its text setting, which brings the naturalness of musical comedy English into an operatic context, but it could be seen as divided stylistically between satire and a moving realism. For example, there is a potential conflict in tone between Dinah's flamboyant, presentational Broadway-style aria, "What a Movie!," which lampoons both America's international arrogance and the way that arrogance is reflected in Hollywood escapism, and her touchingly expressive musings on the psychiatrist's couch. "What a Movie!" embeds its trenchant satire in music of such exhilarating catchiness and verbal adroitness that it becomes celebratory. Bernstein contained too much joy and innate, ingrained optimism to compose a *Wozzeck* or a *Mahagonny* (a fact that helps explain the theatrical failure of his major collaboration with Lillian Hellman). Like Mozart's *Marriage of Figaro*, *Trouble in Tahiti*'s societal critique is tempered by its composer's warmth, sensuality, zest, and desire to entertain. Bernstein dedicated the one-act opera to Marc Blitzstein.

After the premiere of the work at the Brandeis festival, he was back at Tanglewood, where it was performed again, now with an improved final scene. On September 8, 1952, with the birth of their daughter Jamie, the Bernsteins became parents. On October 27 the new father wrote "Jamie's Lullaby." In November he again conducted *Trouble in Tahiti* in a live television broadcast.

No sooner had the broadcast occurred when Bernstein was asked by producers George Abbott and Robert Fryer to compose the score for a musical for which Comden and Green had agreed to do the lyrics. The show was to be based on a series of stories that had appeared in the *New Yorker* called *My Sister Ei-*

*leen* by Ruth McKenney, which had been turned into a play by Joseph Fields and Jerome Chodorov. As Comden and Green later put it (in *The New York Musicals of Comden and Green*), the stories, based on McKenney's own youth, concerned "two girls from Columbus, Ohio, who come to New York in the mid-1930s to seek fame and fortune." The show was in a tight spot; Rosalind Russell had been signed to star in it, but the original composer-lyricist team had failed to produce an adequate score. To keep Russell in the cast, a new score would have to be completed in five weeks. With Koussevitzky now gone, Bernstein must have felt that a barrier to his returning to the Broadway world was removed. Comden and Green were amazed that he agreed to do the show almost instantly, rushing to the piano to play a musical signifier of the 1930s time period—an introductory vamp in 6/8 made famous by bandleader Eddy Duchin. It is a reflection of Bernstein's versatility and temperament that he could so quickly adjust to the aesthetic demands of the show and work so well under intense pressure, shut away for a month with a piano, a typewriter, and his two friends in a smoke-filled room in his apartment at the Osborne near Carnegie Hall. The score was not only produced in time but was one of the most high-spirited, inventive, and melodious of its day.

*Wonderful Town* was a different type of project from *On the Town*.[29] It was a period piece set in the recent past: Greenwich Village in 1935. It demanded a score that could convey a sense of its time and musically embody a variety of personalities: the two sisters just off the train from the Midwest—one a "blond knockout," the other a "would-be writer, attractive but lacking in confidence"; a former athlete who loves domestic chores; a newspaper editor; a "brash young newspaperman"; Irish policemen, and Brazilian cadets. Bernstein enjoyed the assignment, which enabled him to draw on his encyclopedic knowledge of musical styles. He used his version of the Eddie Duchin vamp at the outset of the show and as an underpinning of the opening number, "Christopher Street." (In the score the vamp is marked *molto 'Duchino.'*)[30] He created a delightful Irish barbershop quartet and jig ("My Darling Eileen") for the policemen; an irresistible conga, a party dance that, according to Humphrey Burton, Bernstein "loved to organize at parties from Beverly Hills to Galilee"; and swing music for the Village Vortex (named after the Village Vanguard, where the Revuers had performed). Another reference point was the novelty music of Zez Confrey (whose "Kitten on the Keys" Bernstein had heard in his youth), which lies behind the intricate syncopations-within-syncopations rhythms of the "Wrong-Note Rag," at least as much as actual ragtime does. Bernstein used "Jamie's Lullaby," with its lazy melody in 3/4, as the basis for the lovely song "A Quiet Girl." The songs "Ohio" and "A Little Bit in Love," with their languid, "cowboy" accompaniments and melodies in parallel thirds and sixths, convey the rural origins of the two sisters. The lyrics for *Wonderful Town* are incomparably sophisticated, high points being "Conversation Piece," "Pass the Football," and the comic number, "One Hundred Easy Ways to Lose a Man," still devastating social commentary after sixty years.

Bernstein made a pared-down instrumental adaptation of his still unperformed *Prelude, Fugue and Riffs* for use as a "Courtroom Ballet" to open act 2, but the evening could not accommodate the interruption of an eight-minute ballet.[31] Although there were many purely instrumental breaks in the songs that afforded choreographic opportunities, dance was not used as a means of furthering plot in *Wonderful Town*.

Work on *Wonderful Town* took place against a backdrop of renewed political apprehensiveness. In January 1953 Copland's *Lincoln Portrait* had been removed from the program of President Eisenhower's inauguration, and his music as well as that of other "fellow travelers" (including Bernstein and Virgil Thomson) was banned from Voice of America broadcasts and foreign libraries. After being hounded for several years by HUAC representatives and in the print media, Jerome Robbins buckled in the face of his confrontation with the committee on May 5, offering names of various colleagues he believed were communists (not including his collaborators on *Wonderful Town*). Copland himself was called up on May 26, managing to divulge nothing. Nevertheless, he came away deeply shaken by his encounter with the American right wing at its most thuggish.

The political heat grew more intense for Bernstein himself in July, when the U.S. Passport Office refused to renew his passport, as a result of the voluminous record that had now been compiled on his political affiliations. With a historic debut at La Scala scheduled for the following December, the first ever for an American conductor, he faced a direct threat to his future as a musician. He hired James McInerny, a lawyer known to be expert in clearing political reputations, who had once been on the side of the investigators. The result was a humiliating exoneration that must have both relieved him and crushed his self-respect. The long affidavit he signed made light of all the times he had lent his name to a cause or appeared at a function, saying that he had endorsed letters and petitions casually, without knowing what they contained. He admitted that he was mistaken not to have immediately "made a public disavowal" of the associations implied by photos seen in *Life* magazine or portrayed in the pages of *Red Channels*. He pronounced himself a "foe of communism." The last point was, strictly speaking, true, in that he did oppose the strong-arm tactics of the Russian and Chinese governments, both internally and internationally and, unlike Robbins, had not been a party member. Yet in saying so, he surely must have felt he was betraying those who had stood up under pressure, or those who, like Paul Robeson, had had their international careers ruined because of their views. Signing his name to the document made a mockery of his own contempt for the investigations, which he actually regarded as "a farce," an incursion on free speech, and part of a strategy to undermine support for legitimate revolutions abroad. He wrote to his brother that he had received clearance by the skin of his teeth, but he did not tell him about the contents of the document. The affidavit made possible not only his trip to Milan but also, after he had made additional assurances, cleared the way for his participation as composer in the film *On the Waterfront.*

Bernstein knew he had been lucky, and surely the compromises he had made tempered any tendency to complacency he might otherwise have felt in relation to the behavior of Robbins and others. They also fueled his anger in future decades against right-wing extremism and abuses of power. He was soon to be working in collaborative projects both with those who had betrayed their colleagues and with those who had not.

In the fall of 1953, a year after her own face-off with HUAC, Lillian Hellman approached Bernstein about composing a musical theater work based on Voltaire's satirical novella *Candide*, first published in 1759. Voltaire's picaresque tale takes place all over Europe, in Argentina, and in the imaginary El Dorado. It features a scene in Lisbon taking place during the Inquisition, which gave Hellman a particularly ripe opportunity for satirizing the activities of HUAC.[32] Voltaire's text mixes wit, erudition, grace, headlong speed, radiant intellect, humanity, and wisdom. Among the objects of his scorn are religious hypocrisy, the absurdity of war, imperialism, scientific ignorance and inconsistency, simplistic or overly abstract philosophy, and the idea of the hero. But above all *Candide* is a critique of the philosophy of optimism espoused by Gottfried Wilhelm Leibniz, which Voltaire considered to be a call to passive inaction in the face of the horrors of the world, both manmade and natural. He was shocked by the randomness of the Lisbon earthquake of 1753, in which thousands died, and resisted the facile notion that, as his character Pangloss asserts, "everything is necessarily for the best of ends."[33]

In December 1953 Bernstein was at La Scala conducting Cherubini's *Medea* with Maria Callas in the title role. The experience put him in the center of the opera world, for which *Candide* was ultimately destined. (He would return there in the spring of 1955 to conduct Callas in Bellini's *La sonnambula*, which several critics have seen as an influence on *Candide*'s "Glitter and Be Gay" and the duet "You Were Dead, You Know.") Work on the Hellman project was further interrupted from February to May 1954, when he was in Hollywood composing the music for *On the Waterfront.* The viscerally gripping film stood on its head the experiences that Hellman and even, to a degree, Bernstein himself had had. Father Barry, played by Karl Malden, represents the voice of conscience who advocates that the dock worker played by Marlon Brando should inform on the Mafia thugs controlling the union. ("What's ratting to them is telling the truth to you," he says early on.) In the film it is the police who, ferreting out corruption, stand up for the workers and oppose their violent intimidation. Writer Budd Schulberg and director Elia Kazan, who had been spared blacklisting by informing on others, denied that the film was an apologia for their own behavior, saying only that the film dealt with themes of guilt, split loyalties, and redemption.

Bernstein clearly used Copland as a model for the music, both for its character and in terms of its function. While the orchestral suite drawn from the score is an attractive independent piece, the music's theatrical power emerges far more strongly within the context of the film. The brawny tone of its opening horn melody meshes uncannily with the grittiness of the setting, while the lyrical "underscores" create poignancy, depth, and a sense of vast, lonely spaces in the scenes by the water when Brando and Eva Marie Saint first talk and when they later meet on the rooftop. The stark percussion canon that accompanies the silent opening on the dock creates an indelible impression of violent menace. As the score of *West Side Story* would do two years later, the music evokes the fragility of love across enemy lines, in a setting of urban brutality. It cogently mines only a few motives, which are powerfully combined in the film's final moments when a bloodied, staggering Brando manages to lead his fellow dock workers back to work. In the film Brando and Bernstein's shared qualities create a subliminal chemical bond. Brando was musical in his speech patterns; in the devastating scene in the taxi with his brother (played by Rod Steiger), he almost sings his lines. Like the composer, he exuded a powerful maleness coupled with extraordinary, one might say "female," sensitivity. Bernstein, for his part, was a "method actor" composer and conductor, a musician for whom identification and the personal connection were essential. Noted British music theorist and critic Hans Keller called *On the Waterfront* one of the finest American film scores to date, praising its complex thematic unity, "largely contrapuntal textures" (most unusual in cinema music), and "anti-Hollywoodian instrumentation."[34]

In the summer, while finishing his new *Serenade* for violinist Isaac Stern, Bernstein enjoyed spirited sessions of work on *Candide* with lyricist John Latouche and Hellman in Martha's Vineyard. Latouche had been the librettist for Douglas Moore's successful opera *The Ballad of Baby Doe*. Like Bernstein, Hellman, and 147 others, he had been listed as a subversive in the infamous *Red Channels*.[35] At this point *Candide* was meant to convey a political message. Over the summer much of act 1 was completed, but despite this progress Hellman and Bernstein determined to do the balance of the work by themselves, without Latouche. Meanwhile, the project was again interrupted by the premiere of the *Serenade* in the fall.

The *Serenade* for solo violin, string orchestra, harp, and percussion is based on the *Symposium* of Plato, in which Socrates and six companions discourse on love. There are five movements, representing the seven speeches given at the banquet in the *Symposium*. With the first and last movements each divided into two sections, they are: I. Phaedrus and Pausanias; II. Aristophanes; III. Eryximachus; IV. Agathon; and V. Socrates and Alcibiades.[36]

Phaedrus introduces the solo violin first by itself and then in imitative counterpoint with the strings. Its exquisitely tender melody, which is later used as the accompaniment to the theme of Agathon, becomes transformed into the robust first theme of the Allegro section (Pausanias) that follows without pause. This turns out to be a classically strict sonata-allegro form, though without development section. Its second theme is an expansion of the fourth of *Five Anniversaries.*[37]

The Aristophanes movement skillfully transforms, transposes, and combines two more *Anniversaries* from the same set: no. 1 for Elizabeth Rudolf and no. 2 for Lukas Foss. The Eryximachus movement, perhaps in tribute to the medical profession of its namesake, is a brief, scientifically constructed, contrapuntal whirlwind, lasting only a minute and a half. The solo violin unfurls a quiet, scurrying sequence of sixteenth notes that becomes the basis for a series of rapid exchanges of different lengths between soloist and ensemble. The craft here resembles serialism; the basic form is a kind of palindrome. The middle of the movement is a brilliant *fugato* on the theme.

The beautiful Adagio that then follows, Agathon, returns us to the spirit and themes of Phaedrus and Pausanias. A middle section proposes a new theme and culminates in an anguished solo cadenza elaborating upon it, over held string chords. The music of the first section returns, with the Pausanias theme now emphasized in the first violins.

Socrates follows, continuing the train of thought of the previous movement, with a slow, powerful statement of its second theme.[38] The solo violin enters in the style of a recitative and then reiterates this Socrates theme, ending with a brief cadenza over a held string chord. The buoyant finale (Alcibiades), which follows without pause, is derived from—and eventually incorporates almost in its entirety—the third of the *Five Anniversaries*, for Elizabeth B. Ehrman.[39]

It is striking that, like Auden's *Age of Anxiety*, Plato's *Symposium* describes a party at which philosophical matters are discussed into the night. The general subject matter, and perhaps the very work in question, surely reminded Bernstein of late-night discussions in his dorm at Harvard and at the home of his philosophy teacher David Prall, and his interest in and knowledge of the classics dated back to his days at Boston Latin.

Curiously, in his discussion of the *Serenade*, Bernstein makes no mention of the *Symposium*'s most celebrated passage, and the one with which he would most naturally be associated, given his experience writing theater music at Harvard: the speech of Aristophanes. It is this speech that accounts for the phenomenon of love as the result of the separation of humans into two halves. Aristophanes explains that there were originally three genders: male, female, and a combination of the two.[40] But long ago these four-legged, two-headed humans were punished for their disobedience of Zeus and the other gods by being cut in two.[41] Zeus eventually took pity on the loneliness of the severed humans, who longed to be reunited, and placed their genitals in front, allowing the males and females to reproduce when they came together, and for the others to find physical satisfaction when they did so. Beginning with this longing to join with one's original other half, Aristophanes expounds on his own views of the meaning of love and on the need to please and show reverence to the gods.

The Plato text depicts a world of men—and a world in which homosexual love is accepted. The only mentions of women in the text are in Aristophanes's description of heterosexual longing and, two thousand years before the American debate on same-sex marriage, a matter-of-fact reference to love between women: "Those women who are cut from women are not at all interested in men, but are drawn much more to women." In *Serenade*, as in *The Age of Anxiety*, *Trouble in Tahiti*, *Facsimile*, and the later *Dybbuk*, Bernstein dealt with the theme of trying to connect with others and with oneself, to reassemble a whole self from fragments.

The musical language of the *Serenade* is for the most part delicate and understated. Listening to the piece, one feels close to the composer's essence. The fact that the work makes use of four of the *Five Anniversaries* as source material confirms the importance of these little pieces as doorways into his private feelings. It also suggests that reading the *Symposium*, with its theme of love, inspired not the melodies themselves (which already existed) but a way to combine and link them into a larger form. Yet the inspiration of Plato should not therefore be discounted. On the contrary, it was the *Symposium* and its themes that gave the composer the theatrical image he needed to turn his pleasing fragments into an ambitious statement. And the idea of love surely inspired the Adagio, Agathon, the expressive highpoint of the work, and music not drawn from the *Anniversaries*. A counterpoise to the refined and epicene songfulness of Aristophanes, the bristling intricacy of Eryximachus, and the buoyant exuberance of Pausanias and Alcibiades, Agathon is among Bernstein's most heartfelt outpourings, coming close to the language of Samuel Barber, a composer to whom he is not ordinarily compared. Still in the early days of his marriage, he seems to want to divulge not romantic feelings so much as conflicted ones: loss and the ache of loneliness. There is much joy in the *Serenade*, but at its core this work "about love" has something approaching the tragic in it too. Blitzstein, perhaps the colleague and friend who understood Bernstein's music best, wrote him that it was "just the finest work you ever wrote, and haunts me all the time."[42]

Composed in the same years as Boulez's *Le marteau sans maître* and Karlheinz Stockhausen's second group of *Klavierstücke*, the *Serenade* must have struck most classical music insiders as remarkably old-fashioned. And it was. Alan Rich called it bland "dinner music" for Plato's banquet, "music of such drab, tawdry, derivative tenuosity as to leave a listener with the feeling of having spent time nibbling on dietetic cotton candy. . . . Brahms here, Hindemith there, a waltz by nobody in particular, a little potted palm jazz at the end." Thomson held out some faint hope for the work "with drastic cuts," but ultimately found it "a negligible contribution to music."[43] Howard Taubman believed that the jazzy character of the finale did not belong in the context of the work. Yet it could easily be argued that, in the *Serenade*, operating within the confines of "classical forms," Bernstein loosened his grip on his emotions in the Adagio and in the high spirits of the finale just enough to make the music soar, but not so much that the energy and technical tautness of its inner workings were diffused.

Perhaps critics felt free to dismiss the work simply because its language did not intimidate them.

# 8

## *Broadway and Carnegie Hall*
## *Fall 1954–1957*

Bernstein's life between the years 1954 and 1957 consisted of a dizzying intertwining of many different strands, among them his marriage and expanding family; his increasing fame and affluence; the projects *Candide* and *West Side Story;* the political climate created by the Cold War and the House Un-American Activities Committee; the cementing of his relationship with the New York Philharmonic; and his entrance into the television medium.

His 1954 presentation of Beethoven's Fifth Symphony on CBS's program *Omnibus*, given, amazingly enough, on yet another November 14, inaugurated perhaps the most unexpected aspect of his musical life, if also one that in retrospect seems almost inevitable: his career as a teacher of music on television. The event also had a political aspect that was unknown at the time. The Ford Foundation, which sponsored the broadcast, was willing to break the blacklist "unless an individual was proven a communist" and would even guarantee "any income lost if another sponsor were to pull out" as a result. They were the first sponsor to do this and were powerful enough (and otherwise conservative enough) to set an example that other funders and companies eventually followed. When Robert Saudek, the producer of *Omnibus*, asked Bernstein to appear on the air, it lifted him off the CBS blacklist.

The Beethoven episode, which was followed by "The World of Jazz" (October 16, 1955), "The Art of Conducting" (December 4, 1955), "American Musical Comedy" (October 7, 1956), "Introduction to Modern Music" (January 13, 1957), "The Music of J. S. Bach" (March 31, 1957), and "What Makes Opera Grand?" (March 23, 1958), all programs for adults, gave abundant evidence that Bernstein was a natural for television, paving the way for the airing of the Young People's Concerts that began three years later.

From the first moments of the Beethoven segment, it was clear that Bernstein was not simply good at explicating complex musical matters with clarity, although of course he was. His entire approach was original and was that of a composer. The program restores a sense of shock to the Beethoven work by cutting away the mythology surrounding it, and by extension surrounding all such "masterpieces." Instead of presenting it as a mysterious artifact handed down to us by a demigod, Bernstein draws the audience into the human problem of *making*. Describing Beethoven as "a builder"—something anyone in the audience could relate to—he demonstrates orchestrational choices by having the musicians play the opening of the score in the weaker instrumentation with which Beethoven first orchestrated it. He sifts through and plays rejected pages from the orchestral sketches to speculate on where they were meant to go in the final score. Many are beautiful in and of themselves but do not accomplish what Beethoven needed to accomplish within a given passage and were therefore eliminated. ("I find it's terrible!" Bernstein exclaims about one of them. "I feel that this sketch just intrudes itself into the living flow of the music and stands there grounded, unable to move, until it's over and then the music can take off in its flight again. No wonder Beethoven rejected it, because he of all people had a sense of drive throughout his music that is second to none. But this sketch just doesn't drive.") Particularly revelatory are performances of the exciting passages originally intended for Beethoven's coda and concluding cadence, which are played in context by the full orchestra. Good as these passages sound, Beethoven found solutions that were even better, and Bernstein explains why.

The program is a study in how, brick by musical brick, Beethoven accomplished the gripping momentum, logic, and concision of his final result, giving us insight into the painstaking and inspired work process that yielded what we perceive as the score's "inevitability." And before performing the movement in full, Bernstein delves deeper and more honestly into the wellsprings of art than one would have thought possible in front of a camera in an airless television studio: "Imagine a lifetime of this struggle, movement after movement, symphony after symphony . . . for reasons unknown to him or to anybody else for that matter, he will give away his life and his energies, just to make sure that one note follows another, with complete inevitability. It seems rather an odd way to spend one's life. But it isn't so odd when we think that the composer by doing this leaves [one] at the finish with the feeling that something is right in the world, that checks throughout, something that follows its own law consistently, something we can trust, that will never let us down."

After the Beethoven program there was a flood of critical praise in the press. The fact that the thirty-seven-year-old composer and conductor was "telegenic" didn't hurt, of course. But that was simply one of many qualities that contributed toward his success in the medium. Not the least of them was the fact that he was speaking from the heart and in words that resonated with his own life experiences. When he says, "It seems rather an odd way to spend one's life," one can hear him explaining the purpose of being a musician to his father, a student of the Talmud, who respected learning, philosophy, and things that followed their "own law consistently." Surely Bernstein had the wandering Russian klezmers in mind when he spoke these words about jazz in the second program: "There has always been a shadow of indignity surrounding music and the players of music. This is historically true. It's always gone on. But it's especially true of jazz now, which is almost completely a player's art, depending as it does on improvisation."

While "The World of Jazz" was groundbreaking in its presentation of jazz as a great American art form, and it provided important explanations of its language, there are, perhaps inevitably, aspects of the program that make us deeply uncomfortable today. There is the all-white band; the performance of Bernstein's own composition on a program in which his contemporaries Charles Mingus, Thelonious Monk, and Charlie Parker are not referred to; the fact that Tommy Dorsey and Benny Goodman are named, but the great Duke Ellington is not.

These faults surely reflected the times in which Bernstein lived far more than they did him.[1] The positive aspects of the program are considerable: the love and studiousness he brings to the subject; his revealing discussion of the blues scale and the subtleties of syncopation (both explored in his undergraduate thesis), his superior explanation of the "accidental counterpoint" that results from two or more simultaneous improvisations on fixed harmonies, and his discussion of the continuity underlying evolving jazz idioms; the fact that at least some jazz greats (Bessie Smith, Louis Armstrong, and others) appear in slides and are represented in sound recordings; the discussion of iambic pentameter in blues, and the comparison to Shakespeare; the explicit message that jazz would be regarded as important, serious art were it not for ignorance and snobbery. It is also hard in the end to regret the performance of *Prelude, Fugue and Riffs*, which constituted its belated premiere. (Benny Goodman, who was not in the televised performance, recorded the work the following day with the same band that appeared in the program.)[2]

Transcending its distracting flaws is the program's powerful message, then novel, that jazz is a great art that has permeated Western culture and become a major source of contemporary American concert music's national character (more or less the position taken in Bernstein's undergraduate thesis). Few could have matched the clarity of Bernstein's technical talk or invested it with such personality. The simple point that in blues the flatted third, fifth, and seventh intervals are used melodically, while the I–IV–V harmonies remain major, as they would in a hymn, is worth the whole program.

Bernstein's discussion of the art of conducting was equally exceptional. With the opening of Brahms's Fourth Symphony as his prime example, he was able to convey a sense of why conductors are necessary, how much knowledge and intellectual preparation conducting a score presupposes, and something of the physical act of shaping the music. He shows how different choices about balance, tempo, and manner of playing can radically alter the character of Brahms's opening phrases, while still remaining true to the letter of the score. He explains beat patterns. He talks of the necessity of a conductor's possessing "a great sensitivity to the flow of time" and explains that the ideal conductor "must not only make the orchestra play, he must make them *want* to play. He must make them love the music as he loves it." He cannot do this by "imposing his will" but by "projecting his feelings around them so that they reach way back to the last man in the second violin section." He says of the resulting "current" of emotion, "I would almost call it love": "When everyone is sharing his feelings, when a hundred men are sharing the same feelings exactly, simultaneously, responding as one to each rise and fall in the music, to each little inner pulse, to each point of arrival and departure . . . then there is a human identity of feeling that has no equal anywhere."

Bernstein's discussion of conducting closes with what he calls "perhaps the chief requirement of all": "That he be humble before the composer . . . that he never interpose himself between the music and the audience and that all his efforts, however strenuous or glamorous they may be, be made in the service of the music itself, which is after all the whole reason for the conductor's existence." Here he offers his conducting creed.[3] For a conductor some critics considered prone to self-conscious showmanship—Virgil Thomson once dubbed his podium manner "chorybantic choreography"—it is interesting that the last sentence contains his only reference to the audience.[4] Apparently, from his point of view, his physical behavior was the very opposite of self-consciousness, a spontaneous way of communicating with the musicians, determined by the needs of the score.

Speaking to Jonathan Cott in 1989, he put it this way: "Everything I do is to the orchestra—what the audience sees from their side is their business. . . . I can't be responsible for that. I don't plan any gestures, I've never rehearsed with a mirror. And when my students ask me what they should do to get an orchestra to play a phrase the way I did it, I can't tell them—I have to ask them what I did. . . . I just advise them to look at the score and make it come alive."[5] Philharmonic bassist Orin O'Brien seemed to agree: "I ushered at Carnegie Hall for two years when I was studying at Juilliard (1954–56), and hardly ever missed a Philharmonic concert. From the audience, I found it difficult to take all of Bernstein's gyrations and dancing around the podium, but it was another story from inside the orchestra.

We knew then that his movements weren't put on for the audience's benefit; he was simply living music that he believed in."[6]

Aspects of Bernstein's offstage personality and domestic life came into view in news stories and interviews from the mid-1950s. In a widely syndicated article, Felicia described her husband as "extremely organized—he puts laundry in the hamper every night, goes around emptying ashtrays. . . . And he never forgets an anniversary or a birthday."[7] (She could have added that he methodically answered all his own mail.) On September 23, 1955, two months after the birth of their second child, Alexander, the Bernsteins were interviewed in their nine-room apartment on Edward R. Murrow's *Person to Person* television show. In the first moments Leonard was questioned by Murrow on the contrast between his various musical activities. Wearing a suit (complete with white handkerchief in his lapel pocket), smoking profusely, and seated awkwardly on the sofa next to the gracefully composed Felicia, he seems to radiate a kind of animal restlessness under Murrow's scrutiny. The camera catches a fleeting look of torment in his eyes when he contrasts the conductor's life of "parties, meeting with press agents and orchestra members" with the solitude of the creative person "who communicates with the world in a very private way." His equilibrium returns when he is seated at the two conjoined Baldwin pianos across from Felicia, and they play a bit of a Bach C-major harpsichord concerto. The *New York Post* of November 13, 1955, carried an article about the thirty-seven-year-old composer and conductor that also gave a sense of the bewildering range of activities he was engaged in, returning again to the theme of his duality: "I'd rather do one thing at a time, only the compulsive thing is that I have to go into so many fields," he said, while chain smoking, picking up the laundry, and talking with his daughter Jamie, then three, in English and Spanish. (Four-month-old Alexander was in another room.) "It's like having two different personalities—one as the performer, the other as the creator. A real performer has an outgoing, extrovert personality—he has to see people and be seen by people. The creative life is wholly different. You sit alone in your own little room and commune with yourself or your muse or your God or whatever it is. Usually people are one or the other. I have to be both—that's where the strain comes in almost to a schizophrenic degree."

Particularly striking, in view of what happened over the next fifteen years of his life, is his assertion that he didn't want to be in charge of an orchestra of his own, "because immediately I'd become chained down. I might be able to compose symphonies, but I wouldn't be able to do theater music." The second half of this statement turned out to be true. Between 1957 and 1969, the period during which he was music director of the New York Philharmonic, while he did attempt to work on theater projects, none of them reached the stage.

The fact that he was not yet responsible for directing and planning the work of a symphony orchestra, as he would be from 1957 on, made *Candide* and *West Side Story* of 1956 and early 1957, written at the peak of his fecundity and compositional brilliance, possible. What is remarkable is that, although the two works were written concurrently and cross-pollinated each other musically to a considerable degree, they still seem utterly distinct from each other.

In the summer of 1955, working in yet another vein, the composer wrote incidental music in a late medieval, early Renaissance style for a New York production of Lillian Hellman's version of *L'Alouette* (*The Lark*) by the French playwright Jean Anouilh. *The Lark* opened at the Longacre Theatre on November 17, 1955, and starred Julie Harris, Christopher Plummer, and Boris Karloff. Bernstein's music, which many years later was turned into a *Missa brevis*, consisted of settings of medieval French folk texts and excerpts from the Latin Mass, for seven voices and percussion. The play was very successful and ran for 229 performances. The day after the opening, Bernstein received a telegram from managing director Bruno Zirato of the New York Philharmonic asking him to be a guest conductor at the Philharmonic during the 1956–57 season.

Sometime over the winter Bernstein learned that his Curtis piano teacher Isabelle Vengerova was dying of pancreatic cancer. Because she had not been told how ill she was, she was as surprised to find herself slowly losing weight (something she had always tried and failed to do) as she was by the number of former students who came to call on her. She told Nicolas Slonimsky that, unexpectedly, even Leonard Bernstein had dropped by and helped out by doing the dishes. Vengerova died on February 7, 1956.

In March, on the cusp of renewing his relationship with the Philharmonic, Bernstein suddenly found himself the target of an investigation led by Representative John Rooney of the House Appropriations Committee. Rooney was trying to ferret out suspected communists from the Symphony of the Air, which was scheduled to go on a trip to Asia sponsored by the State Department, and was looking carefully into the past affiliations of anyone associated with it. (Bernstein had conducted the Symphony in the *Omnibus* programs.) Bernstein was in a rare state of panic. He must have assumed that he was finally free from being hounded over his political views. According to biographer Humphrey Burton, it seems likely that John F. Kennedy (then a Massachusetts senator) intervened on his behalf. Kennedy and Bernstein met in connection with an *Omnibus* program about Harvard, took a liking to each other, and had lunch together on March 27, just after Bernstein learned of the investigation. Soon after that, Representative Rooney's investigation into Bernstein's affiliations was called off.

Work on *Candide* continued, with the poet Richard Wilbur contributing lyrics that matched the tone of Bernstein's music so beautifully that one would never guess that there had ever been other lyrics there or that indeed the music had often been written without them.[8] Bernstein's imagination never flowed quite as freely or with as little self-consciousness as it did in the years when he wrote *Serenade*, *Candide*, and *West Side Story*. By the end of the summer of 1956 he had provided a veritable cornucopia of material for the Voltaire project, and in the years to come the various versions created of the work would draw from many crates of music left unused in the original production. This does not mean, however, that he was an easy collaborator on this project. Given Hellman's eventual bitterness, Wilbur's complaints as recorded by Humphrey Burton, and hints conveyed by director Tyrone Guthrie's account ("I wonder whether it was an unconscious reaction to the diamond quality of Bernstein's brilliance? . . . [Hellman] . . . and I . . . seemed to lose whatever share of lightness and gaiety and dash we might possibly have been able to contribute"), we may infer that Bernstein was so focused on his own *Candide* that the others could not find their way fully into the project.

In November 1956 he wrote a "colloquy" in the *New York Times* in which he conversed with his own "id" on the subject of *Candide*, in light of his recent assertions about American musical comedy on *Omnibus*. The self-interrogation results in a determination that *Candide* is essentially an operetta, in the sense that its models are European (opéra comique arias and ensembles, etc.), its settings are mostly European, its period is somewhere between 1750 and 1830, and its language is devoid of jazz and Broadway influence. But its authors are American and therefore their work is American. Hellman, he comments, has "added, deleted, rewritten, replotted, composed brand-new sequences" and provided "a new ending" in a way that "makes it infinitely more significant for our country and our time."[9]

*Candide* is probably Bernstein's happiest score. Despite its reference points in current politics, the setting of the tale outside the United States and two hundred years in the past seems to have given the composer a vacation from his psychological conflicts and issues. Even more than in the musicals that preceded it, he was able to mine his gift for mimicry and his memory for musical genres, table the issue of "originality," and simply enjoy writing. In its surreal deployment of genres often at odds with the locales in which they are placed, and sometimes anachronistic in their musical vocabulary, *Candide* is the sophisticated apotheosis of the Yiddish *Carmen* and madcap *Mikado* of his teenage Sharon productions. Along with a polka and a barcarolle, there is a schottische in Buenos Aires, a Viennese waltz in Paris, and a German gavotte in Venice. There is indeed a tango in Buenos Aires ("I Am Easily Assimilated," to Bernstein's own lyrics), but it is a hundred years too early for one, and it sounds far more Jewish than it does Argentinean (Bernstein's original sketch is marked *Hassidicamente*). Alongside Germanic chorales, the score is filled with echoes of bel canto and coloratura singing (Bellini, Rossini) and reminiscences of Léhar, Mozart, and, most of all, Gilbert and Sullivan. The tonal structure, which is far less dissonant than elsewhere in Bernstein's work, is solidly traditional, but the work's sumptuous vocal lines, sonorous polyphony, and witty accompaniments are never predictable. (The rhythmic and metrical play is far more intricate than in any of the musicals.) Much of the work could be described as Haydnesque, by way of Prokofiev. (The Paris waltz could be an opulent cousin of the Gavotte in Prokofiev's *Classical* Symphony.) In *Candide* Bernstein's wit moves at a slightly accelerated though still essentially eighteenth-century pace. Unlike *West Side Story*, the unity of *Candide* is not achieved primarily motivically (although there are several such connections) but rather through a consistent adherence to operetta conventions in terms of structures, tonality, and meter, which are then subjected to inventive distortion. What motivic connections there are, however, are wonderfully subtle.[10] In her study *There's a Place for Us*, musicologist Helen Smith points out the ingenious derivation of the Westphalian chorale, which serves as a refrain in the work, from the middle section of "Best of All Possible Worlds." An amusing touch is the use of a twelve-tone row in the first and last sections of the trio "Quiet," illustrating the boredom of Cunegonde and the Old Lady in Buenos Aires.[11]

Bernstein's manic ebullience is at its peak in the overture, which eventually became his most performed orchestral composition. It employs a truncated sonata structure formally akin to the Allegro portion of the first movement of the *Serenade*.[12] The second half of the first subject is taken from the "battle music" later in the score, and the second theme is derived from Candide and Cunegonde's duet "Oh, Happy We." The canonic coda comes from the "cabaletta" vocalise at the end of "Glitter and Be Gay."

Bernstein and Hellman may have been attracted to different aspects of Voltaire. She surely relished the opportunity to turn Candide's satire against American targets, while Bernstein may have been inspired more by Voltaire's humanity and the fleetness and exuberance of his style.[13] The composer's ending expresses a heartfelt embrace of life with all its contradictions, while Voltaire's acceptance is quieter and more resigned. Hellman's original words capture Voltaire's muted tone in her own way: "We will not think noble because we are not noble. We will not live in beautiful harmony because there is no such thing in this world, nor should there be. We promise only to do our best and live out our lives."[14]

After a mixed reception in Boston, a trimmed and more focused *Candide* opened at the Martin Beck Theatre in New York City on December 1, 1956. While, with the exception of Walter Kerr's in the *Herald Tribune*, reviews were mostly favorable, box office sales were insufficient to keep the production afloat. It ran on Broadway for seventy-three performances, which, as

Andrew Porter has pointed out, would have been counted a remarkable success in the world of opera but constituted failure on Broadway. In later accounts, Hellman, Richard Wilbur, and Tyrone Guthrie seemed to agree that its elements did not jell. Guthrie called the production "an artistic and financial disaster" and said that his own direction "skipped along with the effortless grace of a freight train heavy-laden on a steep gradient." It had been impossible to find singers who could "do justice to the score" and at the same time "handle the text." He praised Bernstein's "mercurial, allusive score," adding that the composer's "facility and virtuosity are so dazzling that you are almost blinded, and fail to see the patient workmanship, the grinding application to duty which produces the gloss. This may not be an original or greatly creative genius, but, if ever I have seen it, the stuff of genius is there."[15]

Whatever the joyful promise of the original work process, Hellman eventually considered the experience her worst in the theater, and she withdrew her name from all subsequent revivals. Despite the commercial failure of the work, the cast album continued to generate admiration for the score, which Stephen Sondheim has always considered Bernstein's best.[16] Several revised versions followed over the years, most prominently a condensed one with a new book by Hugh Wheeler, which was mounted at the Chelsea Theater in Brooklyn in 1973 and then ran on Broadway for an entire year. This was expanded into a version performed at the New York City Opera in 1982. But not until near the end of Bernstein's life, with the production presented at the Scottish Opera in 1988 using a book by Hugh Wheeler revised by John Wells, was there a version of the work that restored most of the original music to its proper order and reclaimed its identity. There was little left of Hellman in this final version, apart from a few lyrics. Andrew Porter described this incarnation as "the entertaining yet affecting, bubbling yet emotional work that it was always intended to be." In her study of Bernstein's musical theater works, Helen Smith considers it likely that, had he lived longer, Bernstein might have continued to tinker with *Candide*.

Back in October 1956, while work on *Candide* was in production and *West Side Story* was in a temporary holding pattern, Bernstein had been named co-conductor with Dimitri Mitropoulos of the New York Philharmonic for the 1957–58 season. He was scheduled to conduct the orchestra in performances of Handel's *Messiah* starting in late December 1956. But because of the death of conductor Guido Cantelli in an airplane crash in Paris on November 24, he was asked to fill in as conductor starting on December 13 in performances of Ravel's *La valse*, Stravinsky's *The Song of the Nightingale*, Tchaikovsky's Sixth Symphony, and Hindemith's *Mathis der Maler.* As it happened, Cantelli had been one of the leading contenders for the position of music director soon to be vacated by Mitropoulos. The other candidates for the position were European-born giants in their seventies and eighties.

On April 29, 1956, the *New York Times* had carried a full page article by Howard Taubman bemoaning the decline in the quality of the orchestra, arguing that the board and management had become rigid and complacent and that Mitropoulos had allowed its standards to slip. What was needed, he wrote, was a new music director who could restore the orchestra's quality, take "a more vigorous and creative approach to the orchestra's commitments," initiate more integrated and inventive programming representing a wider spectrum of music old and new, and be more "vigorous in reaching a wider public."

Bernstein presented his interesting version of *Messiah* on December 27. He conflated the original three-part structure into two. The work is often given with cuts, but the structure itself has usually been treated as sacrosanct.[17] Part I deals with the Christmas story; Parts II and III with Christ's death and resurrection. In his attention to musical details, in the orchestral and choral forces he employed, and in choosing a countertenor to sing the alto parts, Bernstein was scrupulous in his attempt to honor Handel's musical intentions. But he argued that the text, a collection of passages from the Bible selected and arranged in a certain order by a clergyman named Pooley, and assigned to Handel by a patron named Charles Jennens, did not need to be regarded as inviolable. Part II begins with music and texts linked to the theme of Christ's suffering and death, but then interrupts these with joyful pieces such as "Lift up your heads, O ye gates" and the "Hallelujah" chorus, which Bernstein felt would more properly belong earlier, with the story of Christ's birth. He found that by reversing the order of these sections and making a few judicious cuts, he could divide the work into two parts, maintain Handel's basic key structure, and clarify its dramatic arc. The performance (which was immediately recorded on December 31, 1956) has many beauties and communicates the meaning and dramatic power of a work that can often sound routine.[18]

In January 1957 Bernstein offered several equally interesting programs. Conducting from the piano, he was soloist in Ravel's Concerto in G Major, which he had played since his school days, alongside Haydn's Symphony No. 102, and Bartók's *Music for Strings, Percussion and Celesta;* a substantial evening showcased Isaac Stern in Prokofiev's Second Violin Concerto, sandwiched between Beethoven's "Eroica" Symphony and Sibelius's Fifth Symphony. The young Canadian pianist Glenn Gould performed Beethoven's Concerto No. 2 in B-flat Major on an otherwise all-American program that included symphonies by Roy Harris and Copland and Bernstein's own *Candide* overture.

Jerome Robbins seems to have conceived of the notion of a musical based on *Romeo and Juliet* while he was coaching his friend Montgomery Clift in the role of Romeo in 1948. Some accounts even credit Clift with the idea. The original notion was to set a modern version of the tale among Jews and Catholics celebrating Passover and Easter on New York's Lower East Side. Robbins approached Bernstein with the idea in January 1949, a few months before the premiere of *The Age of Anxiety*, and the two of them then met with scriptwriter and playwright Arthur Laurents four days later, to discuss Laurents's writing the book. Although some work on the show was begun in the next few months, and it was even briefly announced for the 1949–50 season, by April Bernstein was doubting whether they could collaborate on it while he was pursuing such a hectic conducting schedule, and even whether he should cede the project to another composer. Further work commitments and doubts about the project kept the team from concentrating on it until the summer of 1955, when Robbins again brought the subject up and Bernstein and Laurents met in Hollywood. Newspaper accounts of gang violence in Los Angeles between Chicanos and whites proved a catalyst. Laurents suggested setting the work among rival gangs in New York's Spanish Harlem, and Bernstein was instantly drawn to the musical potential of using Latin and South American materials in a show. The basic theme was to be the "futility of intolerance," with the characters and essential structure to be drawn from Shakespeare and transposed to urban, mid-twentieth-century America. The apothecary would become a drugstore; the Capulets' ball a dance at the high school gym. In the first outlines, the characters retained their Shakespearian names: Juliet (not Maria), Romeo (not Tony), Tybalt (not Bernardo), Mercutio (not Riff), and so on. By October there was a new three-act outline with the strife occurring between white and Puerto Rican street gangs. Robbins's letter to Laurents of October 15, in which he argued for a two-act structure, displays his brilliant critical acumen about matters of character, tone, and dramatic structure.

Originally Bernstein was his own lyricist. An Italianate love song for Tony (later "Maria"), written back in 1949 when the project was first proposed, which begins with the three-note germ of the entire score, was set to his own "terrible" words for a long time. (The continuation of the melody after the initial three-note cell comes so close to the orchestral introduction to the dinner party scene in Blitzstein's *Regina*, completed in 1948, that one must assume it is directly influenced by it.) A "D major tune" that had been taken out of *Candide* (where it had once been part of "Oh, Happy We") seemed right for the marriage scene but lacked words. This was to become "One Hand, One Heart." The composer knew that he needed a co-lyricist, and, once he learned that Comden and Green were unavailable, agreed to hiring twenty-six-year-old Stephen Sondheim, who had been suggested by Laurents. Because Sondheim himself was a composer, working with him was a particular joy, "like working with an alter ego," as Bernstein put it years later.[19] (Among their shared enthusiasms was a love of anagrams, at which Sondheim outdid Bernstein.) They worked alongside each other, and in fact struggled "for weeks trying to get the right lyrics for 'Maria,'" breaking the impasse only when Sondheim came up with the poetic concept of the sound of her name. While they often squabbled about the lyrics, both later concurred on the spirit of fun that characterized the collaboration.[20]

By the spring of 1956, much of the first-act music was complete. But since Bernstein was working concurrently on *Candide*, the creative team postponed work until the new year. After *Candide*'s brief and none-too-happy run, work resumed on *West Side Story* in February, with an opening scheduled for the following September, and the team began the difficult process of casting a show that required forty unknown young people, all of whom could sing, dance, and act. In the midst of casting, Laurents received word from producer Cheryl Crawford that she was struggling to find backers for the project and that she herself doubted whether there would be a Broadway audience for something so dark. "I think we are in trouble," she wrote. Laurents defended the show's viability ("Tension, anger, hate etc. all the dark emotions . . . will not depress or repel an audience when they are done in a theatrical, romantic style"), but on April 22 she and her partner Roger Stevens backed out. Sondheim, acting quickly and clandestinely, brought the score to producer Harold Prince and played it for him. He was convinced. When Bernstein played the score officially for Prince and his partner Robert E. Griffith, Prince started to sing along, and Bernstein was thrilled by what he took to be the producer's innate musicality. Before long the show had a new production team and had raised $300,000. (Briefly the show was called *Gangway!* or *Gang Way!*, a title fortunately abandoned.)[21]

This is not to say that the way had instantly been cleared for a successful production. Robbins soon decided to withdraw as choreographer and stay on only to direct, but Prince called his bluff, saying that if he did so the production would have to look for a new producer. Robbins backed down, but in the bargain he secured an eight-week rehearsal period instead of the customary four or five. The extra time enabled him to weld the cast into an ensemble through a combination of method acting techniques, exhausting repetition, brilliant directorial strategy, and sheer terror. At an early meeting with the assembled cast, he told them, "I know I'm difficult. I know I am going to hurt your feelings. But that's the way I am."[22] This proved to be an understatement. Public humiliation and abusiveness were integral to his rehearsal process. So were shrewd methods of creating theatrical realism. He assigned every character a name, separated the two gangs, and forbade them from talking to each other or crossing to the side of the stage occupied by their rivals. (The right side was for the Sharks, the left for the Jets.) There were no ensemble lunches between the gangs, and their real names were not to be used. Furthermore, they needed to thoroughly internalize their characters' personal histories, since he would suddenly turn on them onstage to quiz them about their "parents" or incidents that had marked them. By the end of the rehearsal period, the violence in the show had a palpable underpinning of high tension and anxiety.

Bernstein held Robbins in awe and also, uncharacteristically, was afraid of him. "Jerry was fearlessly insulting," Sondheim remembered. "Very few people can take that. And I saw him humiliate Lenny in [the] dress rehearsal of *West Side* down in Washington. . . . Jerry and Lenny had argued over the orchestration of 'Somewhere.' So when the orchestra was playing it in the pit, Jerry just ignored Lenny, went down to the pit, and stopped the rehearsal, and dictated changes in the music to the conductor, right there in front of Lenny. . . . It was really shocking. And Lenny, instead of confronting him, left the theater. And I had a hunch where he would be, and I went to the nearest bar, and there he was with three or four shots lined up in front of him."[23] According to Carol Lawrence (Maria in the first cast), Bernstein's "nurturing behavior saved us from falling apart." He "too was a genius, but one who was sensitive to the feelings, needs, and anxieties of human beings. Very often after Jerry took us apart, Lenny would put us back together again. . . . He didn't drive us. . . . He led us by believing in us. . . . He would put his arm around me and say, 'Come on, I'll play the balcony scene for you . . . we'll work on it together.'"[24] Despite or because of the brutality, several cast members, Chita Rivera among them, later credited Robbins with teaching them how to act.

In this domain Robbins was the dominant figure, and Bernstein was the creatively accommodating partner. An "enormous excitement" flowed between them (to use Robbins's own words). Robbins found in Bernstein's music a kinetic impulse that instantly inspired movement and that was a joy to choreograph to. He could articulate exactly what he needed from the music, and Bernstein, who as usual didn't sleep much, could provide it for him the next day. Carol Lawrence remembered that Bernstein would bring in new music and play it while Robbins would "stand over him and clutch his shoulders as if he were a musical instrument." Years later Bernstein, too, remembered Robbins's hands on his shoulders.

For Bernstein the collaboration was grueling because he lost much music on the way. As is always the case in theater, numbers went through numerous versions, and whole songs and dance numbers disappeared. An early mambo was discarded, as was a *huapango*. "Mix," originally intended to introduce the Jets near the show's opening, was moved to the rumble at the end of act 1 and subsequently taken out of the score. (Interestingly, it lacks the tritone thumbprint of all the show's songs associated with violence.) A trio for three Jets, "Kids Ain't" (also called "Kid Stuff" and "Like Everybody Else"), meant to inject energy and humor into a first-act lull, was pulled by Laurents for drawing the evening too close to traditional musical comedy. Versions of "A Boy Like That" and "Somewhere" that were more extended, contrapuntal, and operatic than those we now know were sharpened and streamlined. On July 28, 1957, on a flight to Miami, a somewhat discouraged Bernstein wrote to his wife that "All the things I love most in it are slowly being dropped—too operatic, too this and that. They're all so scared and commercial success means so much to them. To me, too, I suppose—but I still insist it can be achieved with pride. . . . I miss you terribly . . . you reside at the very core of my life, my darling."

Yet working with collaborators in such synchrony with each other's aims was bringing out of the composer a score of unity, power, and concision. In fact, he was able to insert into it more of his own preexisting music than the amount he had lost. Bernstein had written the music for "Somewhere" long before; since it lacked a lyric, Marc Blitzstein had given it a temporary one, for fun, that began, "There goes what's his name, / Unhappy what's his name. / I've been wondering who's to blame? / Who's to blame? Huh?"[25] "One Hand, One Heart" was a rejected love duet for Candide and Cunegonde from *Candide*, where it had been followed by a chorale prelude for chorus based on it. The music for "Gee, Officer Krupke," added during New York rehearsals, had been meant for *Candide*'s Venice scene. From his own unfinished Cuban-inspired *Conch Town* ballet, written in Key West in 1941, came the music for "America" and the Coplandesque, rhythmically savage, "Taunting Scene," the show's penultimate number.[26]

Since dance was at the heart of the storytelling, purely instrumental music took on an extraordinary role in the piece. The opening, which had originally been largely sung, eventually set the violent tone with instruments alone. The "Cool" fugue was greatly expanded during rehearsal, no doubt because Robbins wanted to extend the choreography. Nigel Simeone and others consider it the most complex music composed for Broadway up until that time.[27]

The theme for "Tonight" was extricated from its place in the first-act quintet and turned into the love song in the Balcony Scene only after both "Somewhere" and "One Hand, One Heart" were deemed wrong for it. "Something's Coming" was added to bolster the strength of Tony's character on August 7, 1957, only twelve days before the ensemble left for the Washington previews. That day Bernstein wrote to Felicia about the song, saying how much he missed her: "it just wasn't the same not playing it first for you." Bernstein struggled over the ending and continued to believe years later that when Maria gives her speech at the end, holding the gun that killed Tony, "it should be musicalized" and "cries out for music." But many and varied attempts ("a hard-boiled piece," then "something that sounded like a . . . Puccini aria") did not work.[28] The ending he arrived at fused together musical ideas written a decade apart. The funeral cortege combines "Somewhere," "I Have a

Love," and the primary three-note motive of the score into a solemn instrumental passage that somehow manages to convey shock and tragedy, yet also a glimmer of hope.

The orchestration took three weeks. Bernstein called upon his old friend Sid Ramin, who agreed to sign on to the project as long as they could both work with Irwin Kostal, an expert orchestrator involved with *The Music Man* at the time. Negotiations with the producers and discussions between the three of them resulted in a unique ensemble of thirty-one players, including strings without violas, an electric guitar player doubling on the Spanish guitar and mandolin, and five percussionists, one of them playing only timpani. There were five reed players, with one playing eight different instruments, and four of them able to play bass clarinet. From the beginning Bernstein insisted on holding one reed chair for his bassoonist friend Sanford Sharoff, a former classmate from Curtis. Ramin remembers that this "forced us into being very inventive in how we treated the other instruments."[29]

Ramin describes the piano score as the most complete and detailed he ever worked with in the theater. Bernstein stretched the demands on his musicians to the limits but always turned out to be right about what was performable. Bernstein, Ramin, and Kostal would discuss every measure in detail, and while Bernstein's intentions were very specific, he remained open to "popular music embellishments" proposed by his orchestrators, which he would later either approve or change.[30] The music for *West Side Story* capitalized on Bernstein's love of variations in several spots. Two that are particularly delightful are in the dance at the gym: the explosive big-band blues that opens the scene is a variation on the release in the Jets song, in which the lyrics mention the upcoming dance ("Oh, when the Jets fall in at the cornball dance"), and the cha-cha is a variation of the as-yet-unheard song "Maria."[31]

*West Side Story* occupies its own category. The show is a kind of mirror image of Shakespeare, in that the words do not draw attention to themselves but instead project a seemingly artless realism and simplicity. The book ended up being among the shortest for any Broadway musical, a "miracle" of compression, in Sondheim's words. The couple "falls in love in eight lines," he observed, "and you believe it."

It is the music and dance that come closer to Shakespearian intricacy. The show is more dance-driven than any previous musical, with dance furthering the plot, even to the extent of enacting the "rumble" in which Riff and Bernardo are killed.[32] The music is almost Beethovenian in its reliance on a few motives and interval combinations to unify its heterogeneous sections. The story handed Bernstein an opportunity to revel in two idioms that were second nature to him: Latin American music for the Puerto Rican immigrants and a bebop-tinged jazz for the "self-styled 'Americans'" (Bernstein's words), all the while encouraging him to explore his aspiration to an operatic language derived from musical theater. Bernstein's marriage was, in some ways, cross-cultural, and his home life, presided over by Felicia and with a Chilean staff and the ever-present cook, Julia Vega, helping with the children and speaking Spanish with them, was bilingual. He had no personal experience of gang violence, but he certainly knew anti-Semitism and surely, like all of his collaborating team, understood sexual intolerance and the risk of admitting to a love that violated societal norms. And of course he was a child of immigrants, born into an atmosphere of marital strife and tension.

In evoking the world of Puerto Ricans musically, he was not literal. The song "America" exploits the rhythmic ambiguity of the Mexican huapango. Helen Smith notes the use of the Spanish guitar as well as "claves, guiro, maracas (used as timpani sticks), pitched drums, bongos and cowbells" in this number, all associated with Latin American music, as well as the Puerto Rican *seis* rhythms of the song's verse. The mambo and cha-cha at the gym are in the style of Cuban music. At the same time, as Jack Gottlieb has persuasively demonstrated in his book *Funny, It Doesn't Sound Jewish*, a variant of the shofar's call to worship introduces the piece (as indeed another version of it begins *Candide*), and its three-note interval structure (perfect fourth–tritone) permeates many of the principal numbers, including "Maria," "Something's Coming," and "Cool." (He also points out remnants of Jewish liturgical music in many of the songs.) Where other composers can be noted as influences, they have somehow been infused by Bernstein's personality. There are several ostinatos in the prologue, for example, that look Stravinskian on the page. The opening of the "Tonight" quintet looks like a relative of the fast section in Stravinsky's *Symphony of Psalms*. But when one hears these passages, the influences evaporate; nothing could sound more like midcentury, urban America.[33] The score has vocal sections of operatic complexity and substance, most notably the "Tonight" ensemble. It contains more complex musical interrelationships than *Candide*, and contains fascinating near-quotes of music from outside the Broadway tradition. (One of the less frequently mentioned is the reference to Beethoven's *Grosse Fuge* in the "Cool" fugue.)

Such is its unity and reliance on dance that the complete dramatic shape and power of *West Side Story* emerges effectively in the voiceless *Symphonic Dances* extracted from it. Yet *West Side Story* remains a musical both because of its balance between spoken text and music and because of the process of its creation.[34] It is common to remember songs but to forget, or not care, what show they are from. Songs from *West Side Story* are always remembered as excerpts from the larger work, and the musical is referred to as an entity, as one would refer to an opera or a ballet. The integrity and unity of the result had to be, in part, the result of the inner compulsion for order that takes over when an artist is fully engaged with creative work. Although even Bernstein himself eventually referred to the tritone–perfect fifth "Maria" motive as the generative cell behind the entire score, Ramin and Sondheim remember his being surprised and delighted when its prevalence was pointed out to him. Did he consciously plant a suggestion of a phrase from "Somewhere" in measures 101–3 of the show's instrumental prologue?[35] The intelligence of the unconscious mind can sometimes outdo the intelligence of conscious planning, and Bernstein knew how to balance the two.

With their New York rehearsal period drawing to a close, two weeks away from their Washington opening, a first complete run-through was held. It was August 3. On the very same day, Bernstein signed a contract to become music director of the New York Philharmonic, starting in the 1958–59 season, another life-changing development. Frustrated by wrangling between lawyers over a twenty-page document, he tore it up and drafted a one-page letter of agreement that pleased everyone, signed it, and toasted his new position with a chilled bottle of Brut. As he wrote Felicia, who was visiting her mother in Santiago, Chile, with the children at the time, "and I'm in—like for life." The *West Side Story* run-through revealed, he wrote, that although "the problems are many, varied, and overwhelming," there was "a show there, and just possibly a great one. Jerry is behaving (in his own way) and Arthur is doing well. But the work is endless: I never sleep: Everything gets rewritten every day. . . . Some beautiful shots of you and the kids arrived . . . and they melted me."[36]

The signs that others might agree that the show was indeed a "great one" accumulated. The "gypsy run-through" (for fellow actors and show business people) on August 10, their last day in New York, without sets or costumes, left the audience stunned. Then it was on to Washington for three weeks at the National Theatre, where the show opened to mainly positive reviews and was attended by Vice President Nixon and many other dignitaries. (At intermission, Bernstein encountered Supreme Court Justice Felix Frankfurter in tears after the first act.) The day after the opening, *Washington Post* theater critic Richard Coe called the musical "a work of art" and "uniquely cohesive."[37] Music critic Paul Hume weighed in with a measured response to the score, which combined praise for "I Feel Pretty," "America," and "Gee, Officer Krupke" with critiques of "A Boy Like That," "I Have a Love," and the dream ballet. But after the critical failure of *Candide*, the composer was buoyant. When none of the Washington reviews mentioned co-lyricist Sondheim, Bernstein signed over credit for the lyrics entirely to him.[38] Sid Ramin remembers that "every night we would go to the Erlanger Theatre where it was playing [in Philadelphia, after the Washington previews], and there was this little shoeshine boy, this urchin on the street, who must have been about nine or ten years old. And Lenny saw this little boy, and he went up to him and said, 'Would you like to come in and see the show?' And the boy said, 'Oh, yes.' So Lenny took him by the hand, marched into the theater, walked down the aisle, holding this little boy's hand, and the boy had his shoeshine kit in one hand and Lenny's hand in the other, sat down eighth row center, where Lenny was sitting, and they enjoyed the show."[39]

*West Side Story* opened at the Winter Garden Theatre in New York City on September 26, 1957. Most of the reviews were laudatory ("extraordinarily exciting"—John Chapman; "profoundly moving . . . an organic work of art"—Brooks Atkinson), while a few were ambivalent or negative. Visiting British critic Kenneth Tynan found the score "as smooth and savage as a cobra; it sounds as if Puccini and Stravinsky had gone on a roller-coaster ride into the precincts of modern jazz."[40] Walter Kerr praised the "savage, restless, electrifying dance patterns" but found the music "almost never emotionally affecting." Howard Taubman thought that Bernstein lacked a gift for "melodic invention." Playwright Harold Clurman, in the *Na-*

*tion*, attacked the work as a "phony" exploitation of "the pain of a real problem" "for the purposes of popular showmanship," identifying the issue of patronizing exoticism (or "intellectual slumming") that has also been raised over the years in connection with *Show Boat*, *Porgy and Bess*, *South Pacific*, and *The King and I*. He took the talented collaborators to task for wanting "at one and the same time to be progressive and to please several million playgoers, the ticket brokers and the movie companies."[41] The original production of *West Side Story* ran for 734 performances, toured for close to a year, and then returned to New York for an additional 253 performances in 1960.

Having noted that both *Candide* and the *Symphonic Dances from "West Side Story"* begin with transformed shofar "calls to worship," Jack Gottlieb observes that the composer's two best-known compositions could be regarded as symbols of Jewish assimilation every bit as much as was Roxbury's imposing Temple Mishkan Tefila, with its organ and choir loft.[42]

The effect of *West Side Story* on Bernstein's subsequent life and the way he was viewed by the general public, the Broadway audience, and his peers in the classical music world cannot be overestimated. The release of the film version starring Natalie Wood and Richard Beymer on October 18, 1961, made the association between his name and this music a permanent, international phenomenon. As a result, however, Bernstein's other compositional interests were often viewed as secondary or even artificial by those who took him to be, first and foremost, a Broadway composer.

It is no wonder he felt he was leading many lives simultaneously. One day after the heady New York opening of the show, he was on a plane to Tel Aviv with Felicia to conduct the Israel Philharmonic in the gala programs celebrating the completion of their new concert hall. Isaac Stern and Arthur Rubinstein were the soloists. Then he was back in New York on November 20 to be officially named music director of the

Philharmonic, assuming the position previously held by such musical titans as Gustav Mahler (1909–11), Arturo Toscanini, Leopold Stokowski, and his friend Dimitri Mitropoulos.

Although still officially "co-conductor" with Mitropoulos, he now returned to the podium of the Philharmonic in January 1958 as the "music director-elect," and the program he chose contained two of the works he had conducted in his surprise debut with the orchestra fifteen years earlier: the Schumann *Manfred* overture and Strauss's *Don Quixote.* In addition the program included the North American premiere of Shostakovich's Second Piano Concerto, written for Shostakovich's son, Maxim, the previous year, which Bernstein conducted from the piano. This was also the first program he conducted at the Philharmonic using a baton. He had first tried a baton in Israel after injuring his back, and the practice had stuck.

Two weeks later, he gave the first of fifty-three televised Young People's Concerts. These television appearances were marked by a combination of eloquence, learning, glamour, and elegance (that "Harvard" accent), plus a kind of informality that no one before him had associated with "serious" music. His teaching style, like his conducting style, somehow combined discipline and decorum with a startling human immediacy. For better or worse, many in his audience, like the orchestral musicians at the Philharmonic, came to know him as "Lenny."

# 9

## *What Does Music Mean?*

IN WRITING THE text for *I Hate Music* in 1943, Bernstein had not only imagined a child's impressions of concerts. He had also expressed some of his own impatience with the way classical music was presented and perceived. In his Young People's Concerts in Carnegie Hall he was able to address children as an idealized father figure or older brother, while also communicating subliminally that he could still identify with them. An electric current of subversiveness ran through these concerts, as Bernstein seemed almost to reach inside the psyches of his listeners and unlock the barriers between them and music. The concerts created a sense of community, but they were also the exact opposite of "mass entertainment." They addressed the individual, not the collective. Parents who brought their children to Carnegie Hall and later Philharmonic Hall, hoping that their child would receive an injection of "cultivation" and "fineness," and somehow emerge more civilized as a result, were instead confronted by someone who was trying to communicate with a deeper, more philosophical, more emotional side of their children than perhaps they were.

The parents in the audience shown in the concerts' films often look as if they are expecting that Bernstein will explain to their children why classical music is "good." But for Bernstein, "good" is not the point. He wants the children—and their parents—to feel the power, subtlety, and ecstasy of music, to feel why they need it, and to have their experience of life changed. In this he is immeasurably aided by having the New York Philharmonic standing by to play fragments from any music he chooses, and he makes the most of it. The musical moments soak through his words, like drops of blue ink spreading through a page of text. If parents were expecting that this highbrow conductor would explain to the children why "high art" is "high" and "low art" is "low," they were in for another surprise. He actually explains that "high" and "low" are permeable distinctions; that each work of music needs to be evaluated on its own terms.

From the first moment of his first Young People's Concert, "What Does Music Mean?," given on January 18, 1958, Bernstein is tough on his young people. In 1950s America, classical music was often seen as an accessory to a bourgeois lifestyle. And "music appreciation" lectures tended to present it as an ancillary art—as a pendant to the lives of the composers who wrote it, or as primarily an "expression" of something *non*musical—an impression abetted most famously by Walt Disney's animated film *Fantasia*, which presented "fine" music as an accompaniment to brilliantly rendered imagery. Bernstein's opening gesture meets the children on their own turf and dismantles this view. Without a word he turns to conduct the opening of Rossini's *William Tell* overture. Then he turns around and asks the audience what the music is "about." Of course they all shout "the Lone Ranger," to which he answers, "That's just what I thought you'd say."

"Well, I hate to disappoint you. But it really isn't about the Lone Ranger at all. It's about notes—E-flats and F-sharps." (He pauses.) "You see, no matter how many people tell you stories about what music means"—he holds up his hand like a stop sign—"forget them. Stories are not what music is about at all. Music is never about anything. Music just is. Music is notes—beautiful notes and sounds put together in such a way that we get pleasure out of listening to them. That's all there is to it."

He thus launches into philosophy within the first moments of the show. He compares music to language, as he would in a more detailed (but not necessarily deeper) way fifteen years later in his Harvard Norton Lectures. He says that language conveys "ideas." "'Ow—I burned my finger' conveys that it hurts, that I may not be able to play the piano anymore, that I have a loud voice when I scream." But notes (here he plays a few isolated notes) can't be "about sputniks, or lampshades, or rockets." What are they "about"? Then he plays a few phrases of a Chopin nocturne. "Beautiful, isn't it? But what's it about? Nothing." Then the opening of Beethoven's "Waldstein" Sonata ("it's not about anything"), followed by a delightfully elaborate strain of boogie-woogie, which startles and delights the audience. "They're not any of them about anything. But they are all fun to listen to." At this point he makes the distinction between the image formed in your mind by a word ("When I say . . . 'rocket'—bang!—Picture") and the effect of a given note played loudly or softly, higher or lower, played by the piano, or an oboe, or a xylophone, or a trombone. He explains that composers put together notes according to a plan, using musical means. If a story is attached to a composition it is "extra." "Whatever the music means, it is not the story."

He then proceeds to dismantle our associations with *Wil-*

*liam Tell*, explaining that Rossini "had never heard of the Wild West," and that the opera for which the overture was composed actually takes place in Switzerland. Then he discusses the rhythm and orchestration of the work. He has the children sing the opening melody with him to feel the phrase structure, and the way the final phrase rises above the first three and resolves them, "like winning an argument." He has the strings demonstrate their bouncing bow on the opening chords. It sounds marvelous, and we realize that we hadn't noticed it before. We begin to realize that we were not listening closely to the overture at the opening of the program—that it had become more of an emblem than a piece. "It's exciting because it was written to be exciting," he says. "It's exciting for musical reasons and for no other reasons."

All this was a way of saying that music was not a commodity, owned by the keepers of something called "culture," or by the writers of television shows or movies either, but that it was intangible and wondrously complex. It belonged to each individual listener and musical participant.

The Young People's Concerts are educational precisely because they take you somewhere that you are not expecting, and they accumulate depth through a combination of what is said, what is implied, and all that is experienced by seeing and hearing the music played. It is impossible to separate the personality of the teacher from the whole enterprise. If the text were delivered by someone other than Bernstein, the experience would not be the same. The viewer has the strange feeling that the teacher actually needs to share his enthusiasm with us; he seems keenly and genuinely interested in how we are receiving what he is saying. Bernstein's adolescent desire to have "everyone in the world love him" is somewhere in the mix. So is his authentic sense of mission about reaching each person, in the audience and at home, and sharing music with them.

Although there was a performative aspect to the Young

People's Concerts, Bernstein *was* in his natural element when he was teaching. He had taught his sister and brother; he had taught Sid Ramin; he had taught Shirley Gabis and her mother. At Curtis he had usurped the role of instructor in the counterpoint class with Richard Stöhr to such an extent that he had ended up coteaching it. He had taught at Tanglewood. At home he was explaining music to his own young children. In an interview with the *St. Louis Post-Dispatch* on October 23, 1961, Felicia described him as "a marvelous teacher" to young Jamie and Alexander (then nine and six years old, respectively): "He goes straight to essentials and makes everything clear. He gives them tonality and the relationship of chords and all kinds of things children aren't usually taught. . . . He likes to make up songs for them, too. When he was about to leave on a trip a few months ago, he wrote a three-voice lullaby for us to sing: 'Evenings, when it's booze time, that's the time we think of Daddy.'" When he emerged as a teacher on the public stage, he was doing in a scripted and highly controlled way what he had a tendency to do anyway. He was still the boy who had delivered his own bar mitzvah speech, twenty-five years earlier, transforming into a quintessential American delivery something of the rhetorical grace he had soaked up at Temple Mishkan Tefila, drawing on the zeal to instruct handed down from his ancestors and communicated through his father's discourses on the Talmud at the family dinner table.

Continuing "What Does Music Mean?," he plays the *Blue Danube* waltz at the piano ("Now maybe the Danube River inspired Strauss to write that waltz. Maybe—but I have my doubts"), then plays *Tales from the Vienna Woods* and asks why that one couldn't be called the *Blue Danube* or for that matter the *Tennessee Waltz* or the *Missouri Waltz*. He acknowledges that there are works which purport to "tell a story" or "paint a picture." As an example of music in the former category, he makes the children complicit in an experiment involving the score of *Don Quixote*, that challenging work from his Carnegie Hall debut concert in 1944. He asks them to listen to it first picturing a different story than the one that inspired the music, and then with the actual story in mind, demonstrating that their imaginations could make the music seem to fit either scenario. He indulges in a similar experiment with Beethoven's "Pastoral" Symphony ("As you know, 'pastoral' means anything to do with the country") and follows this with three movements from Mussorgsky's *Pictures at an Exhibition* (in the orchestration by Ravel that Koussevitzky himself commissioned). The "Great Gate of Kiev" fills Carnegie Hall with its monumental sound. The eyes of a dark-haired girl in her Sunday dress grow wide, and she takes a big breath and exhales with amazement. "That made you think of a big gate, didn't it?" asks Bernstein. The children are now hesitant to agree. "Well, did it?" There is a weak assent from the audience. "Right. But only because I told you to think about a 'big gate.' . . . The picture that goes with music goes with it only because the composer says so. But it's really not a *part* of the music. It's extra."

Now he is ready to shift his audience's attention to music that has no such "extra" baggage. He has made them attend to notes, bouncing bows, the difference between the same note played on a xylophone and on a trombone, the effect of huge columns of sound filling the hall. But he does not entirely let go of all associations, since he now proceeds to talk about Tchaikovsky's gift for "describing emotions," "feelings like pain, happiness, anger, love." (Ever mindful of the realities of children's lives, he divides the emotions evenly between the good and the bad, boldly starting right out with "pain.") "Have you ever had the feeling that you wanted something so badly that you can't have?" he asks, playing a theme from Tchaikovsky's Fourth Symphony at the piano, to which he sings the words "I want it" again and again, as the sequences climb up and up chromatically, way past the bounds of propriety, finally reaching a climax of anguish—and he stops, saying, "and then something breaks in you, and you cry." Then he turns to the orchestra and has them play the same intense music, which is not just a lesson in sequences and cadences and chromaticism but, of course, also in the inner torments of both Bernstein and Tchaikovsky. And the children in the audience are looking completely engaged, thoughtful, and calm, at forty minutes into a program on classical music. "Pretty emotional stuff, isn't it?" he asks them, rhetorically.

He follows with an example of one theme being employed by Tchaikovsky to depict two different emotions. First there is the opening of the Fifth Symphony—the clarinets in their chalumeau registers accompanied by low strings. His face is almost blank while he is conducting it. "Pretty depressing," he says, his voice trailing off. Then, by only changing a few notes, "what musicians call changing from minor to major—some of you will know what that means," the same tune played at a brisk tempo by the trumpets at the close of the work makes "it all come out joyful and triumphant, like someone who has just made a touchdown and is the hero of a football game." The orchestra soars—Carnegie Hall seems to levitate. "Now we can really understand what the meaning of music is," he says, mopping his brow. "It's the way it makes you feel when you hear it. . . . We don't have to know a lot about sharps and flats and chords and all that business in order to understand music. If it tells us something, not a story or a picture but a feeling, if it makes us change inside—to have all of these good feelings that music can make you have—then you're understanding it. And that's all there is to it. Because those feelings aren't like the stories and the pictures we talked about before. They're not extra, they're not outside the music. They belong to music. They're what music is about. . . . We can't always name the things we feel. Sometimes we can, but every once in a while we have feelings that are so deep that we have no words for them, and that's where music is so marvelous, because music names them for us, only in notes, instead of in words." And then, no doubt while studio executives were crossing their fingers or praying in the television sound booth, Bernstein plays the tiny, incredibly spare third movement (*zart Bewegung*) of Anton Webern's *Six Pieces for Orchestra*, op. 6. It's a brilliant choice, not only because it is only eleven measures long, but because in the middle the flute and glockenspiel etch out a quiet music-box tune that seems to compress Webern's entire childhood into one phrase. (Webern once described his entire pre–twelve-tone output as a reaction to the death of his mother.) "It's so delicate and so deep inside, that you mustn't even breathe while it's going on," Bernstein says. "So you see the meaning of music is *in the music* . . . If you like music at all, you'll find out the meanings for yourself just by listening to it." Without further discussion, he then closes the concert with a rousing performance of Ravel's *La valse*, a work that in its final wrenching and orgiastic pages moves in its own idiom as far past the bounds of courtesy and gentility as Tchaikovsky and Webern did in theirs.

Once he had framed the discussion in his own way, Bernstein could build on the foundation of this first talk in subsequent ones, dealing with musical concepts for their own sake. Sometimes he could seem to backtrack, resorting to a more generically folkloric or narrative approach to describing music, as in his birthday concert for Stravinsky, in which he simply told the story of *Petrushka* and then performed the work. But he would always return to the more mysterious and detailed musical issues eventually, and the concerts continued to surprise by never answering their questions in the way one expected, and by encompassing linguistic, artistic, and personal issues one could never anticipate.

Within the first two minutes of "What Is Melody?" (December 21, 1962), for example, Bernstein is already showing that the word can mean many different things: "It can be a tune, or a theme, or a motive, or a bass line, or a melodic line, or an inner voice." In trying to explain why some people find some kinds of music "unmelodic," he makes the important distinction between a "tune which is complete in itself," the kind one can imagine singing along with, and a melodic idea open-ended enough to become the seed of a symphonic work. Surprisingly, he immediately demonstrates this distinction with the opening of Wagner's *Tristan und Isolde*, a far cry from "Some Enchanted Evening" or whatever music some viewers might have expected to hear in a program called "What Is Melody?" He explicates wonderfully how the two interlocked motives and the chord progressions supporting them at the start of *Tristan*—mere fragments at the outset—generate an almost endless stream of melody in the body of the opera's prelude.

He then shows that counterpoint, which some listeners might at first find "unmelodic," is actually the combination of "many melodies," demonstrating the point with the "hair-raising" climax of the *Tristan* prelude, in which the rising opening motive is played in canon by the violins and cellos, while the chord progression from the work's second measure is intoned repeatedly in the brass—again, not exactly what a viewer might have bargained on hearing in the program. "Don't you ever be scared of counterpoint," he tells the audience. "It's not the absence of melody. It's an abundance of melody." He illustrates this abundance by taking apart a passage in the development section of Mozart's Fortieth Symphony—always a touchstone work for him. The program continues to explore melodic constructions of all kinds. A high point is his discussion of the unrepeating, ever-unfolding melody of the slow movement of Bach's *Italian Concerto*, which he plays on the piano. It is the exact opposite of the kind of song form most of us know best and can remember most easily, but it is certainly the very essence of melody. In the same spirit, he plays a four-minute passage from Hindemith's *Concert Music for Strings and Brass*, in which the strings unfurl a nobly burnished, ever-expanding swath of melody over dark brass chords. "Melody is exactly what a great composer wants it to be," he concludes.

Likewise in a program on "Humor in Music" from February 28, 1959, he opens up the subject rather than closes it down, managing to play a remarkable range of music—from Rameau to Shostakovich—and to make distinctions, to ten-year-olds, between "satire" and "parody," among other things. He emphasizes that "music can only make jokes about music." Extramusical elements—like the shouting and handkerchief waving in the parade of Walter Piston's *The Incredible Flutist*–can delight or make you smile, but true musical humor takes place within the notes and orchestration itself. He plays Haydn as an example of "musical wit." Teaching the word "incongruous" to the audience, the composer of *Candide* demonstrates how Prokofiev's *Classical* Symphony combines an old-fashioned gavotte with "incongruous" "modern musical puns," such as cadences that are prepared in one key but completed in another. Commenting that the essence of humor is "destruction," he plays the Burlesque movement from Copland's *Music for the Theater* (an influence, of course, on his own music for the theater). In humor "something has to go," he explains; something must be made fun of, someone must slip on a banana peel, logic itself must be violated. In the Copland work, it is the sense of an orderly musical progression that is destroyed. The way that Copland's trumpet blues keeps getting stuck on its opening phrase is musically funny. His point about the final cadence of Mozart's *A Musical Joke*, in which each instrument cadences in a different key (and each is given its own key signature) speaks volumes: "The wrong notes must be next to the right notes" in order for us to laugh. Without rules, there can be no transgression, and therefore no humor. Mozart's work is actually a lesson in *style*.

The most surprising moment in "Humor in Music" is when Bernstein introduces "the most incongruous piece of all," the funeral march from Mahler's First Symphony. The idea of humor embedded inside something as mesmerizingly sad as Mahler's minor key canon on "Frère Jacques" is a complex one. But Bernstein has seized on the opportunity afforded by the fact that the children know the round and can understand immediately the "incongruity" of its being used as the theme of a solemn funeral procession.

One of the most remarkable of the Young People's Concerts, broadcast on December 14, 1965, with the unpromising title "The Sound of an Orchestra," takes children into the details of performance practice to a degree one might not think possible in such a format. Like "What Does Music Mean?," there is a bit of educational trickery at the outset, since the program begins, without explanation, with a deliberately poor performance of part of the slow movement of Haydn's Eighty-Eighth Symphony. Bernstein has once again imagined his little girl from *I Hate Music*, who surely feels remote from eighteenth century music and has been brought to Carnegie Hall because such music is supposed to be "good" for her. How can he get her to truly hear it and enjoy it, to be on the inside rather than on the outside of it? He takes a big risk. The performance continues for some time before Bernstein signals a cutoff and turns around to the audience. There is weak applause. "Beautiful?" he asks. "Well, it isn't. I'm not talking about the music, but about the performance. We took an elegant work from the eighteenth century, a graceful monument of the Classical period, and turned it into lush, juicy-fruited music that might have been written a century later by a raving Romantic." He then proceeds to give a detailed lesson in all the musical choices conductors and performers must make to interpret a particular work by a given composer from a specific period. As he had in his *Omnibus* "Art of Conducting" presentation for adults, he brings the audience inside the process of preparing a performance. He spends many minutes having string players demonstrate different styles of vibrato. He points to a moment in the "bad" performance where the violin vibrato is "too fast" and the strings are also "in their highest position, where the vibrato shows up most garishly. . . . Beautiful? Ghastly!" He summarizes the faults of their performance as faults of "exaggeration." While demonstrating excesses in their execution, he quickly explains dynamic markings and what a *sforzando* is, shows how the use of a glissando in the violins might be "a perfect technique for the Supremes or for certain opera singers, but not for Haydn," and demonstrates phrases he conducted with exaggerated rubato. "We've turned Haydn into quite a mess, and to what end? Simply to show off the rich sound of an orchestra, instead of the sound of the composer." He then explains that in his day Haydn probably had at most twenty strings "if he was lucky," and that his orchestras performed in small halls. A proper adjustment to accommodate the acoustics of Philharmonic Hall and still sound like Haydn would be to reduce the Philharmonic string section of sixty-seven players to about forty. This he proceeds to do, and, picking up the movement where the "bad" performance left off, teaches us how, in this particular idiom, restraint, purity, and subtlety lead to a much more nuanced, expressive, and meaningful performance. Bernstein says that he hopes the listeners have "learned the difference between exaggerated sentimentality and real feeling."

During the remainder of the program Bernstein continues to demonstrate how winds and strings and even percussion instruments vary their performance techniques (employing different timbres, approaches to rhythmic inflection, and bowing, even playing pizzicato with different speeds of vibrato) to give us the sound appropriate to French or German or American music. The concert ends with a performance of Debussy's colorful *Ibéria* and with Bernstein reiterating his credo as conductor, which is that the performer's role is to try to realize the composer's intentions and to adapt his sound to the composer's wishes. Therefore there is "no such thing" as "the sound of an orchestra," he says, "or at least there shouldn't be. All that matters is the sound of the composer."

The Young People's Concerts were a historical outgrowth of "family matinees" given by the New York Philharmonic in the late nineteenth century, which then evolved into educational programs specifically geared to children during the First World War. Conductor Ernest Schelling had popularized the series starting in the mid-1920s, and even took the programs on national and international tours. They were offered regularly since that time, but Bernstein's erudition, personality, and commitment to them, along with their dissemination on television, transformed them into a powerful cultural force. The number of people who owed their initiation into the wonders of classical music to these programs must be in the millions.

Bernstein's Young People's Concerts coincided with the years in which he was the father of three growing children. As they aged, his language and teaching strategies changed with them.[1] In the early years, preparation for the noonday concerts could often start at 6 a.m., with an orchestra rehearsal at 8, and a dress rehearsal at 10. The conductor, a night owl by nature and habit, must have been out of synch with his biological clock at the show's outset. In the mid-1960s, when the issue of the quality of television was a matter of public discussion, they were scheduled in evening prime time. At the end of the decade, they were again offered at midday.

The concerts upended cultural expectations that children require speed and obviousness to remain engaged. Instead of hitting them over the head with platitudes, Bernstein appealed to their intelligence. He gave them depth, beauty, philosophy, and real life, along with fun, and it worked.

In an article titled "Speaking of Music" in the December

1957 *Atlantic Monthly*, Bernstein attacked "the music appreciation racket":

> It is, in the main, a racket, because it is in the main specious and commercial. It uses every device to sell music—cajoling, coyness, flattery, oversimplification, irrelevant entertainment, tall tales—all in order to keep the music business humming.

He describes two styles of music appreciation teaching, each one "duller than the other":

> Type A is the birds-bees-rivulets variety. It turns every note or phrase or chord into a cloud or crag or Cossack. . . . It tells us nothing about music. Type B is concerned with analysis. . . . a kind of Baedeker to the bare geography of a composition . . . again it tells us nothing about music except those superficial geographical facts.

He grants that discussions of music for laypersons must occupy some middle ground:

> If we are to try to explain music, we must explain the *music*, not the whole array of extramusical notions which have grown like parasites around it. . . . Obviously we can't use musical terminology exclusively. . . . We must have recourse to certain extramusical ideas, like religion, or social factors, or historical forces, which may have influenced music. We don't ever want to talk down; but how *up* can we talk without losing contact? There is a happy medium somewhere between the music appreciation racket and purely technical discussion; it is hard to find, but it can be found.[2]

To talk about music rivetingly to those who have no training in it, while also teaching and inspiring those with more knowledge, and all the while not falsifying music itself, was a great accomplishment. Bernstein's gift for teaching was acknowledged even by those who were critical of his other activities. In a 1983 letter, Virgil Thomson wrote, "The ideal explainer of music, both classical and modern, has always been Leonard Bernstein."[3]

The conductor delivered fifty-three televised Young People's Concerts between 1958 and 1972. He was proud of them, returning to do them even during his sabbatical year 1964–65 and after his retirement as music director of the New York Philharmonic. Now, in the twenty-first century, they have been translated and shown on television in over forty countries, making players including violinist John Corigliano (father of the composer), oboist Harold Gomberg, and clarinetist Stanley Drucker familiar to millions of people.

# 10

## *At the Center*
## *1957–1964*

Bernstein's educational mission was by no means restricted to the Young People's Concerts. As music director of the Philharmonic he could now plan seasons as a whole and give them a thematic coherence that served an educational purpose and provided a historical and intellectual framework for the music. He also instituted a practice of speaking briefly to the audience on Thursday night preview concerts, in a spirit not terribly different from that of the Young People's Concerts, and when controversial music was to be performed, he sometimes addressed the subscription audiences too.

Furthermore, he was frequently in the position of "teacher" in relation to his orchestras. He routinely took apart contrapuntal strands of a passage during rehearsal so that players could hear their role within a given texture. He often had to win them over to a contemporary composer's idiom, as he did when he explicated Lukas Foss's intentions in the innovative

1967 work *Phorion* so effectively that the orchestra became enthusiastic about realizing them. In later years he had to practically start from scratch in inculcating a performance practice for Mahler in Vienna, where the music had long been banned and misunderstood.

The 1957–58 season had ended with a performance of Arthur Honegger's dramatic oratorio *Joan of Arc at the Stake*, with Felicia speaking the part of Joan. It had been followed by an orchestral tour of Latin America that ended up being a homecoming of sorts for Felicia. The seven-week journey brought the Philharmonic to Panama City, Caracas, Bogotá, and Quito, where the conductor met up with an embattled Vice President Nixon, who had encountered as much hostility in the region as Bernstein had adulation. The two gave a joint press conference at the U.S. embassy, in which Bernstein said that music appeals to human beings at a level where their political differences cease to matter. Felicia joined the tour in Lima and accompanied it to La Paz, on which leg of the journey her husband piloted the plane briefly over the Andes. When he led the Chilean national anthem in Santiago, tears streamed down her face. She had never imagined returning to her homeland in such an extraordinary way. They continued to Argentina, Brazil, Uruguay, and Mexico. At many of these stops, Bernstein stayed up long into the night after the concerts, soaking up the after-hours life and listening to local music. He was particularly enthusiastic about Chilean folksinger Violeta Parra. (According to musicologist Helen Smith, the melody of "The Word of the Lord" from Bernstein's later *Mass* is taken directly from a song of Parra's.)

In his first season as music director of the Philharmonic, Bernstein incorporated a chronological survey of American symphonic music into programs that also included standard repertoire, starting with turn-of-the-century American works, moving on to Ives, Carl Ruggles, John J. Becker, Wallingford

Riegger, Gershwin, Copland, Sessions, Harris, Piston, Randall Thompson, and Virgil Thomson, and then to music of the younger generation: William Schuman, Samuel Barber, Foss, Irving Fine, and Bernstein himself.[1] In the summer he took the orchestra on a historic tour to Europe and the Soviet Union in which he placed American music side by side with great works from the past and in telling juxtapositions with contemporary works from other countries. Bernstein and the orchestra were a sensation in Moscow, Kiev, Leningrad, Stockholm, Scheveningen, Helsinki, Amsterdam, Paris, Basel, Salzburg, Zagreb, Milan, Venice, and London. A highlight of the tour was a poetic and fleet-paced Beethoven Triple Concerto, with John Corigliano on violin, Laszlo Varga on cello, and Bernstein conducting, while providing his nimble and thoughtful pianism. In Salzburg's Festspielhaus the program consisted of Barber's *Second Essay for Orchestra*, the *Age of Anxiety* Symphony, and Shostakovich's Fifth Symphony. In Poland he directed Mozart's Piano Concerto No. 17 in G Major, K. 453, from the keyboard and conducted Piston's Concerto for Orchestra.

The most dramatic and meaningful juxtapositions of all were those presented during the tour of the Soviet Union, where the personal, political, and cultural baggage carried by the events could hardly have been heavier. Concerts such as that given at the Moscow Conservatory (Russian and American national anthems; Berlioz's *Roman Carnival* overture; Ives's *The Unanswered Question;* Ravel's *La valse;* Stravinsky's Concerto for Piano and Wind Instruments and *Le sacre du printemps*) risked discomfiting Soviet officials by introducing music that had previously been banned. Family history was added to the mix when Bernstein managed to convince his reluctant father to join him in Moscow, to be reunited with his brother, Simeon, whom he had left behind in Berezdov forty-nine years earlier (and who had become a bureaucrat). Speaking at the height of the Cold War in the Great Hall of the Moscow Conservatory, the conductor suggested to his listeners that "music can tell us some surprising things that we can't find out from books and newspapers. . . . Americans and Russians simply love each other's music. Each people seems to find something of itself in the music of the other. Somehow we sense a common identity, on the deepest level, in that special corner of the heart where music lives and breathes."

On the orchestra's last night in Moscow (September 11, 1959) Bernstein greeted the audience in a few phrases of Russian, which had been the native tongue of both his parents, and conducted a searing performance of Shostakovich's Fifth Symphony in the presence of the composer, as well as writer Boris Pasternak. The next day, an overwhelmed Pasternak wrote Bernstein in poetic, fractured English: "Art must leave us love-stricken, and sorrow overcome like a deep felt parting or separation. Art is the language of greatness and disclosure, its light, its tragic and suffering being exposed to view."[2]

Bernstein's second season was notable for placing the name and music of Gustav Mahler squarely at the forefront of his audience's consciousness. The year 1960 was the hundredth anniversary of Mahler's birth, and 1959–60 was the fiftieth anniversary of his first season as music director of the Philharmonic. To commemorate both anniversaries, Bernstein programmed a festival that placed a symphony by Mahler on every program between December 31, 1959, and February 21, 1960, with performances of *Das Lied von der Erde* in April. Sharing the programs with legendary Mahler conductors Bruno Walter and Dimitri Mitropoulos, Bernstein himself conducted the Fourth Symphony, the Second Symphony ("Resurrection"), and the *Kindertotenlieder* song cycle, as well as excerpts from *Des Knaben Wunderhorn* and the *Rückert-Lieder*, selections that were close to what Mahler himself had conducted of his own work when he was music director.[3]

Mahler was not standard repertoire in 1960, and he was not

part of the generally acknowledged pantheon of great composers. The larger symphonies, nos. 3, 6, 7, 8, and 9, were still rarities in American concert halls. While all his works were available singly on recordings, it would be Bernstein who would record the first complete set of the symphonies. Mahler had been considered "excessive" and "decadent" by influential critics and performers, going all the way back to the days of his tenure at the Philharmonic.

Bernstein's advocacy of the Viennese master dated at least to 1947, when he had presented the "Resurrection" Symphony with the New York City Symphony as a memorial to the late Fiorello LaGuardia. Responses to the work at that time were decidedly mixed, and several reviews were scornful. In the *New York Sun*, Irving Kolodin pronounced the "Resurrection" Symphony "the most bumptious, empty noise ever contrived," while Howard Taubman in the *New York Times* mixed dislike with condescension: "Those who find Mahler a stirring experience have a right to keep on finding him so; those of us who wish that he had either a good editor or more self-criticism have the right not to listen to him."[4]

Early European performances of Mahler had met with similarly mixed reactions. During the Nazi era (January 1929), a reviewer could simply write that Mahler's work exhibited "the inner uncertainty and deracination of the superficially civilized western Jew in all his tragedy." In the postwar years, when anti-Semitic writing was banned, the standard line that Mahler's was "a tragic case" remained, the cause now being that he was "a man of a more effeminate eastern type . . . [who] had succumbed to the magic of the German national character."[5] These supposed characteristics were still noted in mid-century European criticism, which deployed a kind of code for the presumed inherent weaknesses of people of his background (and which resembled those frequently leveled against Bernstein's music). Mahler biographer Jens Malte Fischer lists them as "eclecticism and triviality, . . . the gap between intention and ability, . . . the hankering after empty effects, . . . the imitation of all forms and styles . . . shallowness and saccharine sweetness."[6]

Bernstein advocated for Mahler with a missionary zeal. He considered him the twentieth century's musical prophet, whose extremes spoke for the times, and thought his symphonies constituted "as sacred a bunch of notes as Brahms's symphonies."[7]

On February 7, 1960, Bernstein presented a Young People's Concert in which excerpts from the First, Second, and Fourth Symphonies, *Das Lied von der Erde*, and *Des Knaben Wunderhorn* were played. It began with his educated guess that not a single audience member knew who Mahler was. Speaking to children with his customary candor, Bernstein presented him as a man torn between various poles: his conducting versus his composing; being a "sad grown-up" while also being an innocent child; being both Jew and Christian, Western European and Oriental; having an "operatic nature" while being a symphonic composer; creating grand orchestral textures at the same time as fine-tuned chamber scoring.

Bernstein in 1960 was in fact struggling with the same musical issues Mahler had faced in his final years: the separation of Western musical language from the wellsprings of its traditional forms, its increasing distance from the folk traditions that had nourished it and rooted it in common human experience, and the consequent distancing of composers from normal concert life. In the spring of 1960 he included a series of contemporary works on his programs to exemplify "Twentieth Century Problems in Music." In the second program of this series, "The Search for New Techniques," he led Henry Brant's *Antiphony One* and the *Concerted Piece for Tape Recorder and Orchestra* by Otto Luening and Vladimir Ussachevsky, and gave the U.S. premiere of Pierre Boulez's *Improvisation sur Mallarmé I* (later known as the second part of *Pli selon pli*), with Marni Nixon as soloist.[8]

Before performing it for his subscription audience, he gave the world premiere of the collaborative Luening-Ussachevsky work at a Young People's Concert called "Unusual Instruments of Present, Past, and Future," which was televised nationally. The Luening-Ussachevsky piece was a surprising success with the young listeners. Luening's brother, who watched the broadcast, wrote to him about how much he enjoyed seeing "the way the kid's eyes sparkled and their smiles broadened when your composition was played."[9] As he had for the young audience, Bernstein later explained some of the basics of electronic music to the adult subscription audience. He demonstrated some of the transformations of real sound of which the tape recorder was capable (the reversal of the sound of a bottle breaking; the reversal played higher or lower, and so on) and the use of an oscillator to create synthetic sounds.

He introduced the Boulez work with the admission that he personally could not analyze Boulez's system without knowing the "mathematical model" upon which it was based. (This was a rare situation for him to be in.) But he proceeded to describe the work of the man who would one day succeed him at the Philharmonic in a way that showed real sympathy and insight. It is rare to see Boulez's idiom depicted in terms any audience member could understand (although it is a task that in recent years Boulez himself has also accomplished).[10] Bernstein explained that the mathematical underpinnings are in service of music that is "unsystematic in its effect," "rather Impressionistic—that is, free-floating, improvisatory, instinctual" and, like Ravel's and Debussy's, reflects an Eastern influence: "This Orientalism is caused not only by the instrumentation (which is indeed very Eastern with its gongs and cymbals, harp and vibraphone, and other mysterious percussion sounds) but also by the treatment of the vocal line, which is full of grace-notes and rapid skips, which inflect very much like far-Eastern music."

Also in common with Impressionism is a kind of "disintegration of meter" resulting from the very complexity of the music's metrical and rhythmic construction. He speculated that this was "a symptom of our age—an age when everything seems to be fragmentized, reduced to molecular proportions."[11] Bernstein then paused to wonder whether contemporary artists' turning inward "toward molecular dissection" didn't reflect the "decline in religious spirit in our time—that spirit that turns outward to the unknown, secure and confident in faith." However, he didn't mean to imply that Boulez's technique marked him as an irreligious man "or anything like that because, curiously enough, the atmosphere he generates in his music is one of great innerness and mystery. Perhaps what it really is, is a new kind of mysticism, born of new scientific insights."

He reprised the Boulez work one year later and would return to the idea that scientific discoveries and new musical methods were linked when he introduced his series devoted to avant-garde music at the Philharmonic in 1963. In subsequent seasons he presented a considerable amount of contemporary music, trying to expand the tastes of his subscribers, and often exploring music about which he himself was ambivalent. This experience left a deeper imprint on his own music than he perhaps ever fully acknowledged.

He had hoped to program Karlheinz Stockhausen's visionary soundscape *Gruppen for Three Orchestras* in these programs, but the structure of Carnegie Hall had made the proper spatial arrangement of the three large ensembles impossible. The German composer had come to meet him and look at the hall, and later wrote, rather astonishingly, of the "postponement": "You should never be sad. You are the only artist since long time ago who gave me the impression to be more than 'serious' one, who can fill a room with life, with *Unbefangenheit* [unembarrassed openness], with *Aufgeräumtheit* [cheerfulness, clarity of mind] just by speaking and laughing about everything. . . . There is a secret relationship between your soul and Mozart's soul."[12]

The 1960–61 season had as a theme "Keys to the Twentieth Century." The programs included Alban Berg's *Three Pieces for Orchestra*, op. 6, works of Stravinsky, Hindemith, Bartók, Ravel, Prokofiev, Chávez, Toshiro Mayazumi (conducted by Seiji Ozawa), and Boulez (conducted by Gregory Millar). In the summer Bernstein began work on his Third Symphony (*Kaddish*), a composition that would occupy him over a two-year period and which bears the imprint of his identification with Mahler in its intensity, overt emotionality, extremes of contrast, and prophetic tone. It may also reflect the impact of his recent experience performing Berg. His rendition of Berg's opus 6 was revelatory, showing a deep understanding of both its impressionistic side and its roots in Mahler, and a shattering identification with its emotional climate.[13] But above all, the *Kaddish* Symphony was his response to the threat of nuclear war.

Bernstein's ascent to prominence coincided with the rise of John F. Kennedy (who may well have removed a barrier to Bernstein's conducting career back in 1956), creating a subliminal connection in the public consciousness between these two glamorous American leaders in their forties, at their peak of popularity and influence, both Bostonians and Harvard graduates, one a Catholic, the other a Jew. One could argue that there were distinct parallels between the personalities of the two men. Both had extraordinary magnetism, a need to have people around them, and the capacity to have many different kinds of relationships. Both combined complexity and high intelligence with a kind of personal directness. Both led extraordinarily public lives and projected an aura of fearlessness. Yet each man remained in some ways private; each was highly compartmentalized; each had sexual secrets. In an archival interview about the president from July 1965, the conductor described Kennedy as having a "remarkable combination of informality and stateliness—that's not precisely the word—casualness and majesty. . . . It's very hard to come by—that combination; I don't know many people who have it. Utter informality, great readiness to laughter, very quick perception, immediate understanding of anything you say, even if it's veiled or is only suggested, not actually stated, and yet an ability to juggle various matters in his mind simultaneously."[14]

On the evening of the 1961 Kennedy inauguration, Bernstein conducted his new fanfare especially commissioned for the occasion, as well as Handel's "Hallelujah" chorus and "The Stars and Stripes Forever," and he attended a presidential party in which he made the faux pas of cutting in on Kennedy himself, who was dancing with an old friend of his. (The woman was furious, while Kennedy "paled for a moment, but . . . got over it," according to Bernstein.) After watching Bernstein adroitly improvise his way through a long evening as master of ceremonies at a benefit for the National Cultural Center on November 29, 1962, Kennedy quipped that the conductor was the one person he "would never run against for political office." Felicia and her husband dined alone with the president and First Lady and another couple on November 14, 1961, the day after attending a White House dinner in honor of the great cellist Pablo Casals. Bernstein recalled the evening as exhilarating fun; the president, uncharacteristically, stayed up until 2 a.m.

Burton Bernstein recalls learning of an occasion later in the Kennedy presidency when Felicia implored the president not to listen to the generals urging him to get deeper into the Vietnam War. Kennedy apparently told Felicia that he agreed with her, that in fact he believed he had been "hoodwinked by Westmoreland" and needed to find a way to exit from a potentially hopeless situation.[15]

The year 1961 saw both the premiere of the orchestral *Symphonic Dances from "West Side Story"* by the Philharmonic at a gala concert on February 13, and the opening of Robert Wise's film version of the musical on October 18. Although the film differs structurally and musically from the original stage show (it further reduces some of the operatic complexities and changes the order of some numbers), it solidified the perception of the work as a "classic" and made its music almost universally known. The film received ten Academy Awards.

The 1961–62 Philharmonic season focused largely on French or French-influenced music in the fall ("The Gallic Approach") and turned to Middle European music in the spring ("The Middle Europe Tradition"). Bach's *Saint Matthew Passion* was given in English (April 19–22), and the two Bartók Rhapsodies for Violin and Orchestra were performed with Isaac Stern and later recorded, in electric, impassioned renditions.

February 28, 1962, saw the arrival of the third Bernstein child, Nina, which brought the family to its final complement of five. Daughter Jamie describes the family as the conductor's refuge: "It was the safe place, the warm place, the fun place, and we grew up with the sense that the family was the place where it was all going to be okay, for the most part. We had our bumps in adolescence, of course, but in general it was a very happy place to be, and a lot of that had to do with our mother, who created this warmth and stability, this lovely atmosphere." With his family, Bernstein was as animated as he was with an orchestra. Even buying a sweater would turn into an occasion as he made friends with the taxi driver, with the shopkeeper, and with complete strangers at the store. When he wasn't working, he was still in motion, answering all of his mail in sessions with Helen Coates, producing poems, doggerel, doing crossword puzzles, playing games, having visitors over, and participating in home movies. Among the most memorable of these was a comic rendition of *Tosca*, dubbed to Callas's first recording, with Felicia in the title role and Leonard as Scarpia, and "Call Me Moses," a parody of the film *Exodus*, with Burton as Moses, Leonard as Pharaoh, and Marc Blitzstein as a slave master.

In April 1962 an austerely contemplative performance by Glenn Gould of the Brahms Piano Concerto No. 1 in D Minor caused a scandal in the New York press, in part because of Bernstein's comments to the audience beforehand. The ruckus contributed to Gould's growing determination to withdraw from concertizing. Bernstein and Gould were enormously fond of each other. The pianist, who had limited enthusiasm for most popular music, called *West Side Story* "a masterpiece." Bernstein revered Gould's playing. He and Felicia had listened repeatedly to Gould's first Goldberg Variations recording when she was in the final month of her pregnancy with Jamie. The two musicians had previously collaborated on a performance of Beethoven's Second Piano Concerto and had given a riveting account of the first movement of Bach's D-Minor Harpsichord Concerto on television in 1960. As the 1962 season approached, the pianist telephoned the conductor several times to prepare him for a rendition of the Brahms that reduced the external drama, slowed the tempos and put them in exact proportional relationships, and shed an "analytical" light on its contrapuntal inner workings. Although Bernstein saw the work in a more traditional manner, he accompanied Gould's performance with conviction. The result had a sublime, almost Baroque clarity. In his customary Thursday preconcert remarks, however, he wryly explained that he was bowing to the soloist's wishes, despite his own differing conception of the work. In the *Times* the following morning, Harold Schonberg lambasted Bernstein for his "betrayal" of Gould, and the pianist himself for his slow tempos, which he suggested stemmed from his poor technique. Other reviewers followed suit, and Bernstein's "discourtesy" even made the German papers. Yet Gould had read and approved the comments beforehand, finding them good-humored and charming. Neither man ever backed away from their assertions that they had made their musical differences public by friendly mutual agreement. Gould's letters to Bernstein continued to be as affectionate and funny as ever, and Bernstein visited the pianist in his Toronto apartment after his withdrawal from concert life in 1964.[16]

In April and May of 1962 Bernstein made the first of many recordings of Haydn with the New York Philharmonic, recording Symphony No. 82 in C Major ("The Bear") and Symphony No. 83 in G Minor ("The Hen"), composed for large Paris orchestras in 1785 and 1786. It was no coincidence that Bernstein had put Haydn at the center of his Young People's lesson in style, "The Sound of an Orchestra." He had showed an affinity for the composer's music as far back as 1945. Indeed, one could argue that if Mahler was his principal alter ego, Haydn was a secondary one. If his self-confessed aim as a conductor was to fully realize the composer's intentions and to embody their spirit—to *become* them for the duration of the performance—he seemed to come close to doing so in his measured, radiant, witty Haydn renditions, which brought out important elements of his own personality: lucidity, humor, and tenderness.[17]

In November 1964 Bernstein would receive one of the great compliments of his life in an article in *High Fidelity* written by H. C. Robbins Landon, the foremost living Haydn scholar. Calling Bernstein's recording of the first two Paris symphonies "among the great Haydn recordings of history," he praised the conductor both for his "obvious sympathy for and knowledge of Haydn's style," for the meticulousness and rightness with which he chose his edition, judged tempos, differentiated between movements of like but subtly different character, and "the almost incredible pains" with which he addressed small details of performance practice, such as the correct handling of trills. Saying that this care would still be for naught were it not also combined with musical depth, he extolled Bernstein as "one of the greatest, if not *the* greatest" living Haydn interpreters in America or Europe.[18]

While Bernstein did not perform nearly as much Mozart as he did Haydn, he had a deep connection to certain works (including Symphony No. 40 in G Minor) to which he returned repeatedly. He recorded four of the piano concertos as pianist/conductor, as well as the G-Minor Piano Quartet with the Juilliard Quartet.

As a conductor of Beethoven, perhaps his favorite of all composers, many reliable observers considered Bernstein uneven in his years with the Philharmonic. For example, Paul Robinson, in *The Art of the Conductor*, calls his performance of the Fourth Symphony "not very convincing. The introduction is too fast, lacking mystery. . . . The fast movements are energetic but monotonous. . . . In the slow movement the upper strings are thin, lacking richness of tone, and the brass is noisy but has no nobility." Yet the consensus is that many of the New York cycle and most in the Vienna Philharmonic's have the depth and power of the very greatest Beethoven recordings.

On the night of September 23, 1962, Bernstein led the Philharmonic in its premiere concert in its new home, Philharmonic Hall (later named Avery Fisher Hall), the first completed building in the new Lincoln Center for the Performing Arts. The event, broadcast live coast to coast, had the aura of a state occasion. New York Governor Nelson Rockefeller, Ambassador Adlai Stevenson, UN Secretary General U Thant, and Secretary of State Dean Rusk were in attendance. The entire audience rose and applauded when Jacqueline Kennedy, looking radiant in a black-and-white gown, appeared in her box facing stage right. The program began with "The Star-Spangled Banner," proceeded to the "Gloria" from Beethoven's *Missa solemnis*, and ended with Vaughan Williams's *Serenade to Music* and the first part of Mahler's Eighth Symphony ("Symphony of a Thousand"), "Veni, creator spiritus," for which more than three hundred people were assembled onstage. This was another of the important public occasions in which Bernstein made Mahler's music central. Before the intermission came Aaron Copland's harshly eloquent *Connotations for Orchestra,* which the sixty-two-year-old composer, in remarks recorded for the television audience, explained was a reminder that the center was "dedicated not only to rehearing the great works of the past but also to the more challenging music of our own day." The piece was the composer's first twelve-tone work for orchestra, and neither the audience nor the critics cared for it much. But at its majestic close, Mrs. Kennedy beamed and seemed to exclaim out loud. During the intermission, the viewing audience watched Felicia, her hair elegantly tied in a bun, escort the First Lady to the greenroom, where the exhilarated conductor kissed her on the cheek like an old friend, and Copland, clearly buoyed by the expert performance of his new work, smiled at her as if she were an angel. The evening was a triumphant moment for American music and music making, and surely one that must have made the members of the board of the New York Philharmonic believe that they had indeed succeeded in "reaching a wider public" and placing their orchestra at the center of the nation's cultural life.

In October Bernstein conducted a program of works by Honegger, alongside the rarely performed *Le martyre de Saint Sébastien* by Claude Debussy, with Felicia delivering the speaking part of the saint with sincerity, conveying the protagonist's inwardness, strength, and vulnerability. On April 10, 1963, Bernstein accompanied clarinetist Benny Goodman at Carnegie Hall in the posthumous premiere of the Clarinet Sonata by Francis Poulenc, who had died suddenly on January 30.

In the summer of 1963, Bernstein had resumed work on his *Kaddish* Symphony. He finally completed the short score in August in Fairfield, Connecticut, apparently much to the relief of his entire family, who had watched him brooding over it for two long years. When he emerged from his studio waving the score above his head, shouting "I finished it!," Felicia joyfully jumped into the swimming pool with her clothes on.[19]

The Kaddish text is a traditional daily prayer that is both a hymn of praise and a supplication for peace. Although it does not literally refer to death, it is also the principal prayer recited at the graveside in the Jewish funeral. For most people it therefore evokes mourning above all, even though its message is one of renewal. It is mostly in Aramaic, the language of common people in the time of Jesus (and the language in which he spoke his sermons), and most of it dates from the first or second century. Passages in Hebrew, including the plea for peace at the end, were added to it centuries later. The Kaddish prayer begins:

> Magnified and sanctified be His great name
> Throughout the world which He hath created according to
> His will.

In Bernstein's work, the Kaddish text, which is traditionally recited by men, is sung three times through by the soprano solo, chorus, and boys' choir. His treatment of the prayer, which is already both an affirmation of life and a requiem, both praise and supplication, and written in two languages, explores additional dualities. There are two soloists: one a speaker, the other a singer. The score combines the traditional prayer, in Hebrew and Aramaic, with a personal mediation upon it in English. There are both sacred and "profane" elements in the score: choral singing suggestive of Jewish cantillation, alongside jazzier, American-sounding music. There are dueling musical idioms: anguished, highly chromatic segments using twelve-tone rows, alongside tonal and modal music. There are dual resonances within Bernstein's written text: the "father" can be viewed both as the "father of us all" and also, in places, as the composer's own father, Samuel. Written at the height of the Cold War, the text addresses not only personal death but also planetary death and the threat of human extinction: "I want to say Kaddish. . . . I have so little time, as You well know. Is my end a minute away? An hour?" By this time, the composer was an active member of the Committee for a Sane Nuclear Policy (SANE) and an advocate of disarmament. He had been alarmed by his children's casual references to their expectation of a nuclear war that would end human life.[20] And then there is the duality of God and man—man, who risks perishing if he cannot maintain the "spirit" (God) within him; God, who cannot continue to exist unless he accepts man.

Like the later *Mass*, *Kaddish* approaches religion from the vantage point of skepticism. Like *The Age of Anxiety* and *Mass*, it presents the idea of faith as something lost but still attainable. If there is a musical parallel to be drawn to the retrieval of this faith, it is in the retrieval of the diatonic scale accomplished in the score's more tonal passages.

Skepticism is intrinsic to Judaism, which embraces the paradox of an unknowable, unfathomable God—"That which cannot be named"—to whom one can also voice doubts and make complaint. This is exemplified in the Book of Job: "Thine hands have made me and fashioned me together round about; yet thou dost destroy me" (Job 10:8–10).[21] With *Kaddish*, Bernstein risked offending the religious with his personal take on the prayer and his musical settings of it; he challenged an audience happy with his Broadway music with a dark and often acerbic work; and he courted mockery from critics and academics for his blending of twelve-tone elements with melodic, diatonic music, no matter how artfully linked they were. Bernstein entered new territory in this work, inaugurating a "later" musical period in which he attempted to grapple more frankly with serious extramusical subject matter, while creating a synthesis out of his many musical influences, including atonality. Coincident with the evolution of this phase of his work, composers as different as George Crumb, Frederic Rzewski, George Rochberg, Philip Glass, Steve Reich, David Del Tredici, John Adams, Alfred Schnittke, Toru Takemitsu, Mauricio Kagel, and Louis Andriessen were also finding ways to accommodate tonal elements and nontonal ones within a single work.[22] Parallels to what Bernstein was doing can also be found in the music of Britten and Shostakovich from this time.

In its less tonal sections, such as the mysterious opening, and the savage Allegro in Kaddish I (with its twelve-tone ostinato figures in regular alternations of 7/8 and 3/4 time, and its angular fugue), the symphony contains some of Bernstein's most arrestingly intense music. Tonal passages such as the soprano lullaby and the bold, pealing entrance of the boy sopranos in G-flat major in Kaddish III are also remarkably beautiful. (Both passages anticipate the music of *Chichester Psalms.*) Shorn of its speaker, the symphony would simply be a three-fold Kaddish setting, and a high point in the composer's mature output.

But whether one can fully appreciate the superb music alongside the spoken text is another matter. For example, the effect of the orchestral outburst in "Din-Torah" before Kaddish II, with its intricate percussion music and lucid, intense contrapuntal writing for strings and brass, which has a focused rage rare in Bernstein's output, is vitiated by the literalness of the words preceding it, making it seem bombastic: "Tin God! Your bargain is tin! It crumples in my hand! And where is faith now—Yours or mine?" The finely written scherzo, with its delightful wind writing and ingenious manipulations of the row from the Kaddish I Allegro, the "Kaddish melody," and other figures, is reduced to being an underscore, trivialized by the superimposed narration describing God's dream ("I'll take you to your favorite star").

Bernstein's text has found few enthusiastic partisans. The passages expressing anger at the Almighty may have offended those who found the work blasphemous, but it is the more optimistic and sentimental sections that seem weakest today. The lines that attempt to comfort God ("However great Your pain I will help You suffer it. O God, believe. Believe in me. And you shall see the Kingdom of Heaven") have a narcissistic and simplistic ring to them, regardless of the complexity of thinking behind them.

The monologue form is by its very nature a perilous one. Even the speaker's parts in Schoenberg's *Ode to Napoleon*, Stravinsky's *Oedipus Rex*, and Copland's *Lincoln Portrait* are difficult to perform convincingly. Monologues that work, such as Prokofiev's *Peter and the Wolf*, William Walton's *Façade*, or Schoenberg's half-sung *Pierrot Lunaire*, meld music and text so well that one can't imagine them separated. The role of the speaker in *Kaddish* was originally taken by Hanna Rovina in the Israeli premiere, then by Felicia Bernstein in the United States, thereafter by Michael Wager, and finally left open to speakers of either sex by the composer. Yehudi Menuhin performed and recorded the speaker's part with consummate restraint. The work has also been performed by the composer's daughter Jamie with her own text, and by Samuel Pisar, a writer, lawyer, and Holocaust survivor who received permission from Bernstein to incorporate his own harrowing narrative into the speaker's part. Bernstein somewhat pared down his text after Felicia's performance. But it is her heartfelt, sincere, and anguished reading of the original words that leaves the most moving impression, and it is her fragile, sometimes strained voice that seems to be the best timbral match for the music her husband wrote. Bernstein had originally felt that a woman's voice could best represent "that part of man that intuits God."[23] Perhaps he was right.[24]

On November 22, shortly after completing the final touches on the orchestration of the work, he was at a staff meeting in Philharmonic Hall, planning a Young People's Concert, when he heard the news that President Kennedy had been assassinated. That afternoon the *Kaddish* Symphony became a posthumous tribute to the slain president. That night was the first time that Jamie Bernstein ever saw her parents cry. An unusually somber Bernstein conducted the Philharmonic in a televised memorial concert on Sunday, November 24, bringing Mahler's "Resurrection" Symphony once again into the center of American consciousness, at a time of collective shock and grief.

Speaking the following night at a Madison Square Garden benefit for the United Jewish Appeal, Bernstein told an audience of eleven thousand people that he had chosen the Mahler work "for the resurrection of hope in all of us who mourn him." He spoke of Kennedy's "reverence for the life of the mind," citing words from a speech Kennedy was to have delivered on the day of his death: "America's leadership must be guided by learning and reason." "Learning and reason," Bernstein continued, "precisely the two elements that were necessarily missing from the mind of anyone who could have fired that impossible bullet. Learning and reason: the two basic precepts of all Judaistic tradition, the twin sources from which every Jewish mind from Abraham and Moses, to Freud and Einstein, has drawn its living power. Learning and reason: the motto we here tonight must continue to uphold with redoubled tenacity, and must continue, at any price, to make the basis of all our actions."[25]

A few months after the assassination, Jacqueline Kennedy brought her children John and Caroline to Fairfield to get away and relax with the Bernstein family. There was mutual affection and a natural sympathy among them and, one could speculate, an intuitive feeling of kinship between Jacqueline and Felicia.

The 1963–64 season at the Philharmonic contained a mini-festival of music of "the avant-garde," which gave the concerts an extraordinary range, placing the two twentieth-century masters closest to Bernstein's heart, Stravinsky and Copland, alongside music by younger composers. Bernstein gave even more informal talks to the audience during these programs than had been his custom. In one of the early talks he commented, "That music has a future nobody will deny, but the nature of it is a question perhaps more crucial now than at any time in the history of music." A sense of what he was up against can be gleaned from the spirited ovation that greeted his announcement in his final talk that "this week we are presenting the last group of avant-garde works in this series." It is likely that more audience members walked out during these programs (and while the music was being played) than in the entire history of the orchestra. Still, whatever the ambivalence of the music director—and Bernstein admitted to having mixed feelings about some of the works he was conducting—or the distaste of the subscribers, the season was a shot in the arm to living composers. On the more accessible side, it included an all-Stravinsky evening, presenting the three symphonies in honor of the eighty-two-year-old composer, the American premiere of Bernstein's own *Kaddish* Symphony with Felicia as speaker, and a performance of Copland's Piano Concerto, with the composer as soloist. Alongside this fare was music by Edgard Varèse, Luigi Dallapiccola, Stefan Wolpe, György Ligeti, Iannis Xenakis, Earle Brown, Morton Feldman, and John Cage.[26]

The story behind the performance of Wolpe's Symphony began in the spring of 1962, when Bernstein asked his former assistant conductor Stefan Bauer-Mengelberg to visit Stefan Wolpe at his Seventieth Street brownstone walk-up, to explore the possibility of renotating the ferociously complex three-movement work, so that the Philharmonic could give the piece, composed in 1956, its belated premiere. There was no question of altering the sound content in any way; it was a matter of translating the mathematical proportions of the meters and note values Wolpe intended into notation that was more practical. Bauer-Mengelberg was a mathematician as well as a conductor, and Wolpe was persuaded. The work required twenty-three work sessions between Bauer-Mengelberg and the composer of several hours each, which Bernstein paid for out of his own pocket. He then asked his former assistant to conduct it, since Bauer-Mengelberg now knew both Wolpe's wishes and the work itself inside out. Unfortunately, the parts (also paid for by Bernstein) turned out to be unacceptable when they arrived at the Philharmonic and had to be redone, with the result that the musicians only received them two and a half days before the concert. Even after significant extra time had been borrowed from a Beethoven rehearsal, only two of the movements were ready for performance. In introducing the work, Bernstein apologized to the audience for presenting only two of the three movements, calling the Symphony "astonishing" for its "intensity, musicality, and originality." The work was warmly received by the audience, but reviewers considered it a scandal that Bernstein had not conducted the piece himself and that the Philharmonic could not learn the entire work. In the *Boston Globe* Michael Steinberg wrote scornfully that Bernstein had "abdicated" the task of conducting it and had undermined the work's reputation in his pre-performance remarks.

Bernstein spoke to the audience at considerable length about aleatoric ("chance") music, making distinctions between indeterminacy of different kinds. Commenting on the rising "involvement of the performers in the creative process" in the music of Stockhausen, Lukas Foss, and others, he demonstrated what it was like to have the entire orchestra improvise following a few prearranged signals. (One suspects, from the variety of instrumental colors and techniques of playing heard in this and several other engaging group improvisations later recorded by the Philharmonic, that there were more "prearranged signals" in operation than the conductor let on.) Varèse's *Déserts* was strategically placed after Vivaldi's popular

"Summer" from *The Four Seasons* and before Beethoven's "Eroica." György Ligeti's *Atmosphères* and Iannis Xenakis's mind-bending *Pithoprakta* were performed alongside Beethoven's Second Symphony and Ravel's *Tzigane*. Both the Xenakis and the Ligeti were U.S. premieres. (Composer David Schiff has written that he never forgot the spellbinding Xenakis performance. In 1968 George Balanchine choreographed *Pithoprakta* next door at the New York City Ballet.)

The Cage work was *Atlas Eclipticalis*, in which notes, rhythms, and dynamics were derived from superimposing transparent music paper onto a map of the stars (the "atlas" of the title), following imperfections in the music paper itself and using changes determined by the *I Ching*. On the surface, at least, one would be hard-pressed to think of a composer at a further remove from Bernstein than John Cage. Cage questioned the very notions of intentionality and deliberate communication in art that were core principles for Bernstein. But Cage had started life as a musician in the same way that Bernstein did, as a pianist (an early enthusiasm was for Grieg) with a desire to compose. Perhaps some commonalities could also be found between the two men in their desire to break down barriers between genres and to welcome nonacademic listeners into their music (in his early twenties Cage gave lectures on music and painting to housewives to earn money); in their literary gifts; in their quest for spirituality. Cage didn't like art that deliberately communicated emotions, art that "pushes you around." He once said, "I am as angry at the 'Hallelujah Chorus' as I am with 'Attica.'"[27] (*Attica*, named for the 1971 prison uprising, was a composition with a political message by Frederic Rzewski.) Cage's works for percussion, "prepared piano" (in which objects are placed on the piano strings to transform its tuning and timbres), and voice and piano, and later those organized through chance procedures of many kinds, were of a piece with the Zen Buddhism and Asian philosophy that had taught him how to "let go" of his own thoughts and emotions. It was a huge leap from Bernstein's emotive and traditional musical world to Cage's one of accepting whatever sounds occur within a predesigned structure, almost a leap from *doing* to simply *being*.[28]

According to which account you read, either the orchestra was disrespectful to Cage in rehearsals but properly behaved in the concerts, or their lack of understanding of the work's seriousness of purpose carried over into the performances themselves. In his biography of Cage, *The Roaring Silence*, David Revill writes that, by the third night's performance, the "orchestra laughed and talked among themselves, played scales or melodies instead of the notes in their parts, sang or whistled into the contact microphones." "Bernstein seemed unable to control the situation," and at a meeting afterward "castigated them for their behavior." Although a sold-out house had heard the music's opening measures, by the end of the piece "half the audience had left," and at the end, when Cage came out for a bow, hisses were heard even from the stage. This kind of combined performer/audience rejection was not unusual for Cage at the time (a Venice performance of the same work "provoked a near riot," according to Revill), but he was deeply upset by it.

Bernstein co-conducted Earle Brown's *Available Forms II* alongside the composer. The work is scored for two conductors leading two orchestras (seated not separately but intermingled), each of which has nineteen fully notated fragments ("events" in Brown's terminology), which it plays when signaled to do so by its conductor. The work combines careful composition (Brown had an exquisite ear) with the element of improvisation on the part of the two conductors. In a memoir, Brown's wife (dancer Carolyn Brown, from Merce Cunningham's company) took Bernstein to task for treating the piece as a kind of "competition" rather than as a sonic dialogue.[29] Writing in the *Herald Tribune*, Alan Rich called it "dense, fascinating, intensely colored and full of creative fire." Yet Rich also castigated Bernstein for attempting to "kill off" the avant-garde with his preparatory remarks to the audience. The New York Philharmonic's archive suggests otherwise. Again and again subscribers and listeners on radio wrote in, requesting copies of the remarks and expressing appreciation for how helpful they were. A remarkable number of letters expressed gratitude, even "everlasting gratitude," for a chance to hear the music. (A clear favorite, indicative of the prescience of many listeners, was Ligeti's *Atmosphères*.)

On January 23, 1964, the American musical community was shocked to learn of Marc Blitzstein's violent death the previous day in Martinique. Blitzstein biographer Howard Pollack recounts how the fifty-eight-year-old composer was attacked and robbed by three fishermen with whom he had been out drinking—apparently after he had "slipped into a deserted alley with one of the three for some sexual encounter." He died in the hospital of a ruptured liver the following day. A devastated Bernstein, due to conduct the Philharmonic in a performance of Beethoven's "Eroica" Symphony that night, dedicated it to his friend's memory. In the *New York Herald Tribune*, Eric Salzman wrote that the Beethoven performance was one of "wild, relentless drive" that left "detail, clarity, accuracy and indeed everything but anguished, frenetic intensity far, far behind."[30] In the following months, Bernstein conducted a memorial concert for his friend and started to work on a restoration of Blitzstein's opera *Regina* with a young conductor, John Mauceri, which bore fruit twenty-five years later.

# 11

## *Chichester, Vienna, Mount Scopus 1965–1969*

Bernstein combined introspection and extroversion in equal measure, but his public side was so strong it was sometimes hard to believe that it wasn't the whole man. In a sense, he needed an audience for his introspective side and, unlike the classic introvert who gets energy from solitude, needed to store that audience within him when he retreated to his inner world to compose or study music. When he reemerged into the public sphere, he had a burning need to discuss the joys of complex art and poetry, to share his internal states and mystical longings, to make the internal external. Although interaction with collaborators was essential to him when he was writing his theater music, he seemed to need to enter a special, private state of mind to produce other works. On many occasions he described ideas coming to him while lying down in contemplation, or sitting at the piano for hours on end in a kind of trance, from which he would awaken to find pages and pages of notes before him. These visionary trance states resembled those he entered while conducting, and from which he would have to return at the end of a performance.

For Bernstein, music was an interactive, social art. Addressing a hypothetical posterity was antithetical to his nature. Although sympathetic to his colleague's frustrations and to his artistic idealism, he would certainly have differed with the brilliant composer Milton Babbitt, who wrote, "The composer would do himself and his music an immediate and eventual service by total, resolute and voluntary withdrawal from [the] public world to one of private performance and electronic media, with its very real possibility of complete elimination of the public and social aspects of musical composition."[1]

Bernstein's 1964–65 sabbatical from the Philharmonic afforded him, at least theoretically, an entire year to compose. The fall was taken up with work on a musical based on Thornton Wilder's *The Skin of Our Teeth*, with Jerome Robbins, Betty Comden, and Adolph Green. When that project ran aground, he turned his attention to a sacred commission from the Very Reverend Walter Hussey, dean of the Chichester Cathedral in England. In his first letter approaching the composer about a work for the cathedral, Hussey had mentioned his devotion to the arts, specifically his having previously commissioned a Madonna and Child from sculptor Henry Moore, and a cantata from Benjamin Britten. After Bernstein agreed to compose a work for performance in summer of 1965, Hussey wrote expressing his delight and added that Bernstein should not feel stylistically encumbered in any way, even going so far as to say, "I think many of us would be very delighted if there was a hint of 'West Side Story' about the music."[2] In late February, the composer wrote Hussey that he planned a setting of three psalms, with additional verses from three more as commentaries —the only "hitch" being that he could "only think of these Psalms in the original Hebrew." Hussey agreed to the use of

Hebrew, merely requesting that the words be written phonetically for the choirs. The eventual instrumentation was for brass (three trumpets and three trombones), strings, two harps, and a large percussion battery. Bernstein stipulated that the long alto solo always be sung by a boy alto or countertenor.[3]

With the composition of *Chichester Psalms*, Bernstein attained a perfection of form and stylistic focus that link it to his abstract "classical" works, such as the Clarinet Sonata and the *Serenade*. (Alex Ross's word for the piece—"immaculate"—is apt.) Yet almost all of it derives from music intended for the Broadway stage. The piece represents an oasis of calm in his stylistic development, reconciling his theatrical and concert music and offering an unforced affirmation of the optimism and religious faith his other works aspire to. In it he managed an act of alchemy by adapting songs and choral music from the aborted *The Skin of Our Teeth* as well as not just "a hint" of *West Side Story* but an entire deleted song from it to fit the Sephardic Hebrew texts. What perhaps made this possible was the fact that, in their theatrical contexts, these songs had expressed themes analogous, however distantly, to those in the psalms to which they were ultimately linked. As he always did when adapting previously composed ideas to new purposes, he modified, expanded, and transformed them.

In his book on the work, Paul Laird shows just how much of *Chichester Psalms* came from music intended for the Thornton Wilder show. The fragment from Psalm 108 that begins the work ("Awake Psaltery and harp. I will rouse the dawn!") is derived from a *Skin of Our Teeth* chorale, and the exuberant 7/4 allegro music that follows it sets Psalm 100 ("Make a Joyful Noise") to music from what was to be the song "Here Comes the Sun" in the show. The use of bongo drums in the movement, along with the kind of dancelike asymmetrical meter so favored by Bernstein (and used in many of the *Anniversaries*,

*I Hate Music*, *Kaddish*, and many other works), gives the music a popular flavor that the psalm text could be seen as inviting ("Serve the Lord with gladness: come before his presence with singing").

The second movement is a plea for peace. Psalm 23, "The Lord is my shepherd, I shall not want," the psalm most commonly recited at the Jewish funeral, is set for boy alto to the serene music of the song "Spring Will Come Again" from *The Skin of Our Teeth*. As Paul Laird suggests, the orchestration for two harps now associates it "with King David, the most famous harpist of the ancient Hebrews."[4] But the masterstroke here is the use of the abandoned music of "Mix," which was to have been sung by the Jets in act 1, scene 1, of *West Side Story*, now adapted to fit words from Psalm 2, "Why do the nations rage, and the people imagine a vain thing?"[5] This violent interruption by the lower voices and percussion, and the ensuing counterpoint between the two contrasting types of music (with "Mix" being sung at exactly twice the speed of Psalm 23), changes the meaning of the peaceful psalm sung by the innocent boy alto, so that when it resumes its course it feels undermined. Indeed, on his final held tone, fragments from the "Mix" music again intrude quietly, as if in warning, and then there is a last outburst from the bass drum on the initial rhythmic figure of "Mix"/Psalm 2.[6]

This lack of resolution prepares for the dissonant, emphatic opening of the third movement for strings alone, a chordal treatment of the *Skin of Our Teeth* chorale that is strikingly theatrical. Midway through this introduction, an Ivesian echo of two fragments from the boy alto melody of the second movement is heard on muted trumpet, supported by harp harmonics. The passage encapsulates the two previous movements and prepares for the tranquility of the flowing 10/4 choral music that follows, a setting of Psalm 131 ("Lord, My heart is not haughty. . . . My soul is even as a weaned child") with, as a final pendant, verse 1 from Psalm 133 ("Behold how good, / And how pleasant it is, / For brethren to dwell / Together in unity.").[7] The main melody of this movement comes from another sketch for *The Skin of Our Teeth* (the "War Duet"), but somehow here its Hebraic character seems palpable, and everything about its flowing, contrapuntal elaboration suggests the humility and spiritual letting go of the psalm text. The chorale motto that began both the work and the final movement returns at the end, sung quietly by the choir *a cappella* and then echoed by muted trumpet and harp.[8]

Bernstein achieves a happy synthesis here. The work grows out of its Broadway materials yet beautifully fits them to the new religious context. Unlike the *Kaddish* Symphony or the later *Mass*, the work sets scripture without personal commentary. *Chichester Psalms* became one of Bernstein's most frequently performed and popular works. But the solace reached in its ending could only be provisional for someone as creatively restless as he was.

In April 1965 Bernstein took advantage of being on sabbatical to perform in the Schumann Piano Quintet with the Juilliard Quartet, which included his old friend Raphael Hillyer. In the summer he conducted *Chichester Psalms* in New York and attended its official premiere in England.[9]

He returned to the New York Philharmonic in the fall, still preoccupied by the issue of the future of tonality and of symphonic music. On October 24 he aired some of the inner musings of his sabbatical year in an almost Talmudic article for the *New York Times:*

> The classical concept of a symphony, depending as it does on a bifocal tonal axis, which itself depends on the existence of tonality—that classical concept is a thing of the past.

> Does that mean that symphonies can no longer be created? No; in a loose sense the word "symphony" can be applied to all sorts of structures. On the other hand, Yes; in a strict sense the decline of the symphony can perceptibly be dated back to the beginning of the century . . . what will happen to our orchestras?

For the next two seasons he programmed a revelatory survey of "Symphonic Forms in the Twentieth Century," including works by Mahler, Sibelius, Schoenberg, Webern, Carl Nielsen, Shostakovich, Prokofiev, Albert Roussel, Hindemith, Ives, and Vaughan Williams, while also in his public comments raising the issue of whether tonality was really exhausted. He added Ives's Third Symphony to the Philharmonic's repertoire on a program with Mahler's Ninth Symphony, and in December he conducted Mahler's Seventh Symphony on a program with the Webern Symphony, op. 21. The Webern performance may have been one of the most natural, varied, and movingly musical renderings of the work ever given, and one that made the link to the world of Mahler most unmistakably. For once the players were clearly exhorted to really "sing" the melodies in Webern's *Klangfarbenmelodien*, and the rhythms have a Viennese suppleness. Audience noise on the recording of the concert is noteworthy, but so is the sound of appreciation in the applause.[10] Nevertheless, the rendition initiated a complaint from a subscriber, to whom Bernstein wrote this reply on January 18, 1966:

> Dear Miss Selman,
> It is the duty of any Symphony Orchestra—particularly that of a cultural capital like New York—to keep its audiences abreast of main currents in the development of 20th century music. The truth is that the Philharmonic does not go far enough in this obligation, out of consideration for its large subscription audiences. If the Webern symphony, already some forty years old, already a classic, and a mere eight min-

utes in length, cannot be comfortably absorbed in a season of more conventional music, then I am at a loss for an answer.

Sincerely,
Leonard Bernstein[11]

In the fall of 1965 he presented the Seventh, Eighth, and Ninth Symphonies of Gustav Mahler. Many observers noted the depth of Bernstein's identification with the composer, and in letters he himself described his uncanny feeling, when he was leading Mahler, that he was performing his own music. The entire programs of December 9, 10, 11, 13, and 15, 1965, were devoted to performances of Mahler's Eighth Symphony ("Symphony of a Thousand"), of which the first half had been presented at the inaugural program at Lincoln Center. The work requires a gigantic orchestra, a chorus, a children's choir, and eight vocal soloists. A correspondent from the *London Times* called the performance "one of the towering moments in my life in the concert hall." Despite his personal conviction that the Eighth was the weakest of Mahler's symphonies (because it was the least "autobiographical"), Alan Rich, writing in the *New York Herald Tribune*, called it "a striding, dazzling, pounding evening. . . . Bernstein had obviously laid himself bare in the service of the score, and the cohesion, the motoric energy, the pure driving brilliance of his conception can stand as a landmark among many in his musical career."[12]

Harold Schonberg's reviews of Bernstein began to shift during this period, and his responses to the Mahler symphonies programmed in 1965 and 1966 reflected his perception that Bernstein was becoming a more judicious orchestral leader who had "learned to pace himself and the music much more convincingly." In September 1965 he wrote of a performance of Mahler's First that it was for the most part well-planned and straightforward, and that when it deviated from the letter of the score it did so persuasively. His basic criticism of the conductor had always tended to be that he was a didactic leader with a tendency to exaggerate elements and distort the music in order to emphasize to the audience how it was made, or convince them how beautiful it was, and that in the process the long line of the music was lost. By the end of the 1965–66 season, he expressed the view that Bernstein had returned from his sabbatical a more mature musician and that in a few years he would no longer be called "Lenny" but rather "Maestro."

The year 1965 was the hundredth anniversary of the birth of Jean Sibelius and of the then rarely played and recorded Danish master, Carl Nielsen. Bernstein performed a series of works by Sibelius in his "Twentieth Century" cycle, including his Third and Fourth Symphonies, and devoted a Young People's Concert to him. Sibelius was another composer with whom he had an individual connection. His performances showed a deep sympathy for the inner logic of Sibelius's musical train of thought, a grasp of his vast architecture, and an ability to find the through line and momentum in his strangest passages, such as the conclusion of his Second Symphony, a veritable sinkhole in some renditions. But more historically significant, given the composer's relative obscurity, were the presentations of major works by Nielsen, including his Third Symphony (*Sinfonia espansiva*, op. 27) and the Concertos for Clarinet and Flute. Bernstein had performed and recorded Nielsen's Fifth Symphony with the Philharmonic two years earlier. In the *New York Times* of November 14, 1965, Richard Freed described Bernstein's new recording of the Third Symphony with the Royal Chapel Orchestra of Copenhagen as "electrifying" and "one of the conductor's finest recordings to date, as well as the strongest argument yet for Nielsen." Eventually the Philharmonic released recordings of Nielsen's Second, Third, Fourth, and Fifth Symphonies.

In May 1966 Bernstein had his first encounter with the Vienna Philharmonic, conducting a new production of Verdi's

*Falstaff* at the Vienna State Opera, which proved to be a career milestone. Conducting in the same opera house where Mahler had created legendary performances before coming to New York, he fell in love with the orchestra and, against all odds, with the city. (Because of his "marriage" to the New York Philharmonic, Bernstein called the relationship "an illicit affair.") The production, directed by Luchino Visconti and with baritone Dietrich Fischer-Dieskau in the title role, galvanized audiences and critics, as well as the cast. "You have the feeling that he's not out there on the podium," said Fischer-Dieskau. "You feel he's on the stage with you. He catches everybody with his eyes and his stick." *Falstaff* was followed by a week of concerts that included *Das Lied von der Erde* with James King and Fischer-Dieskau and a performance, conducted from the keyboard, of Mozart's Piano Concerto No. 15 in B-flat Major, K. 450. Viennese music critic Joseph Wechsberg described Bernstein as the only living conductor with "the ability, authority, and musical sex appeal" to rival Herbert von Karajan.

In the fall of 1966 Bernstein started to plan his exit from the New York Philharmonic. At a press conference in early November, it was announced that he would retire from his position as music director after the 1968–69 season, after which he would maintain close ties with the orchestra as its laureate conductor for life. Even Bernstein, with his titanic energy and limited need for sleep, could not sustain his compositional productivity while being music director of the Philharmonic and conducting it week after week, appearing regularly on television, and traveling all over the world as a visiting conductor. By assuming the position at the Philharmonic, he had seized the opportunity to be at the center of American concert life and to live with many of the greatest works of music ever written, even if it meant producing little music of his own. While not exactly a Faustian bargain, it was still a gamble that he could ascend to music's greatest heights while keeping his musical soul—his ability to compose. At the end of the summer of 1967, he told biographer and art critic John Gruen:

> It is two years since I wrote my last note, the *Chichester Psalms.* Since June 1965, I have not been able to begin to form a composition. You now find me—August 15, 1967—in the position of starting all over again from where I was then! It's very difficult. I mean the muscles that were all exercised then and ready for use have now gone slack. I don't know where to begin. I pick up a pencil and think, "Now what do you do when you write a piece? What do you do first?" . . . There were two years between *Kaddish* and the *Psalms.* There were six years between *West Side Story* and *Kaddish.* Nothing in between![13]

The 1966–67 season at the Philharmonic saw Bernstein conducting Schoenberg works with the orchestra for the first and only time. He directed the Chamber Symphony No. 2, op. 38, and *A Survivor from Warsaw*, op. 46, both in October, and the great Violin Concerto, op. 36, in January, all works from the composer's American years. Robert Craft found the Violin Concerto performance "astonishingly accurate and perfectly within the idiom." The narrator in *A Survivor from Warsaw* was Vera Zorina, an actress and ballet dancer who had once been married to George Balanchine and was now Mrs. Goddard Lieberson (and mother of future composer Peter Lieberson). The spring season included a memorable Verdi Requiem and an unforgettable performance of the Schumann Cello Concerto played by twenty-two-year-old cellist Jacqueline du Pré.

In July Bernstein was back in Israel, conducting three concerts in the aftermath of the Six-Day War.[14] East Jerusalem was the home of the Wailing Wall and what had been, before the partition of 1948, the old Hebrew University, including the amphitheater on Mount Scopus. For a Jew to be able to walk through East Jerusalem seemed like a miracle. Bernstein sided with those hoping that the end of the war would begin a new life of peaceful coexistence between Jews and Arabs in the newly unified city. He prayed and cried at the Wailing Wall, visited wounded soldiers in the hospital, and played Yiddish songs for them. His concert with the Israel Philharmonic at the Mount Scopus amphitheater on July 9 presented Mendelssohn's Violin Concerto in E Minor, performed by Isaac Stern, and the final three movements of Mahler's "Resurrection" Symphony in a performance that overwhelmed the massive audience. Proceeds were donated to the Jerusalem Foundation for the Development of Jewish-Arab Activities. After leading the orchestra and chorus in "Hatikvah," the Israeli national anthem, Bernstein turned to speak to the tearful audience. Looking serenely confident in his white suit and Nehru jacket, with the sun setting over the desert behind him, he called Jerusalem a "city united and at peace . . . a city of infinite possibilities. This golden city can and should become a model for the whole world. Why not? This is no ordinary city—this is the very center of faith. Let it spread, and let the walls come down."

In mid-July he joined the rest of his family in Ansedonia, Italy, a small fishing village between the imposing Monte Argentario and the Tyrrhenian Sea, for their first vacation away from the United States. The family was also visited by writer John Gruen and a photographer. They were preparing a book with a self-contradictory title, *The Private World of Leonard Bernstein*, which the composer eventually came to regret. Sam Bernstein was once heard to remark that it was fortunate that his son was not a woman, since he seemed "incapable of saying 'no.'" Although the photos taken for the book by Ken Heyman preserve a joyful sense of the Bernsteins' family life that summer, one can't help wishing that the conductor had said "no" to the coffee-table book and left their vacation time truly "private." It seems to have been the verbal contents that disturbed him, and these provide interesting insights into his state of mind at the time. In one of his characteristically late-night conversations with Gruen, he said it depressed him that the "best works of art are works of despair now. . . . The plays of Pinter, Beckett . . . The music that is good is of despair. It's fragmented, it's atomized." The irony was that the aim of "nobility" had been left only to "Soviet tractor art," with the result the last noble strains of symphonic music had been written by a great composer able to rise above the limitations of Soviet strictures, Dmitri Shostakovich. But this meant that there were no new composers to champion in the way Koussevitzky had been able to champion Copland, Harris, Schuman, Prokofiev, and Stravinsky, and this had been a factor in his deciding to leave his position at the Philharmonic.[15] Relating this situation to the social and political realm, he said that "what the present crisis really boils down to is not only a crisis in faith. . . . It's a crisis of world revolution . . . based on the right to eat. And we of the West, who insist on the right to eat at other people's expense, seem to be doing everything we know to prevent this revolution from taking place. Instead of aiding it, and making it happen in a positive way, lending our money and power, we are using our money and power to prevent its happening."

Felicia was suffering that summer. She had painful rashes from the sun and slept apart from Bernstein because of his snoring. On his forty-ninth birthday, she threw the paintings she had been working on into the Mediterranean, from which they were rescued by twelve-year-old Alexander.[16] To be Bernstein's sibling, spouse, or child had to be a mixed blessing, and extremely difficult at times.

Felicia was a quiet activist. She was a founder of the women's branch of the American Civil Liberties Union, had been deeply involved in the civil rights movement, marched against the Vietnam War, and raised money to help the impoverished in Chile, among many other causes. When liberal Senator Eugene McCarthy announced his candidacy for the presidency on

November 7, 1967, Felicia and her husband were quick to offer their support. Bernstein contributed the song "So Pretty," with words by Comden and Green, to a "Broadway for Peace" fund-raiser and later introduced the senator at rallies in New York and Boston, while Felicia worked privately raising money for his antiwar campaign. The Vietnam War raged on, and the United States narrowly avoided being overrun in Saigon by the Tet Offensive, signaling that no end to the war was likely if the United States continued to pursue a military victory. The spring of 1968 became one of almost unprecedented domestic turmoil, including the arrest and incarceration of the "Boston Five" (including pediatrician Benjamin Spock and Yale University chaplain William Sloane Coffin Jr.) for conspiring to illegally assist people seeking to avoid the draft; Robert Kennedy's entry into the presidential primaries; the My Lai massacre; the assassination of Martin Luther King Jr. in Memphis on April 4; President Lyndon Johnson's decision not to seek a second term; student takeovers of buildings at Columbia University, and their violent ouster by police; protests in Berkeley, coinciding with antiwar demonstrations in London, Paris, Berlin, Rome, and Japan.

In May, as France was coming close to revolution and Prague was having its brief moment of political reform and artistic openness before the Soviet crackdown, Bernstein was in Vienna for a month, continuing his love affair with the orchestra and with Austrian audiences. He conducted the most Viennese of all operas, *Der Rosenkavalier;* played and conducted Mozart's Piano Concerto No. 17 in G Major alongside the *Chichester Psalms;* and appeared as pianist in a recital of Mahler songs with singers Walter Berry and Christa Ludwig. Then from America came the news that Robert Kennedy had been assassinated. The senator had been gunned down at 12:13 a.m. on the morning of June 5, at the end of a speech to his supporters at the Ambassador Hotel in San Francisco, following his victory in the California primary. A memorial service was scheduled to take place at St. Patrick's Cathedral in New York, and once again Jacqueline Kennedy asked for Bernstein's musical assistance in honoring a murdered Kennedy.

On the morning of the funeral, the Bernsteins received a call from the police reporting that there had been a death threat on the conductor's life, and that therefore a police detail would accompany them to the cathedral. At St. Patrick's Bernstein conducted the hushed middle section from the finale of Verdi's Requiem and, as the Kennedy children, dressed in white, filed past the coffin of the slain senator, the Adagietto from Mahler's Fifth Symphony.[17] As the senator's body was transported by train from New York to Arlington National Cemetery (a normally four-hour trip that took eight hours because of the hundreds of thousands of people who lined the route as the train passed), the Bernstein family headed north. Thirteen-year-old Alexander never forgot the fear he felt nor Bernstein's composure as the two of them, no longer protected by police detail, drove through the streets of New York toward Connecticut in his father's convertible. "My father put the top down, while I spent the whole trip looking up at the buildings we went by, looking for snipers."[18]

At 4 a.m. the following morning, Jacqueline Kennedy, still not asleep after the painfully solemn day, wrote a letter to Bernstein:

> Everyone has gone to bed, but I just wanted to stay up by myself to think about so many things, and about today. In awful times, I think the only thing that comforts you is the goodness in people. I wanted to write you that tonight—or this morning, or whatever it is—because when I come home I will be so tired and I may start thinking about the badness in people. When your Mahler started to fill (but that is the wrong word, because it is more this sensitive trembling) the Cathedral today, I thought it the most beautiful

> music I had ever heard. I was so glad I didn't know it. It was this strange music of all the Gods who were crying and then, if only you could have seen it, it was the time when Ethel had thought of the most touching thing: having the littlest nephews and nieces, small children, before that terrifying array of cardinals in gold, and gothic vaults, carry all the little vessels for communion up to the high altar, so that they could have some part in the farewell to the Uncle they all loved so much. They were so vulnerable, and your music was everything in my heart, peace and pain and such drowning beauty. You could just close your eyes and be lost in it forever. I think your goodness and those few soaring moments of Mahler together are more beautiful than if you had played the most beautiful Requiem all the way through. And it was so much more appropriate for this Kennedy . . . and his wife who loved him mystically.[19]

Over the summer Bernstein resumed his role as an advocate for McCarthy's candidacy. At one point he became so carried away in a public speech that he argued that if Hubert Humphrey were selected at the Democratic convention, it would be better to vote for Nixon and thereby bring about a violent backlash.

In October Bernstein was excited and heartened by the premiere of Luciano Berio's tumultuous *Sinfonia* for eight amplified voices and orchestra (dedicated to Bernstein), which the Italian composer himself conducted at the Philharmonic. The work's sheer musicality, intimations of tonality, and sweeping historical and social vision gave Bernstein a sense of optimism about where music might be headed.[20] The two composers were good friends and could communicate easily on political and musical levels. *Sinfonia* honored Martin Luther King Jr. in its time-suspended second movement, a meditation in which the words "O Martin Luther King" serve as the sole text. The third movement uses the scherzo of Mahler's "Resurrection"

Symphony as the foundation for a wild musical collage reviewing the entire history of music, which rides, as it were, on the flowing "river" of Mahler's music. (The association between this music and a river is grounded in the fact that Mahler based the scherzo on his song "Saint Anthony of Padua's Sermon to the Fishes" from *Des Knaben Wunderhorn.*)

In November Bernstein was the pianist in a recital of Mahler songs given by Dietrich Fischer-Dieskau as a benefit for UNICEF. The great baritone later wrote that his accompanist lived in the moment: "He will always let his hands glide silently across the keys while the audience is still applauding. . . . But then there is one electric shock after another, always surprising coloration, something exceedingly intimate and yet extending far beyond the edge of the stage."[21]

Bernstein presided over a series of extraordinary programs during his final months as music director of the Philharmonic. In mid-January he combined Bach's Brandenburg Concerto No. 5 (with Julius Baker, Isaac Stern, and the conductor at the keyboard), Prokofiev's Piano Concerto No. 1 in D Major, op. 19, and Mozart's Violin Sonata No. 26 in B-flat Major, in which he accompanied Stern, with the premiere of Milton Babbitt's *Relata II.*[22] Later that month he conducted Bruckner's Ninth Symphony, and this was followed the following week by Beethoven's *Missa solemnis.* Then there was the Verdi Requiem in April.

In early April, Samuel Bernstein, then seventy-seven, experienced several heart attacks. On April 28, 1969, he died, holding his wife's hand. His son changed the programs of May 8, 9, and 10 to include his *Jeremiah* Symphony (dedicated to his father) and, one of Sam's favorites, the Schumann Second Symphony, with its extraordinarily beautiful slow movement. Bernstein had long advocated for the eloquence of Schumann's orchestrations, a view not universally shared. His recordings of the Schumann symphonies are arguably among his finest. One can only imagine the deep emotion he must have felt while conducting these two works he had played in his father's company in Tel Aviv in 1947.

Bernstein's last concerts as music director, conducting Mahler's Third Symphony, followed only one week later on May 15, 16, and 17. During the ovation on the night of the final performance, according to music critic Leighton Kerner, "Mr. Bernstein did not turn to the audience, but stood facing his orchestra for what seemed like more than a minute."[23]

# Part III

# 12

## *Questions and Declarations*
## *1970–1973*

THE CONFLICTS BETWEEN Bernstein's many gifts, interests, and needs could not be resolved simply by his leaving his position at the Philharmonic. By 1969 he had already founded Amberson Productions (named for the German equivalent of his name) to film and videotape his concerts, and he was embracing his new relationship with the Vienna Philharmonic by committing himself to a series of conducting and film projects there, including performances of Beethoven's *Fidelio* and the Ninth Symphony, Strauss's *Der Rosenkavalier*, tours of Germany, Switzerland, England, and Italy, and much more. Furthermore, he would be maintaining his close ties with the New York Philharmonic, as well as with the Israel Philharmonic, the London Symphony, the Bavarian Radio Symphony, the Royal Concertgebouw, and the Santa Cecilia Orchestra in Rome. Over the next twenty years he would conduct forty-two different orchestras.

According to his children, the process of decompressing from the heady, demanding, and ultrasocial public realm of conducting to the quiet, private inner world where the notes came from was increasingly difficult. As daughter Jamie put it, "It stripped his gears every time." Looming over him as he departed his full-time role at the Philharmonic was Jacqueline Kennedy's commission to compose a work for the opening of the new John F. Kennedy Center in Washington in 1971. He also had several "smaller" composing projects in the works, including writing music for a film on the life of Saint Francis of Assisi to be directed by Franco Zeffirelli. The night after his final Philharmonic appearance as music director, he attended a Jimi Hendrix concert. Then he was off to Europe.

Bernstein's new freelance life began with a few monumental performances. The first was a rendition of Verdi's Requiem given in Christopher Wren's magnificent St. Paul's Cathedral in London, with Martina Arroyo and Placido Domingo as soloists. This was also the first of his many filmed performances, at the time a risky financial gamble to undertake, but in the end remarkably valuable. The films disseminated music to vast new audiences, while preserving live performance practices of their era and the interpretation and artistry of all involved in a more comprehensive and authentic way than modern studio recordings do.

From London, Bernstein traveled to Paris, Rome, and Tel Aviv before going to Vienna, where he performed and conducted Beethoven's First Piano Concerto, led the Ninth Symphony, and delivered an inspired performance and production of *Fidelio.* It was an extraordinary honor to participate in the celebration of the Beethoven bicentennial in such an important way, and the depth and excitement of the performances changed the way he was perceived even in America. In early February 1970 he returned to the New York Philharmonic to conduct Elliott Carter's new Concerto for Orchestra, a Philharmonic commission, along with Haydn and Tchaikovsky works. He helped the orchestra master the intricate rhythmic language of Carter's remarkable work, which was inspired by a long poem, *Vents* (*Winds*), by the French poet Saint-John Perse, concerning the regenerating and devastating power of winds. The concerto seemed to simultaneously evoke the winds of political change sweeping the United States in the late 1960s and those occurring within the art of music. Carter called for the orchestra to be divided into four ensembles, which played music of highly contrasting characters, making use of the composer's "metrical modulations" and exploiting the talents of individual musicians such as pianist Paul Jacobs, whose artistry Carter deeply admired. Even each bass player had his own individual part. The musicians grew increasingly enthusiastic the more they conquered the score's challenges, and a decision was hastily and unexpectedly made to record the work. The recording session grew festive when Aaron Copland unexpectedly joined the conductor, composer, and many of the musicians in the sound booth to listen to the spatial separation of the four large ensembles. Bernstein's rendering of the work was dark, turbulent, and expressive. Carter later said that Bernstein conducted it "very well—without that marvelous attention to detail that Boulez gave it later, but he did succeed perfectly in capturing its broad line, that long breath running through the piece."[1]

The early 1970s represented a period of exploration and branching out for Bernstein. Many observers believed that he was becoming an even better conductor. His two major creative accomplishments of the period—the musical theater work *Mass* and the Charles Eliot Norton lectures (*The Unanswered Question*) he gave at Harvard, which later became a book and a series of videos—seem to have been attempts to synthesize everything he had ever done and thought.

Bernstein's experience of his European tour had been marred

by the publication of a scathing article in the June 8, 1970, *New York Magazine* by Tom Wolfe, and a controversy surrounding his "relationship" with the Black Panthers had awaited him back in New York. In April 1969 there had been a series of police raids on members of the Black Panther Party in Harlem that had uncovered stockpiles of arms and pipe-bomb materials. Twenty-one Panthers were charged with "plotting to kill policemen . . . and [to] bomb police stations, department stores and railroad facilities," charges that eventually did not add up in court. The suspects were being kept in solitary confinement, and bail had been set at such exorbitant amounts that civil libertarians considered that they were being subjected to "preventive detention." Solidarity of any kind with the Black Panthers, who were opposed to the Gandhian principles once espoused by Martin Luther King Jr., the Congress of Racial Equality, and the NAACP, entailed considerable risk.[2] But in January Felicia Bernstein organized a legal-defense fund-raiser to be held at the Bernsteins' Park Avenue apartment, with the goal of providing funds to ensure that the Panthers had a fair trial and that their wives and children were taken care of while they were being detained. When Bernstein arrived at the party, the center of gravity shifted to his interactions with the single representative of the Panthers who was present.

Unfortunately for the Bernsteins and their cause, two members of the press who attended the event incognito, Wolfe and *New York Times* columnist Charlotte Curtis, ridiculed their efforts in a damaging way. Curtis reported sarcastically on the evening in a full-page article on the social page on January 15, Martin Luther King Jr.'s birthday ("Black Panther Philosophy Is Debated at the Bernsteins"), and the paper followed with a blistering editorial the next day, declaring that "the group-therapy plus fund raising soiree at the home of Leonard Bernstein . . . represents the kind of elegant slumming that degrades patrons and patronized alike. . . . Responsible black leadership is not likely to cheer as the Beautiful People create a new myth that Black Panther is beautiful."[3] William Buckley followed suit with a humorously derisive column in the *New York Post*, "Have a Panther to Lunch," and in June, Wolfe's 25,000-word article ("Radical Chic: That Party at Lenny's") made the event and Wolfe's catchphrase world-famous, and the Bernsteins subject to mockery, hate mail, and picketing outside their apartment building. The conductor was even booed at the Philharmonic. Many of those who attended the event later received letters outlining the anti-Semitic positions of the Panthers, anonymously signed "A Concerned and Loyal Jew." The "Loyal Jew" was none other than FBI director J. Edgar Hoover, who had compiled a list of those present and instituted a letter-writing campaign designed to discredit the Bernsteins. Lost in the shuffle was the fact that the fund-raiser didn't represent an espousal of armed violence, let alone of anti-Semitism, but a defense of due process. The Wolfe article proved highly effective in squelching events of this kind. Its arch and flowery prose managed to wound the Bernsteins, and it particularly upset Felicia, whose activities on behalf of others were normally so private.

Nevertheless, the couple hosted another potentially controversial fund-raising party on May 10, 1970, for the legal defense fund of Philip Berrigan and Sister Elizabeth McAlister, two members of the Harrisburg Seven, voices of conscience against the Vietnam War, who had been charged with plotting "to kidnap Henry Kissinger and blow up Washington's underground heating tunnels" (charges that were pure fantasy on the part of the FBI). The complicated story behind their case is brilliantly told by Barry Seldes in his book *The Political Life of Leonard Bernstein*.[4] After reading a 1970 sermon written by the imprisoned Daniel Berrigan, in which he drew parallels between the American Catholic left and the clergy of Nazi-occupied Denmark, and attending Berrigan's play *The Trial of the Catonsville Nine*, the composer went to see him at the Danbury Penitentiary on May 24, to ask for his advice about *Mass*. Berrigan later described his visitor: "He seemed tired and harassed but gentle as a lamb. He said the press had coined a new word, 'Catholic Chic' to describe the meeting last wk, at which they raised 30 grand for the cause. . . . He seems quite awed by the prison thing. . . . Almost like someone waiting in a novitiate or an old time rectory."[5]

While the meeting did not engender any specific text for *Mass*, it may have influenced its urgency of mood and strengthened the composer's sense of mission about its communal tone. Berrigan believed that Bernstein would be using his sermon as the basis for lyrics, and clearly the FBI did too. They soon issued a memo making sure that Bernstein would be denied a second planned visit to Danbury Penitentiary in July, and cautioning President Nixon not to attend the premiere of *Mass*, lest he be seen applauding an attack directed at him in Latin. In the end, despite its outbursts of anger against the powers that be and its fiercely antiwar mood, *Mass* seems more the eclectic expression of a world that has lost its spiritual center than a specifically political statement.

*Mass* is a succession of linked musical numbers in a nearly bewildering variety of musical idioms. Even today it remains a bumpy ride, with reminders of the rock and pop idioms of the time, musicals such as *Jesus Christ Superstar* and *Hair*, brass band music, and composers as different as Ives, Carl Orff, Copland, Stravinsky, and Krzysztof Penderecki. It remains difficult to have a consistent, settled opinion about a work so wildly heterogeneous in its materials and performance styles. Of course, Bernstein had proved himself a master of synthesis before. Listening today, when such a variety of reference points is quite common, the work is exciting, moving, and full of good music, but it also seems uneven.

As in the *Kaddish* Symphony, *Mass* juxtaposes a sacred text and contemporary reflections on it. While the Celebrant, with the support of the chorus, sings through the entire Mass text, soloists from the congregation offer skeptical commentary in vernacular styles. When eventually the Celebrant has a breakdown, a boy soprano takes up the song of praise that the Celebrant has lost, leading him and the congregation to gradually join in a hymn of peace that is passed along to the audience. The ending has the tone of equivocal hopefulness that is not unlike that of *The Age of Anxiety*, suggesting that each individual is responsible for preserving the spirit of worship embodied in the liturgy. Bernstein biographer Humphrey Burton convincingly traces the concept of *Mass* to three sources: work on Franco Zeffirelli's film about Saint Francis of Assisi, *Brother Sun, Sister Moon*, for which "A Simple Song" had been intended (as the music of Saint Francis's creed); the experience of conducting at Robert Kennedy's funeral at St. Patrick's Cathedral; and the Beethoven centennial in Vienna in 1970.[6] The composer began by writing the vernacular lyrics himself, but six months prior to the premiere of the work he was still way behind in the composing process, and he sought help in finding a co-librettist. His sister Shirley, who was now an agent for playwrights and lyricists, recommended that he see the musical *Godspell*, which had lyrics by her client Stephen Schwartz, and in the spring of 1971 Schwartz began working with him on the text. (There was also a small, memorable contribution from Paul Simon.)[7]

*Mass* begins strikingly with a pileup of six voices and seven percussion instruments, all in competing meters and keys (aptly described by Robert Craft, in a negative review, as "*Les Noces*, as it might have been recomposed by Berio"). This is then "answered" by the Celebrant's "Simple Song." Both are true aspects of Bernstein—the opening in fact resembles the cacophonous eight-voiced "Amen" just before Kaddish II in the Third Symphony—but the "Simple Song," because of its words, reads like a commentary on the "crazy modern music" of the work's introduction. Throughout *Mass*, idioms bounce off each other in similar ways, fascinatingly but not always convincingly. An attractive aspect of the work is that the purely instrumental passages—which are in Bernstein's late, nearly atonal idiom—have the function chorales do in the Bach *Passions*. They provide moments of reflective commentary. Ironically, it is at these moments, when the voices are silent, that the piece conveys the strongest religious quality, and perhaps the deepest feeling. They include not only the three Meditations Bernstein later extracted from the work as an orchestral group, which are positioned at key points in the structure, but also connecting passages of solo wind writing. The first Meditation, one of the best things in *Mass*, originated as a poignant piano *Anniversary* dedicated to Helen Coates on July 17, 1970, and published after her death as a memorial to her in *Thirteen Anniversaries*. The second is a short series of variations on the unharmonized atonal eleven-note "row" in the finale of Beethoven's Ninth Symphony, which occurs when Schiller's "Ode to Joy" describes the human race bowing down to the Creator in the starry sky. (Along with the variations in the second movement of his early Violin Sonata, this is the composer's strictest set of variations.) The second variation is only three measures long and piles Beethoven's row into giant dissonant chords. The third Meditation, which would not be out of place in the *Kaddish* Symphony, expands canonically on an angular theme that includes all twelve chromatic half steps.

In the days leading up to the premiere of *Mass*, Bernstein was urged by Felicia, Schuyler Chapin, and others to make cuts in the score. He complied for one performance but then restored all the deleted music. Certainly he was right, in the sense that the work's problems do not originate in its length (it lasts roughly two hours), and cuts would only damage the carefully planned structure. Each of the five sections of the *Mass* has its own key and tempo relationships. Once again, a "chain reaction" principle often links one section to the next. For example, in the second introit, the theme of the Middle Eastern–sounding Acolytes' music in 9/8 (in rhythmic groupings of 3/8 + 3/4) becomes transformed into the melody of the calm chorale "Almighty Father" in 4/4 that follows it; after an interruption by solo oboe, the cadential harmonies of the chorale are then turned into the ferociously dissonant chords (C minor above A major) of the Confiteor, at the end of which these same dissonant chords, now played in groups of six, generate the accompaniment and some of the harmony of the Trope that follows, "I Don't Know." This kind of linkage between sections could be likened to the connections between "blocks" in early Stravinsky (such as *Le Sacre du Printemps*), were it not for the fact that here there are also 180-degree shifts in idiom from one passage to the next.[8]

Near the end of the evening, the fervent gospel chorus that erupts on the words "Dona nobis pacem" (Give us peace), and repeats with increasing intensity until vocal improvisations are added (replicating the spirit of the ending of *Prelude, Fugue and Riffs*, but this time with actual improvisation), cannot help but be stirring to anyone who experienced the Vietnam War era. The eruption (which several writers think was influenced by Beethoven's use of "warlike" music at the same point in the *Missa solemnis*) almost seems to cause the Celebrant's breakdown near the end, a passage the composer was still working on almost up to opening night. This fifteen-minute "mad scene" is a moving stretch of music that recapitulates thematic material from throughout the score, beginning with the second Meditation (with the Beethoven row in both the vocal and instrumental parts) and culminating in the theme from the first Meditation.

Helen Smith rightly draws parallels between the roles of priest and conductor, noting that Bernstein's three symphonies share *Mass*'s subject matter of a "crisis of faith" and likewise feature "the presence of a solo voice." She also observes that, while the presence of rock instrumentation serves as a timbral reference point to the music of the 1960s, the music the rock instruments play is more rooted in "blues, soul and jazz."

The opening-night audience of 2,200 included neither President Nixon nor, in the end, Jacqueline Kennedy Onassis.[9] But the rest of the Kennedy family, including eighty-year-old Rose Kennedy and Senator Ted Kennedy, were there, as were many ambassadors, dignitaries, and, surprisingly, Henry Kissinger. Also in the audience was Aaron Copland, who later proposed the work for a Pulitzer Prize, which it did not receive.

The first-night audience applauded for half an hour, and many of the Washington reviews were wildly enthusiastic. Some others focused on the personality of the composer rather than on the music, even referring obliquely to the Tom Wolfe affair. For example, in the *New York Times*, the distinguished drama critic Eric Bentley called *Mass* "ideology" and "group therapy at a bargain rate." Also in the *Times*, music critic Donal Henahan praised the work's ambitions, calling it "a major effort by a protean composer" and observing that in American music "no one since Ives has felt quite so much at home in the skin of his own culture while at the same time possessing the historical and intellectual breadth to move outside that skin when he thinks it suits his purposes. . . . This sounds like a work wrenched out of the artist almost against his will, like something he had to do for us, whether we like it or not." In the same paper, Harold Schonberg described the piece as a "mélange of styles," "slick, chic, sentimental . . . a combination of superficiality and pretentiousness." In the *New Yorker*, music critic Winthrop Sargeant, an expert on Mahler and Bruckner and a Sanskrit scholar who had translated the *Bhagavad Gita*, was roused by *Mass* to one of the most enthusiastic reviews he ever accorded a contemporary work: "The message seems to be that religion may go into eclipse in a materialistic age but that it never dies. As for the music Bernstein has written for this spectacle, I find it sincere, moving, and often subtle. . . . In fact I was surprised by the real originality of the score. . . . He utilizes the whole array of musical resources available in his time. It is, I think, quite a feat for a contemporary composer to evolve a style that is both a personal medium of expression and a wholly communicative one for the audience."[10] Stephen Sondheim admired Bernstein's chutzpah and the fact that his mistakes were "not just little errors, not just a dog piddling in the middle of the carpet," but on a gigantic scale. That said, he found the work "a huge, titanic disaster."[11]

In *Mass* Bernstein approached the issue of what Copland once called "style and consistency" by rebelling against it, choosing to link musical numbers through internal means and a tight theatrical structure rather than by style. He never went as far in this direction again.

In the spring of 1972 Bernstein led the Vienna Philharmonic in the Third, Fifth, and Ninth Symphonies of Mahler. In the fall he directed a new production of *Carmen* at the Metropolitan Opera, in the original version with French dialogue, with Marilyn Horne in the title role. He guided a superbly shaped and tragic reading, in which his restrained tempos brought out the vitality and tension in a work he had loved since his adolescence.

Later that fall, Bernstein moved into Eliot House at Harvard University and began recording music with the Boston Symphony to serve as examples in his forthcoming Norton Lectures, scheduled for that term. He loved being back at Harvard so much and became so engrossed in the project that he ended up staying an entire year, giving the first lecture the following fall. To Bernstein's children, the lectures were a natural outgrowth of the Young People's Concerts, for which they had always been the sounding board. Since they were now college age, it was logical that the talks had grown up, too. Jamie Bernstein was then a junior at Harvard, and she naturally found her father's year-long presence a mixed blessing. "Whatever slim hopes I had of finding out who I was as an autonomous person were dashed the moment he arrived," she said, laughing. "On the other hand, it was exciting having him there, and thrilling to experience the lectures in real time." Each of the six talks was offered at Harvard Square Theater and then filmed, with an on-stage audience, two days later at a WGBH studio in Boston.[12]

Like *Mass*, the lectures were fascinating but also uneven. Bernstein's reading of Noam Chomsky's book *Language and Mind* had suggested to him an intellectual armature on which he could hang his discussions of music and the question of its direction. In contemporary linguistics Bernstein found the provocative hypothesis that humans have both the innate capacity to produce certain speech sounds (phonology), such as "Ma," and also an innate linguistic capacity to derive language from these elements. Chomsky postulated inborn, genetically endowed, structural linguistic parameters loose enough to account for the varieties of human languages, but restrictive enough to explain how all languages work. The presence of these parameters would explain why children can develop the ability to speak after exposure to only a limited field of model sentences. Chomsky outlines in minute detail the ways in which an almost infinite variety of different linguistic "surface structures" can be derived from the same "deep structures." He calls the innate ability to invent these derivations (the ability to construct sentences based upon deep structure in innovative ways that do not need to be taught) "transformational grammar."[13]

This gave Bernstein a model for postulating a similar underlying universal human predisposition for music: the idea that we are born both with an instinctive understanding of sound ("musical phonology"), and with a basis for deploying these sounds in structures that convey specifically musical meanings ("musical syntax" and "musical semantics"). But, of course, being Bernstein, he tried to wed this notion of a universal musical substructure to his views of music's current predicament and where music might be headed. The title of his lectures, *The Unanswered Question*, referred both to Ives's composition of 1908 and to the question of music's future.

Bernstein had always believed that human biology and the laws of physics accounted for the universality of tonal/modal scale patterns in all musical cultures, and lay behind the fact that children instinctively sing along with adults in their own range, without knowing what an "octave" is, and dance to a beat without knowing what "rhythm" is. In his Young People's Concerts, he operated on the assumption that musical comprehension has a strong instinctive component, that, given the opportunity to listen to works by Beethoven, anyone could eventually learn to follow their syntax and semantic processes, just as, under the proper conditions, anyone could eventually learn any of the human languages.

Using analogies from linguistics to examine the way Western music's many languages evolved, the lectures began with an explanation of the overtone series and then reviewed music history from the Middle Ages to the present day. Among the high points were Bernstein's analyses of Beethoven's Sixth Symphony; his comparison of the actual opening of Mozart's Fortieth Symphony to a four-square hypothetical "deep structure" he had the orchestra perform; his discussions of poetry as the linguistic equivalent of music, including his digressions about Mallarmé, T. S. Eliot, and E. E. Cummings; his insights into Stravinsky's aesthetics; and the fine performance of *Oedipus Rex* he offered as a pendant to the final lecture. As an application of Chomsky's ideas to music, the lectures were inevitably flawed and could not possibly match Chomsky's rigor. But as a more intuitive response to Chomsky on the part of a musical thinker, the lectures were fascinating and musically illuminating.

Bernstein's proposition that the structures of musical grammar point to an innate human musical capacity was provocative enough for some scholars and music theorists to take up the challenge of looking further into the matter, most notably linguist Allan Keiler, and the team of linguist Ray Jackendoff and composer Fred Lerdahl. Bernstein's conclusion that some form of tonality is essential to musical coherence may be problematic, given how mutable and subjective the concepts of "tonality" and "coherence" appear to be. But he may have meant the word "tonal" in a broad, almost metaphorical sense. In a period in which serious music seemed in danger of becoming disconnected from its social purpose—to become a form of pure research—he was arguing that good composers should not abandon the aims of the giants of the past who had created art on the highest level that still resonated with the intuitive understanding of lay listeners. By speaking of musical fundamentals within the context of linguistics, he was arguing for a complex music that builds its cosmic edifices on the "nya, nya" taunts of children on the street, the lullabies sung by mothers to infants, and the festive dances of folk traditions. Seen in this way, the lectures seem prophetic.

When he had spoken of Beethoven's "universality" in his 1970 film made during that composer's 200th birth year, Bernstein was also speaking of his own goals as the composer of *West Side Story* or *Chichester Psalms:* "That dubious cliché about music being the universal language almost comes true with Beethoven. No composer ever lived who speaks so directly to so many people. . . . It has a purity and directness which never becomes banal. It's accessible without being ordinary."

Perhaps Bernstein's lectures communicated some viewpoints that he was already outgrowing. Aligning himself, as if by habit, with the Boulanger school of thought, recommending, as he had at the Young People's Concerts, great works of

Stravinsky's such as *L'Histoire du soldat* and the *Symphony of Psalms*, and espousing "tonality," he speaks with brisk assurance but not much emotion. But when he is discussing Schoenberg, we feel in his manner and voice, and in the sound of his piano playing, how intrigued and involved he is, note by note, phrase by phrase, even as he voices skepticism about the numerical schemes lying behind Schoenberg's twelve-tone music. At the very moment he was speaking these words he was moving closer to Schoenberg's sound world, or at least to that of Berg, in his music. In his later work, he occupied a territory halfway between the rigors of the academics who paid little attention to his music and the open-hearted expressivity of his own previous theater and concert music. But he was now rather far from the world of early Copland, Roy Harris, William Schuman, and Stravinskian neoclassicism. In his later years he also performed the music of his American friends far less frequently, and felt increasingly at home both in Vienna and in the works of the great European tradition.

# 13

## *Dybbuk*
## *1974–1979*

After *Mass* Bernstein created only one more work in the show business tradition, or at least only one more that came to fruition and opened in a theater. Although he still had Broadway in him and could write a popular song when the occasion moved him to, he was now primarily a different kind of composer. It would be convenient to give this period its own name, to call it his "Amber period," say, so that one could more easily accept it on its own terms and not expect the music to suddenly turn into *Candide*. It is tempting to associate a lot of this later work with the side of his personality that was more like his father, the serious, brooding side. Nowhere is this more the case than in the music he composed for Jerome Robbins's ballet based on *The Dybbuk*, a 1914 Hasidic play by the Russian writer Shloyme Zanvl Rappoport (1863–1920), better known by his pseudonym S. Ansky. Robbins had been hoping to create such a ballet ever since the era of *Fancy Free* and had proposed it to the New York City Ballet in 1951. Although estranged from the Judaism of his parents, he had never forgotten a trip with his sister and mother to Poland as a child, which had ultimately led to his conception of *Fiddler on the Roof.* Like Bernstein an outsider to regular religious observance, Robbins somehow found himself deeply connected to his religious ancestors when he made his art.

"Dybbuk" means "attachment" in Hebrew and denotes a tormented soul who possesses a living person and must be exorcised.[1] Written simultaneously in Yiddish and Russian, Ansky's *The Dybbuk* takes place in a Hasidic village community and explores Jewish mysticism and numerology, explicitly hovering between the worlds of the dead and the living and dealing with the tension between the more rational Talmudic study and the rituals, spells, wordplay, and sorcery associated with Kabbalah. It tells a tragic love story about a pledge made by two friends that someday their children, Channon and Leah, would marry each other, and of the pledge's violation by Leah's father, who betroths his daughter to a wealthy man when she is of age. Ignorant of this history, Channon, now a young yeshiva scholar, falls in love with Leah and invokes spirits to win her. But at the moment when "the secret of the Double Name of God is revealed to him," he dies. He then possesses his beloved as a dybbuk, and, at the moment she is about to be married, speaks through her mouth, saying that he will not abandon her. An exorcism of his spirit appears to succeed, and the wedding is reconvened. But right before the wedding, Channon's ghost reappears to Leah, and she approaches him in her white wedding dress, merging with him in the other world.[2] George Gershwin at one time planned to compose an opera based upon *The Dybbuk*. Copland was inspired by it to compose his 1929 chamber work *Vitebsk*.

Bernstein's score is one of his most consistent, subtle, and mysterious. Nothing could be farther from *Mass.* Integrated, focused, and as inward-looking as his grandfather's daily life, it should be heard in its entirety rather than in the two suites it was eventually carved up into. At fifty minutes, it does not feel long; it occupies its form well and interestingly. It maintains a dark palette throughout, both instrumentally and musically. It is superbly orchestrated, containing some particularly haunting writing for solo oboe, solo trumpet, solo strings, and delicate chamber groupings. Although for the most part rhythmically restrained, almost reined in, there are animated, characteristic Bernstein dance passages in the 5/8, 7/8, and 9/8 meters he was so fond of, but even these sections remain either dark-hued, ghostly, or harsh and biting. The score's melodic materials, often in the Jewish "freygish" mode, with its prominent augmented second interval between the second and third note, are not as overtly tuneful as one normally expects from this composer. That is part of the work's style.[3] Unlike *Mass*, *The Age of Anxiety*, or *Kaddish*, *Dybbuk* does not have an ending that shifts to an optimistic tone in its final section. It even lacks *Jeremiah*'s poignant resolution, closing cyclically with a return to the macabre march heard near the beginning and then fading to quiet fragments that pierce the silence a few last times before disappearing. An atmosphere of resignation hangs over *Dybbuk*.

The score has a large component of serial and numerically derived material. The letters and words of Hebrew are considered to have numerical equivalents ("gematria"). For example, the number for "life" in Hebrew is 18. In the Ansky play, much is made of the fact that Leah's letters add up to the magical number 36 (two times 18) and Channon's are three times that, and that therefore they are mathematically matched. Bernstein made use of 18s and 9s in his score, and used nine-tone scales. There is a kabbalistic tree of life sketch in his hand among his papers, and he made the assertion in the *New York Times* that "every note in the ballet was arrived at by Kabbalistic or mystical manipulation of numbers. That includes numerology, conversions, anagrams."[4] However, he also suggested that the process was in part instinctive, that many of the score's rows, intervals, scales, inversions, and retrogrades were arrived at intuitively. Steeped in kabbalistic readings and procedures while composing, Bernstein appears to have derived his own procedures from them. There are a few hints of Stravinsky in the rabbinical singing, in the first orchestral passages (which are slightly reminiscent of Stravinsky's *The Flood*), and in instrumental touches throughout the score.[5]

Robbins created an abstract work, not a retelling of the story. For him, as for Bernstein, the ballet dealt with "the visions, hallucinations, and magical religious manifestations of an oppressed people."[6] But for Bernstein it was also a return to an unspoken theme from Plato's *Symposium*, the fusion of male and female into one being, as well as to the theme of star-crossed lovers that had animated *West Side Story*. The premiere of *Dybbuk* was given on May 16, 1974. In her review in the *New Yorker*, Arlene Croce rebuked the team for deliberately avoiding "the explosive, archaic passions" of the play, and asked of Robbins, "Is this what he's been waiting thirty years to do—to cut the guts out of a great old Russian-Yiddish primitive beast?"[7]

In June 1974 the Bernsteins moved from the protected elegance of their Upper East Side neighborhood to a slightly smaller apartment in the Dakota, known for its distinguished artistic residents, on the Upper West Side. Within days of the move, Felicia was hospitalized and underwent a mastectomy. Characteristically, she kept her breast cancer a secret from Jamie until the day after her graduation from Harvard, and from twelve-year-old Nina until after the surgery itself. It marked the beginning of a painful era for the entire family. During the next two years, as Bernstein worked on a new musical, *1600 Pennsylvania Avenue*, with writer-lyricist Alan Jay Lerner, there was an erosion in his sense of discretion about his relationships with men. He was at a point in life when people often rebel against their own aging, and perhaps his wife's illness added to his own intimations of mortality. He had been in a losing struggle to maintain his monogamy for many years, but he had maintained the marital understanding that he be discreet and apparently never became involved in any relationships that threatened the family's stability. That had changed during the final stages of his work on *Mass*, when he fell in love with a lively twenty-four-year-old man, Tom Cothran, a music director at a Los Angeles radio station, who played the piano and was literarily and musically brilliant. Soon Cothran was in New York, on the Bernstein payroll, and a friend of the family. (He proofread the entire score of *Mass*).

In May 1976 Bernstein experienced a major disappointment when *1600 Pennsylvania Avenue* failed with both critics and audiences, closing after only seven performances. The concept itself did not bode well: a show spanning a hundred years of U.S. history, with the presidential occupants of the White House and three generations of black servants as the central characters. The composer wrote more music for the work than for any of his other theater pieces. As in *Candide*, the language lies somewhere between musical theater and operetta. After the collapse of the show, Bernstein reused some of the material in other ways. But as with *Candide*, there were also later attempts to rescue the score in its original form. Since a good deal of it can now be heard in *A White House Cantata*, created eight years after the composer's death, some musical passages now exist in two different contexts. The *1600 Pennsylvania Avenue* music heard apart from the drama rises to a high level in three extended numbers that writer Helen Smith characterizes as "scene-songs." It is hard to think of another contemporary composer who could have written these pieces—so fluent, engaging, tuneful, and utterly tonal, yet also full of harmonic and rhythmic inventiveness and mischief. One of them is a nine-minute "Sonatina," sung by British soldiers in 1812, that tells a complicated story while also fulfilling the expectations of a five-part Classical structure, consisting of an introduction; sonata-allegro; *fugato;* minuet and trio; and concluding rondo, in a captivating tonal idiom.

After the closing of *1600 Pennsylvania Avenue* there was an unpleasant incident at Sardi's restaurant in which Bernstein reduced Felicia to tears by blaming her for suggesting he work with Alan Jay Lerner in the first place. But the context of the outburst was far larger than the show. In the same month Bernstein took Tom Cothran along with him on a six-week New York Philharmonic tour. Any romantic connections with men had previously been kept offstage. Cothran read anthologies of American poetry along with the composer and helped him choose the poems he would set in his new *Songfest* cycle. Bernstein's performances in London of Gershwin's *An American in Paris* and *Rhapsody in Blue* filmed during this time revealed, according to Humphrey Burton, "an astonishingly downcast" conductor and a distracted, inaccurate pianist. The crisis deepened in July, when Bernstein moved out of the family home and rented a house with Cothran in Carmel, California, in which he stayed for six more weeks, far from New York gossip. It was there that he composed four songs for *Songfest* within one week: "A Julia de Burgos," "Music I Heard with You," "Zizi's Lament," and "What Lips My Lips Have Kissed."[8] Later that summer at Tanglewood, in the midst of the family turmoil, Bernstein led a magisterial and electrifying performance of Liszt's great *Faust* Symphony, which was recorded at Symphony Hall soon after. From the blazing first movement, to the serenely gentle Andante (named for Gretchen in Goethe's play), to the skittering, triumphant finale, with its syncopated *fugato* that is almost Stravinskian in its angularity, this was a performance that plunged one into the heart of nineteenth-century romanticism while remaining architecturally crystal clear.

Back in Martha's Vineyard, a devastated and humiliated Felicia was smoking more than ever, hardly sleeping, and telling friends that her husband was away working with Arthur Laurents. In the fall Bernstein rented a room in the Navarro Hotel, near the Dakota, and then went to Europe, at which point a trial separation between the couple was announced publicly. In Vienna, traveling with Cothran, he completed his filmed Mahler symphony cycle with Symphony No. 6, sporting a short-lived beard, and in France he recorded Bloch's *Schelomo* and the Schumann Cello Concerto with Mstislav Rostropovich, in performances so compelling that the cellist believed he could never surpass them.

In the winter of 1976–77 Bernstein and Cothran spent time together in Palm Springs, with Bernstein finishing *Songfest* and starting to think about an opera based on *Lolita* (in which Dietrich Fischer-Dieskau would play Humbert Humbert). But things with Cothran did not truly jell into a satisfying way of life. Although they remained close friends, their romance ended, and by spring Bernstein started to see more of Felicia again. In July 1977 the family was at Tanglewood together and planning an Austrian holiday to coincide with a Bernstein festival there. However, the reconciliation virtually coincided with a return of Felicia's illness, now in a different form. She was diagnosed with lung cancer (like her husband, she had always been a heavy smoker). As she began to undergo radiation and then chemotherapy treatments, Bernstein moved back into the Dakota.

Bernstein had conducted an excerpt from *Songfest* at the Jimmy Carter inauguration concert in January, but the complete work was given its premiere in Washington on October 11, 1977, by the National Symphony, conducted by Rostropovich in his first concert as music director of the orchestra. It was an all-Bernstein program. Although debilitated by chemotherapy treatments, Felicia was able to attend the performance.

*Songfest* is a cycle of twelve songs for six singers and orchestra, a stylistic quilt celebrating America's ethnic, poetic, and musical diversity. Beneath the surface it is also a musical and personal self-portrait. "Storyette H. M.," set to a text by Gertrude Stein, dovetails explicitly with Bernstein's life situation at the time of writing ("One was married to someone. That one was going away to have a good time."), but in a tongue-in-cheek fashion. As set for two singers (soprano and bass), the music emphasizes both the fractured wit of the prose poem and its divided sympathies ("I am content, you are not content"). Its steadily off-kilter seven-plus-five meter and pentatonic blues scales are musically irresistible. Rarely has pain been suggested so seductively. (The pentatonic tune recalls the fake-Hollywood Tahitian music in "What a Movie!" from *Trouble in Tahiti*, composed in the first months of the Bernstein's marriage.) Bernstein combines two meditations on being black, Langston Hughes's "I, Too, Sing America" (a Whitmanesque affirmation) and the ironic "Okay 'Negroes'" by Jamaican American poet June Jordan, in a powerful, jazzy duet of contrapuntal musics and attitudes. (Elliott Carter's dualistic mesh of verse from ancient Greece alongside words by American poet John Ashbery was written a year later in 1978.)

While the professional excellence of Bernstein's music is impressive throughout, the songs heard individually cut more deeply than they do in context. Few composers have set American English with his skill. The personal and compositional intensity lavished on Lawrence Ferlinghetti's "The Pennycandystore beyond the El," Walt Whitman's "To What You Said," Conrad Aiken's "Music I Heard with You," and Edna St. Vincent Millay's "What Lips My Lips Have Kissed" show a mature, literate composer exploring an idiom on the borderline between tonality and atonality, supremely able to embody and project a text in a way that is convincing, flexible, moving, yet unsentimental. The one piece that may fail to read as intended is the opening, "To the Poem," which is musically memorable but unconvincing as an expression of the irony the Frank O'Hara poem, with its odd verbal accentuations, suggests.

The haunting Aiken setting—an aria in search of an opera—sets its outer portions in a Barberesque A major tinged with a Lydian D-sharp, and its central stanza conveys the emptiness of the beloved's absence ("Your hands once touched this table and this silver / And I have seen your fingers hold this glass") in a pointillistic, twelve-tone idiom, delivered as if in a trance of memory. Throughout the song the missing beloved casts a constant canonic shadow. In "To What You Said," which is derived from the prelude to *1600 Pennsylvania Avenue*, an unvarying fixed tone (middle C) persists from first measure to last as the harmonies continually shift around it, a fascinating model of composing tonally, yet freshly. The constant tone poses a riddle, as does the poem. Does it represent the persistence of desire, or the persistence of aloneness? (Whitman's second line reads, "Though you have strayed hither, for my sake, you can never belong to me, nor I to you.") The sardonic and poignant Ferlinghetti song, with its jazzy bass and swinging baritone melodic line, explores tightly knit twelve-tone territory with consistency, while still managing to suggest blues and a tonal center of C minor.[9] The affecting Edna St. Vincent Millay setting, another "aria," anticipates the idiom of the opera Bernstein would write six years later.

*Songfest* begins and ends on a public, festive note, but what one remembers best from it are its plaintive, private moments. The poetic lines that linger in the mind are Millay's:

> I cannot say what loves have come and gone,
> I only know that summer sang in me
> A little while, that sings no more.

In January 1978, despite having undergone a serious operation on her now damaged heart in November, Felicia was able to accompany her husband to Vienna and Milan for his performances of *Fidelio.* She then returned to New York for further chemotherapy treatments. That spring Bernstein canceled his remaining concerts to stay with her. The couple had purchased a house on Long Island, overlooking the ocean, and it was there that Felicia spent her final weeks and died on June 16, 1978, at the age of fifty-six. At the end she had returned to the Catholic faith and was given last rites. There were two services, one Catholic, the other Jewish. At the shivah held at the Dakota, Jacqueline Onassis was the first mourner to arrive. Felicia was buried at the Green-Wood Cemetery in Brooklyn.

Shirley and Burton Bernstein tried to distract their brother with a trip to Greece two weeks later, but mainly he sat by himself, staring out to sea, inconsolable. He wanted to cancel the enormous sixtieth birthday tribute planned for him at Wolf Trap Farm Park that August, but it would have meant denying the National Symphony much-needed funds. The televised event was attended by 6,500. One musician in the orchestra described Bernstein as having "aged ten years in a few months." Another friend found him "one of the saddest human beings I ever experienced."[10] Amid the many tributes and performances at Wolf Trap, Lillian Hellman's painful words honoring Felicia must have left the most lasting impression on him: "Leonard Bernstein will have to live with the memories of their many good times and also with those of the last horrible months. . . . Perhaps he will be the wiser for it, and the memories will lead him to create even greater things."[11]

Felicia's death left Bernstein in a depressed, rudderless, undisciplined state. No one who was not a family member had ever loved Bernstein as Felicia had, and the reverse was also true. They had anchored each other, and the family life they had created together had anchored, fulfilled, and immeasurably enriched Bernstein. In a 1970 film he had once described Beethoven's contradictory personality: "Out of notes he could create a beautifully ordered world, but in everyday affairs he was a hopeless mess. . . . He got on everybody's nerves. . . . It was impossible for him to settle down. . . . He was always looking for something else." Those close to Bernstein during the period following Felicia's death agreed that he could often be "a hopeless mess." Despondent, needy, guilt-ridden, lonely, he held himself responsible for his wife's illness and death, and told anyone who would listen that she had been the greatest love of his life.

His children now had to cope both with the loss of their mother and with their father's guilt and depression. He particularly relied on his youngest child, Nina. Preoccupied with his own mortality, discouraged about not having accomplished what he had hoped as a composer, and holding himself accountable, however irrationally, for Felicia's early death, he would say, "I'm all wrapped up in elf's thread." ("Elf's thread" is an anagram for "self-hatred.") His wife and children had kept his ego and tendencies to tactlessness or self-dramatization in check. "Now, Lenny," Felicia would exclaim when something he said at dinner seemed over the top. His children had nudged him in the direction of humility by making fun of his fame, his insatiable need for attention, and his ability to become emotional on his own behalf, to "move himself." The normalcy of family life had given him a sorely needed sense of order, about which he could then complain, and against which he could privately, and sometimes publicly, rebel. But without Felicia, he seemed to have lost his center, his sense of boundaries, and sometimes even his customary consideration for others. Although he could pull himself together for most occasions and performances, when he drank he could painfully embarrass his family, friends, and colleagues. (And of course he continued to smoke as heavily as ever.) At the same time, he was the hub of an enormous industry predicated on his continuing to maintain a grueling schedule of public appearances, concerts, and recording and video sessions, meticulously organized for years in advance by Harry Kraut at Amberson Productions. Although he was more than merely complicit in setting such a life in motion, he complained about it as if it had been imposed upon him. "Sometimes I feel like I am working for Harry," he would say. He wished he could escape from all of it and write that one great work that he could be remembered for. He worried that *West Side Story*, good as it was, would be his only legacy. "I am so tired of being Leonard Bernstein," he told his son, Alexander.

# 14

## *In the Garden*
## *1980–1985*

Miserable though he was in 1979, Bernstein was fortunate on most levels, and he knew it. He had his children; his brother, sister, and even his mother were still alive; he had his métier and his many gifts; he had the love and admiration of millions; he had worldly security. He had lived more fully than most people could ever imagine doing. Yet many of his own inner conflicts had now caught up with him. His composing may have often taken a backseat to his life as a performer, but it must have become painfully obvious to him by this time that his nature compelled him to do both, and that the option that he could chose a private life over his public one had been an illusion.

After Felicia's death, Bernstein showed no inclination to settle into any new stable domesticity. While he was now "free" to lead what was in 1980 called a "gay lifestyle"—frequently surrounded by groups of adoring young men, he also had a number of fulfilling, deeper relationships—he was neither a happier nor a more unified person as a result. He still relied heavily on those who had always been at the center of his life: his children, whom he had taken with him all over the world when he could, and his brother and sister. Yet his new way of life also had the effect of alienating those who cared about him most, not because of its homosexual aspect but because the atmosphere of unalloyed adulation he was surrounded by obscured the private man they loved. Without the rudder of his marriage he became more extreme and more insecure. Even an admirer such as composer Ned Rorem was taken aback by his friend's self-absorption and need to be reassured and flattered during this time. In public, Bernstein's physical demonstrativeness—which was not always entirely consensual—was sometimes too much of a good thing. As one old friend put it, "He had his tongue down everyone's throat—men and women. He wanted to French kiss the world." Copland, Blitzstein, and Laurents had cautioned him about the destructive and drug-like properties of fame. Writer and composer Paul Bowles, a friend since the 1930s, told a biographer that fame had made Leonard "smarmy and false." Yet this was only one side of him. After they had visited together in Tangier, Morocco, in 1977, Bowles described him in a letter to a friend as "exactly the same as he had been" when they first met, and wonderful to be with: "we talked for three days. . . . I can't see any difference except in appearance."[1] A literary friend of Felicia's, who did not know Bernstein's musical side (she describes herself as "unmusical") and tended to see him when he was not at his best, remembers being startled by glimpsing the power of his mind when she sat next to him on a plane and watched him complete the formidable *London Times* crossword puzzle in a flash, "almost without thinking."

Despite his complicated personal life, Bernstein continued to grow as a musician and was able to rise to extraordinary achievements in his final decade, both as composer and conductor. Nor did he ever lose his curiosity, generosity, superhuman energy, or capacity for joy. But from a personal point of view, it seems fair to say that his happiest years were behind him. His grief over Felicia stayed with him for the rest of his life.

In September 1979 he conducted and recorded the musicians of the Vienna Philharmonic in the string orchestra version of Beethoven's String Quartet No. 14 in C-sharp Minor, op. 131, which he had first heard forty years earlier at Mitropoulos's American debut. Several orchestra members had written him that it was a foolhardy idea—that achieving unanimity of bowing, phrasings, and articulations in a work of such intricacy and virtuosity, intended for single players, was impracticable. But he was of the opposite opinion, that it was easier than playing the piece as a quartet, since a conductor with a single conception of it was there to shape it, and he had persisted—buying fifteen sets of quartet parts, plus extra ones for the basses, marking the bowings and the places to be played and not to be played. He was prouder of this recording than of any he had ever done, and he dedicated it—an unusual thing to do with a recording—to Felicia's memory. In Vienna he not only performed Mahler, standing where the composer had once stood, but Haydn and Mozart, in the city where each composer had spent their last years. In conducting, he said, "one rides something like waves of love which are created by the composer whom we happen to be playing." He still performed as a pianist, although now increasingly with what he called "popsicle fingers" (stiff from stage fright and insufficient practice).

In July 1980 he fulfilled a commission from the Van Cliburn International Piano Competition. (Works are often composed specifically for recital competitions to test the ability of performers to quickly prepare and memorize music for which there is no performance tradition.) Bernstein composed a compact ten-minute work that explores an enormous range of moods, characters, and piano textures. He titled it *Touches*, dedicating it "To my first love, the keyboard."

Bernstein's memory of the arrival of his Aunt Clara's piano fifty years before was, in fact, tactile: "I remember touching this thing the day it arrived, just stroking it and going mad." Perhaps composing *Touches* gave him momentary refuge from the tormented state he was in that summer, reconnecting him with memories of childhood and with his undergraduate days, when, full of youthful ardor and still relatively anonymous, he had last written an extended work for solo piano. Like that 1938 Piano Sonata, *Touches* has a solitary, even bleak quality, suggesting in its fleeting chain of associations the nocturnal ruminations of an insomniac. It is a more modest offering than the youthful sonata, not a declaration of artistic ambitions but a tentative starting from tabula rasa. However, as he had so often before, Bernstein "started again" with a preexisting kernel of music, an intimate, spare, one-page meditation ("Virgo Blues") he had written for his daughter Jamie's twenty-sixth birthday on September 8, 1976. To this "chorale" he added eight variations and a climactically resonant restatement of the theme that subsided into a quiet ending. But only the second and ninth sections, which are nearly identical, qualify as variations in the traditional sense, in that they retrace, in quirky fits and starts, the exact pitches and phrasing of the theme. The other sections behave like the variations in *The Age of Anxiety*, each evolving from features in the preceding one. The "chorale" somehow evokes both a blues and the opening of *Tristan und Isolde*. Although there is no underlying tone row, the way the notes appear individually, one at a time, suggests one.[2] The fifth variation resembles the music of Leon Kirchner and could almost be a part of that composer's song cycle on Emily Dickinson's poetry written at about the same time. (Both composers were fond of the eight-note octatonic scale.) The outburst of the climactic restatement of the theme at the end occurs at the second phrase of its return, not its first, giving the impression of a sudden welling up of feeling in midthought. Bernstein's assistant Jack Gottlieb suggested that perhaps there might be one more variation before this one. While Bernstein appeared to agree, he never altered this rewarding little piece.

Amazingly, the spirit of entertainment still coursed through him, like a stream buried under ice. He had written an orchestral work in a pops vein in 1977, *Slava!*, dedicated to Mstislav Rostropovich and reusing the rousing numbers "Rehearse!" and "Grand Old Party" from *1600 Pennsylvania Avenue*, and he composed a second one in 1980, *A Musical Toast*, dedicated to conductor André Kostelanetz. But his full-length *Divertimento for Orchestra* for the Boston Symphony, completed in September 1980 for the orchestra's centenary celebration, was a more substantial contribution to the long tradition of elegant suites written in a spirit of fun. The eight movements in assorted idioms are linked by the recurring use of the notes B–C, standing for "Boston Centennial," and of the fanfare motive that opens the first, "Sennets and Tuckets." The ensuing movements include a Schubertian Waltz for muted strings in 7/8; a mysterious slow Mazurka for double reeds and harp, which is interrupted by the oboe solo from the first movement of Beethoven's Fifth Symphony; a rousingly balletic Samba; an amusing Turkey Trot in alternating 4/4 and 3/4; a short interlude, Sphinxes, in which two lugubrious twelve-tone rows resolve tonally; a fine twelve-tone Blues, orchestrated in the style of Miles Davis and Gil Evans's *Sketches of Spain* album; and a finale that begins with a beautiful canonic threnody for three solo flutes (marked "In Memoriam") and resolves into a raucous March (entitled "The BSO Forever") in alternating meters of 2/4 and 5/8.

In October 1980 Bernstein received a letter from a twenty-seven-year-old writer and editor named Stephen Wadsworth, asking to do an interview with him for *Saturday Review*. It included a strategically placed mention of the possibility of "a game of anagrams" (something Bernstein might have found hard to resist) and ended with a postscript: "P.S. Interested in librettos?" Bernstein agreed to meet him, and even to being interviewed, on condition that Wadsworth bring along an outline for a sequel to *Trouble in Tahiti.*

Bernstein had dreamt of a follow-up to *Trouble in Tahiti* for many years, envisaging it as a serious opera in a completely different idiom, part freely atonal, part strictly twelve-tone, part diatonic, free of the stylization and satirical edge that had made *Trouble in Tahiti*'s characters somewhat two-dimensional. He was frankly tired of Broadway, of pleasing producers, of thinking in terms of "formulas" and of conventional rhyming, strophic "numbers written to boost the show at 10:30." He imagined a story occurring thirty years after *Trouble in Tahiti*, which would include Dinah's death and the family's reunion at her funeral, and which would deal with family life in a manner that was "strong, sad, even depressing and deeply investigatory of interpersonal pain."

Wadsworth, who had met Bernstein's daughter Jamie at Harvard, turned out to be a handsome, literary young man who was then managing editor of *Opera News.* He too was grieving, having recently lost his sister Nina in a car accident. In his outline for a sequel to *Trouble*, he independently included a central scene that was a funeral. Almost immediately, the idea of an interview was forgotten in favor of discussing an actual collaboration.

In the spring of 1981, with the new opera in its early stages, Bernstein composed *Halil* ("Flute" in Hebrew). The fifteen-minute work, scored for solo flute, string orchestra, and percussion, was written in memory of a nineteen-year-old Israeli flutist, Yadin Tanenbaum, who had been killed in 1973 while serving as a soldier in the Sinai. Like many of Bernstein's compositions from the *Kaddish* Symphony on, it combines music derived from a twelve-tone row with tonal music growing out of related interval patterns. The form is dreamlike and episodic, with a theatrical element created by music suggesting the soldier's death. There is a distant dramatic link to the Berg Violin Concerto in its musical evocation of youthful vitality cut short—here suggested by the Gershwinesque dance music midway into the score—and the peaceful, tonal close. The composer conducted the premiere in Tel Aviv on May 27, 1981, in the presence of Tanenbaum's parents, with Jean-Pierre Rampal as soloist.

But it was the opera *A Quiet Place* that would most powerfully bring to fruition the eclectic explorations of Bernstein's later years. As he had when he composed *Mass*, the composer again found creative inspiration in working with a young man who had been introduced to him by a family member. Wadsworth was a writer and singer who had fallen in love with opera as a child and teenager growing up in the New York metropolitan area. Much like his mentor, he had an "erratic and grudging relationship with American theater music," believing that too much on Broadway was unadventurous and inauthentic, and that most American operas were remote, neo-European constructs painted in pastels, not urgent musical and theatrical expressions of American issues and problems.[3]

The concept of using an existing opera as the basis for a new one was the culmination of Bernstein's lifetime practice of carrying forward ideas from one work to another. It was the ultimate "chain reaction" variation. Since Bernstein was thirty years older than he had been when he composed *Trouble in Tahiti*, the work would necessarily be a reflection on his own aging. By turning to the one-act opera for his source material, he would be revisiting music he had been working on when he was first married to Felicia, on their honeymoon in Cuernavaca, and would be musically recalling their life together. The opera became a way of reviewing the two families in his life: the one he had been born into and the one he had created with Felicia.

The man Wadsworth met at first gave him pause. "He was a complicated guy at a complicated juncture of a complicated career, and still in mourning for Felicia," he later said. But by himself, apart from admirers who expected him to behave like the public Bernstein, "he was a gem. Incredibly dear, respectful, kind beyond words, deeply funny, the best intellectual companion imaginable, interested in truth, and brilliant with words. It was exhausting just keeping up with his mind." For obvious reasons both men were initially apprehensive about undertaking the huge project. At first they spent a great deal of their time together studying musical works, everything from jazz and popular song to Britten's *Owen Wingrave*, which Bernstein was very taken with at the time, and to Leoš Janáček's *The Cunning Little Vixen* and Berg's *Wozzeck*. The challenge of setting vernacular American English was uppermost in their minds. In their first conversation, they had talked about Janáček and Bartók (whose centenary would be celebrated in 1981) and their shared "passion for the inflections of language as it was spoken rather than as it was idealized in song." "We worked hard to avoid writing in schemes, to avoid the disease we coined 'schematoma,'" Wadsworth later wrote. "Rhyme schemes, meter schemes, closed forms, 'well-made play' schemes were viewed suspiciously and only grudgingly allowed."[4]

Wadsworth did some writing in December 1980 in New York, and the composer wrote some music by himself the following summer. Then they had a period of working side by side in a Massachusetts farmhouse, which was sufficiently productive for them to decide to look for a commission for the work. The moment of truth arrived when they were preparing for a workshop of the piece at Indiana University in Bloomington. First Bernstein fell ill and was bedridden for nine days. Then, with Wadsworth near at hand crafting the text and the vocal structure (and literally dragging him out of bed and pushing him to the piano at times), he drafted most of the first-act music in one extended work period. With Wadsworth taking an increasing role as a sounding board for the music, and Bernstein participating in every aspect of the libretto, they wrote much of the opera without yet knowing where it would end.

To the characters of Dinah, Sam, and Junior from *Trouble in Tahiti*, the collaborators added Junior's sister, Dede, and her husband, François (who is also the former lover of Junior), along with several important subsidiary characters, including the Funeral Director, the Analyst, and Doc and Mrs. Doc. Bernstein had in mind a "troubled Junior," with a "possible boyfriend," but Wadsworth made him psychotic and gave him incest fantasies about his sister. Wadsworth created Mrs. Doc out of vivid memories of dyspeptic, alcoholic women he had known as a child. (He didn't know Lillian Hellman, whom some writers later speculated was the model for the character.)[5]

The original production, which was given its premiere by the Houston Grand Opera in June 1983, followed through on the original premise: *Trouble in Tahiti* was presented first. After an intermission, *A Quiet Place* moved the action forward thirty years. The second opera, in four scenes lasting roughly two hours, covered a twenty-four-hour period (as *Tahiti* had) from the afternoon funeral to the fragile family peace achieved in the garden the following afternoon. Several reviewers described the plot as a gloomy soap opera about uninteresting characters, with an emphasis on incest and homosexuality. Donal Henahan in the *New York Times* wrote, "To call the result a pretentious failure is putting it kindly." Only Leighton Kerner of the *Village Voice* and Andrew Porter of the *New Yorker* responded enthusiastically. Porter in particular valued the score's remarkable setting of American English. "The melodic lines are as sharp-eared as Janáček's in their transformation of speech rhythms and speech inflections," he wrote.

Before the two scheduled subsequent productions at Milan's La Scala in June 1984 and at the Kennedy Center in Washington in July, the authors, along with conductor John Mauceri, revised and trimmed the work to give the evening a more satisfying structure and to more convincingly link the two operas. The solution, suggested by Mauceri, was to embed the entirety of *Trouble in Tahiti* into the second act of *A Quiet Place* as a flashback (divided into two parts), triggered by Sam's reading of his dead wife's journals from early in their marriage. The new version was better received, although there remained many, including the *New York Times*'s Bernard Holland, who simply didn't care for the music or its text at all. For the Bernstein family members who attended the premiere, the opera stirred too many unsettling memories of the sorrow they had gone through at the time of Felicia's death, and of their father's pain, to be easily enjoyed.

The three acts of the revised version have three distinct profiles. The entire first act takes place in the funeral home after Dinah's death and is the single longest continuous stretch of music Bernstein ever wrote, not counting the *Dybbuk* score. Here friends and acquaintances mingle around Dinah's coffin, while Sam remains mute and immobile at the side of the stage until he finally explodes in rage in a confrontation with his children at the end of the act. The libretto in this extended scene, Joycean in its layered overlapping dialogue, is also reminiscent of a Robert Altman film. Exceptionally beautiful hymnlike chorales sung by the chorus give the act a religious aura. Otherwise the subsidiary characters often sing twelve-tone music, creating a dark, disturbing backdrop, against which the more tonal "arias" sung by Dede, François, Junior, and finally Sam are vividly differentiated, encouraging emotional identification.

The first-act orchestral prologue evokes the car accident in which Dinah was killed, using as a source a principal motive from *Trouble in Tahiti* that stood for the couple's anguished attempts at connection, and the notes of which formed that work's final chord. *A Quiet Place* begins with this same chord. The prologue suggests, at least subliminally, that Dinah's accident was in some sense deliberate, the ultimate outcome of her marital unhappiness.

The twelve-tone music in the funeral home seems to represent the mystery and violence of her death and is also used when conversation is forced, ironic, or ritualized. There are passages, such as the dialogue between the Funeral Director and Dinah's brother, Bill, that are strictly twelve-tone. At other times, versions of the row are used almost like a leitmotif or cantus firmus, in conjunction with ideas not derived from them. Both the chorales and the music of Sam incorporate parts of the row. Throughout the act, which is among the most musically striking in American opera, death itself seems ever-present in the gigantic twelve-note chords that punctuate the proceedings, the hushed, chromatic chorales intermittently sung by the chorus, and the tolling, repeated-note motive that, first heard near the opening as the car crash in which Dinah is killed is evoked in the orchestra, subsequently returns periodically, sounding like the beep of a heart monitor in an intensive care unit.

The second act, which takes place in the family home that night, also carries poignant autobiographical overtones, as Sam and Dede go through Dinah's things while, simultaneously in another room, François tries to console Junior. As Sam reads from Dinah's diary, *Trouble in Tahiti* emerges from his present reveries as a flashback.[6] Multiple cross-references to both *Trouble in Tahiti* and to the row forms and new materials of *A Quiet Place* proliferate in this scene, making it like a development section. Here the family members connect to each other musically, if not humanly.

The third act is set outside the house the next morning. Amid family games and childish taunts, tensions erupt again, but a reading of a letter from Dinah results in Sam's finally reaching out to his son, and the work concludes on a note of fragile peace. Dede's third-act aria, perhaps the most excerptable vocal music in the opera, subtly builds on motives from Dinah's "There Is a Garden" aria in *Trouble in Tahiti* and also incorporates a slowed-down version of the song "This Time" from *1600 Pennsylvania Avenue*. (There is also a hint of "Maria" near the beginning.) It is Dinah's own voice, heard near the very end of the third act, that leads to the concluding gesture toward healing between father and son. Surely this moment must have had an aching significance for the composer.

In *A Quiet Place*, the principal characters are all haunted by their memories of Dinah, and their music is haunted by her music in *Trouble in Tahiti*. Dede's opening waltz (marked *Valse manique* in the score) carries her mother's musical DNA melodically and harmonically, as well as in its 3/4 time signature.[7] Junior's instability is first rendered in music of vacillating eighth-note patterns. His memorable and quintessentially Bernsteinian blues melody, subjected to many variants over the course of the work, was originally intended for Fischer-Dieskau to sing as Humbert Humbert in the abandoned opera based on Nabokov's *Lolita*, but it also has audible roots in Dinah's garden aria.[8] Sam's long tirade, first directed at Junior and eventually ranging over his whole life, uses aggressively shifting accents that recall the rhythms of the ambitious young Sam from the earlier opera. When he breaks down in tears of recrimination, grief, and guilt, he is answered in a trio of internalized reminiscences, "Dear Daddy," which is sung by the younger protagonists over an accompaniment derived from the street scene in *Trouble in Tahiti*.[9] Junior's mocking striptease in front of his mother's coffin near the end of the act is sung to his *Lolita* tune in pure show-business G major. The orchestral postlude that brings the act to a close sounds a third version of the melody: first quiet, exquisitely harmonized in muted strings, and then reaching a powerful orchestral climax reminiscent of Berg. Bernstein infuses Wadsworth's Junior with his own swagger, and both the striptease and its brief big-band orchestral answer provide the work with a surprising jolt of musical joy. It is hard not to read these jazzy outbursts against Sam as the composer's irreverent nose thumbing at the father figures in his life who had disapproved of his popular vein.

Despite the deep links between the music in the new work and the older one, it is perhaps not entirely believable that the stylized period piece *Trouble in Tahiti* represents the actual past behind such a searingly realistic present.[10] But like Baba the Turk or the bread machine in Stravinsky's *The Rake's Progress,* this theatrical difficulty can be overcome by imaginative direction. Many operas are flawed. The mastery, vitality, and beauty of this one puts it in a very rare category.

In May 1983 an article by musicologist and conductor Leon Botstein appeared in *Harper's Magazine* that may well have been the single most devastating critique to date of Bernstein's career. While Tom Wolfe had ridiculed Bernstein's political positions, and Harold Schonberg and others had often derided his conducting; while his compositions had sometimes had a mixed reception, and his Norton Lectures had been disparaged by some, the Botstein article was the first to portray the entire course of his professional life as a "tragedy" and cautionary tale. The article was all the more effective because it came from a scholar who could cite chapter and verse in making his case that "the most gifted musician of twentieth-century America," as he described Bernstein, had failed to develop a personal voice in his compositions and had vitiated his teaching and performing gifts in a "celebration of personality, fame, and publicity, at the expense of art." If Botstein's article had only been unremittingly negative, it would have carried less weight than it did. But by first acknowledging Bernstein's accomplishment as the composer of *Candide*, his gifts as a pianist, his occasional successes as a conductor, and his impressive achievements in the Young People's Concerts, Botstein established a credible basis for then attacking what he called the "overwrought efforts at self-proclaimed profundity" of the Norton Lectures and the "pedestrian," "disappointing" level of most of Bernstein's performances as a conductor, whose dullness stemmed sometimes from a lack of discipline and "the overeagerness to display feeling," and at other times from simply being "unexceptional in tempo, phrasing and balance" and therefore lacking a distinguishing point of view. Perhaps most woundingly of all, Botstein was disparaging about the derivative, middlebrow nature of most of Bernstein's compositions. Of Bernstein's Broadway work he opined that "theatricality . . . is both the source of his wide popularity and the root of his triviality. . . . Like Kurt Weill, but with less originality, Bernstein studied the techniques of 'serious' composers and adapted them for the popular stage." He was no fan of *West Side Story*, describing it as "a danceable, decorative, frenetic journey—with maudlin pauses—through a condescending urban version of *Romeo and Juliet*." And in detailing the limitations of such later Bernstein works as the *Kaddish* Symphony, *Mass*, and *Halil*, Botstein, perhaps unconsciously echoing Copland's censure of twenty-five years earlier, stated that "All you hear is the overworked emulation of how a musical idea might be pursued and developed if it existed." Then he added, even more damagingly, that "Bernstein's inner necessity is not really musical. Rather it is to register, grandly, how he feels about serious life-and-death matters." The article ended by pointing out that conductors live a long time, urging the sixty-five-year-old musician to "seize the opportunity to change." "He should discipline himself," Botstein wrote, "stop being a corporation and become an artist again."[11]

The article articulated what was in fact a common view

among intellectuals, fellow composers, and musical academics of the time, or at least what they often said publicly. Bernstein seemed to some to have become emblematic of the commoditization of serious music and, as a conductor, of the celebration of the performer over the composer. It was hard to keep up with him; he appeared to be scattered compositionally, almost desperate. Other composers must have envied the facts that his musical theater works were known and loved throughout the world, and that every one of his concert works had been performed instantly upon completion and was available on recordings. (By contrast, to take two examples, neither Roger Sessions's ambitious opera *Montezuma* nor Leon Kirchner's *Lily*, based on Saul Bellow's *Henderson the Rain King*, has been recorded to this day.) Surely many in the shadows resented his seemingly unapologetic position in the limelight, even when he used it to promote their music.

Many saw him as a "popular" composer who was trying to prove that he was "serious." But the opposite was true. He wrote his first musical only after consolidating his own serious idiom with three fine sonatas, his first symphony, and the ballet *Fancy Free*. Another myth was that he couldn't orchestrate. Yet the time constraints of putting together a Broadway show are such that orchestration is almost always delegated. Because of his hectic schedule (the result, of course, of his own decisions), he also availed himself of orchestration help when he was writing *Mass*, *A Quiet Place*, and also parts of *Jubilee Games*. But as *Fancy Free*, his three symphonies, *Serenade*, *Prelude, Fugue and Riffs*, *Songfest*, *Dybbuk*, and many other works demonstrate, Bernstein was a superb orchestrator. The one skill in this regard he may have lacked was that of creating the lush big-band sound of Broadway—a specialty of Sid Ramin (a lifelong Count Basie fan) and Irwin Kostal, orchestrators of *West Side Story* and other works.

Comments coming from Copland and Virgil Thomson,

the former referring to "conductor's music" and the latter to criticisms about Bernstein's technical inadequacy, also affected the way his concert music was viewed. For whatever reason, Copland, who was usually so astute, didn't hit the mark in his early comments about his friend and ally. Bernstein's music is theatrical but it is not merely a music of effects; its sounds and gestures are achieved through the careful accretion of its smallest elements. Like all good music, it is just as interesting, sometimes even more so, when it is played at the piano, apart from its orchestration.

But while no one would describe Bernstein as excessively modest, one could be justified in calling him uneasy, even awkward, in his relationship to his own concert music. When he turned from the security of conducting the greatest of all musical works to the loneliness of composing, Bernstein suffered the same terror all composers do. When he resurfaced, he did not comfortably reconcile his inner world with his outer one. His titles, public comments, and program notes all betray insecurity. His description of *The Age of Anxiety* was distractingly grandiose; his accounts of *Chichester Psalms* and *Trouble in Tahiti* too glib; in the *Kaddish* Symphony, he undercut his powerful music with an overwrought spoken text. This most confessional, sociable, and seemingly shameless of beings was, I believe, unsure how much value to place on his music and remained vulnerable and insecure about it, even while circling the globe and basking in seemingly universal acclaim. In addition, when he tried to explain himself as a "dual personality," as he frequently did, it somehow rang false. Yet the self-description was undeniably accurate.

The gulf between his versatility as a composer and the expectations of even those who admired him was particularly large because, at least in the United States, no one audience exists that could encompass the catholicity of his musical interests. The Broadway audience did not know or care for the music that inspired or gave a context to his less accessible works, and the academics, who were often snobs about his show music, stopped paying attention to his concert music. Fortunately, he never had to read director Jonathan Miller's description of him as "a wonderful show-biz composer whose talent rather inconveniently overflowed into other areas." Yet the "Broadway" Bernstein and the "concert" Bernstein were the same man, exploring different sides of life in different musical contexts. None of the shows are without music adapted from earlier classical projects, and few of the major concert pieces lack material derived from the musicals.[12]

Bernstein the man was hip and bold, but his music was steeped in tradition and often reflected the innovations of composers from a generation before him. Even the jazz that most marked his own "jazzy" music was not new, and his twelve-tone and "avant-garde" explorations postdated those of his peers by twenty years. But, as twentieth-century composers as diverse as Sergei Rachmaninov, Jean Sibelius, Frank Martin, Maurice Duruflé, Henri Dutilleux, Francis Poulenc, Grażyna Bacewicz, Samuel Barber, John Harbison, and many others have reminded us, originality is not the same thing as history-making innovation. Bernstein's life was original, and the way he put together the elements of his musical language was as well. His music is melodically, harmonically, and rhythmically distinctive. Heard apart from the publicity surrounding the man and his public life, it is personal, moving, ingeniously constructed, musically substantial, and fresh. It has remained captivating long after the music of many composers he championed, and many once deemed "significant," has begun to sound historical. Even a work such as *Fancy Free*, in which the influence of Copland and Gershwin is palpable, and which was comparatively old-fashioned when composed, still retains the imprint of its composer's personality and the musical vitality it had seventy years ago. Perhaps each aspect of Bernstein's kaleidoscopic musical life would have been easier to understand by itself than it was alongside everything else. Had composing been his only art, had he labored in obscurity as a professor in some small New England college, say, or been an unglamorous, timid, and laconic solitary, his compositions' many virtues and their unprecedented range might be more readily acknowledged.

One member of the musical intelligentsia able to take the long view on Bernstein's career was Elliott Carter. Carter nominated his friend for membership into the American Academy of Arts and Letters in 1981 (Carter himself having been elected in 1956) and wrote the following words: "Leonard Bernstein is America's most renowned musician because he has gained a universal reputation as a conductor of classical music, as pedagogue, and as a composer of outstanding scores of concert music and of music for the theatre. His concern with broad communication has led him to write very telling, highly imaginative works for Broadway that have freshness and newness and yet wide appeal. His concert works of wide variety have captured musical audiences everywhere."[13]

# 15

## *Regrets, Celebrations, and Goodbyes*
## *1986–1990*

In the fall of 1986 Bernstein toured two continents with the Israel Philharmonic in celebration of their fiftieth anniversary, bringing along a new two-movement work entitled *Jubilee Games.* The first movement applied many techniques he had first explored as a conductor in the early 1960s, when he conducted such works as Earle Brown's *Available Forms II* and Lukas Foss's *Time Cycle* and led the New York Philharmonic in controlled group improvisations. The seven-and-a-half-minute structure is a kind of rondo in which the recurrent theme is a rhythmic percussion refrain, accompanied by shouts and whispers of the Hebrew words for seven (*sheva*) and the jubilee number, fifty (*hamishem*), which Judaic tradition views as attained after seven cycles of seven. Interspersed with these recurrences are brass fanfares suggestive of shofar calls; improvisational passages assigned to different orchestral choirs; and a slow, dissonant chorale played first by brass alone (where it sounds like Carl Ruggles's *Angels*), then by brass with the percussive refrain, and finally by the entire orchestra (at which point it sounds like a mammoth orchestral hymn by Messiaen). The second movement, Diaspora Dances, has the musicians whispering *hai* (alive) and *hayim* (life) to buoyant dance music in eighteen beats, made up of groups of nine (2 + 3 + 2 + 2). (The numerical equivalent of the Hebrew *hai* is eighteen.) A figure reminiscent of the whistle call of the Jets occasionally breaks through the texture. The middle section is a gentler, Hasidic dance in the vein of *Dybbuk*. When the opening eighteens return, they are given a jazzy new twist, and sent into further contrapuntal adventures.

In December, for the reopening of Carnegie Hall, Bernstein composed a six-and-a-half-minute hymn for baritone and orchestra, using a prayer in Hebrew from the Book of Numbers ("May the Lord Bless You and Keep You"). The hymn opens with brass music anticipating the prayer's melody. What follows is closely modeled after a lyrical *Anniversary* written a month earlier for the composer's friend Aaron Stern. The first half of this *Anniversary* is played by oboe, accompanied by other winds. Then the trumpet intones a bit of the prayer again, after which the music of the *Anniversary* resumes in the strings. Finally the baritone voice enters for the last minute and a half, intoning the peaceful message. The trumpet is heard again at the final cadence, which mixes major and minor in a telling way.

After the first performances of *Jubilee Games*, Bernstein added the Carnegie Hall hymn to the work as a slow movement. Not until he had added a further movement in 1989 did he consider the work complete, at which point he retitled it Concerto for Orchestra ("Jubilee Games").

In May 1987 Joan Peyser's biography of Bernstein became a best seller. While it made valuable points about the music world and showed insight into Bernstein's musicianship and his work as a composer, the book seemed to interpret his every personal gesture and undertaking in the most venal way possible, portraying him as a man of personal excesses, hypocrisy, and monstrous egotism. It also managed to be unkind to Felicia. Bernstein's children made him promise not to read it, and it is possible he never did. Perhaps in reference to the Peyser volume, his friend Lukas Foss, who had known him for fifty years, commented, "People who have many contradictions are much harder to understand. In Lenny's case, the books written about him do a lot to make him less understood than before."[1]

In August Bernstein was conducting the Vienna Philharmonic in Salzburg, where he celebrated his sixty-ninth birthday. On his evenings off he went with Betty Comden to see James Levine conduct Mozart's *The Abduction from the Seraglio* and Strauss's *Capriccio*. Most memorably of all, Comden sat with Bernstein at a performance of Schoenberg's towering *Moses und Aron:*

> Lenny told me he had heard it only once before and was not sure how he felt about it, that it might be rough going, and we might want to wander out at some point. We sat there totally mesmerized and deeply moved. The prologue was a brief reenactment of Kristallnacht with Jews hunted and cemeteries and synagogues defiled and destroyed. Onstage through the whole opera there was a menorah, overturned and broken, lying on its side. During the Golden Calf scene, they ingeniously used the arms of the candelabra to construct the golden horn of the idol. At the end Lenny turned to me and, visibly shaken, said that that was the opera he wished he had written.[2]

But while *Moses und Aron* is built entirely from one twelve-tone row, in his own music Bernstein continued to explore an idiom that straddled the line between the tonal and the nontonal, and in which twelve-tone rows rub shoulders with passages firmly in a key. His rows characteristically comprised primarily half steps and major and minor thirds, which make them singable and chromatic rather than angular. In his 1988 *Arias and Barcarolles*, a cycle of eight songs originally for four singers and piano four-hands (later reduced to two singers, mezzo-soprano and baritone, and piano four-hands), he explores twelve-tone writing in three of the pieces. For a person as brash and public as Bernstein, the work might at first seem a surprising summation. It is pervaded by a sense of nostalgia and remembrance, and its texts, like the libretto of *A Quiet Place*, are focused on family relationships. Unlike *Songfest*, the cycle is deeply unified not only in terms of its musical materials but also in its subtle, haunted tone and in the familial connections embodied in its texts and encoded dedications. Later orchestrated twice, first by Bright Sheng, and then by Bruce Coughlin, the cycle loses some of its poignancy on a bigger scale. The sound of the work in its original form conveys the voice of the private man. The piano writing has the quiet clarity of the *Anniversaries*, while inevitably stirring wistful memories of Bernstein's piano partners in youth: Mildred Spiegel, Harold Shapero, Annette Elkanova, and others. Accompanied by piano alone, the singers can remain intimate.

The cycle's fifth song, "Greeting," dedicated to "J. G." (presumably his assistant, Jack Gottlieb), has a tender, paternal simplicity. The narrow range and purity of its vocal line and accompaniment recall Bartók's folk song settings for children, or Ives at his most consoling. The world of *Trouble in Tahiti* is not far away from the two "couple" duets, the first of which could be heard as a dialogue either about a marriage or about the music being sung ("Funny the way it goes . . ."), as it wanders from key to key. The duet "Mr. and Mrs. Webb Say Goodnight," the penultimate number in the cycle, is a kind of scena depicting a couple trying to go to sleep and drifting in and out of memories as their children make a racket in the background.

The chatty, witty lyrics suggest a seven-minute cabaret scene in nine sections. Here the composer expresses his lifelong "fascination with matrimony," to use Harold Shapero's phrase, and, behind a protective shield, his own memories of marriage and being the parent of small children. "Little Smary" sets to music a bedtime story his mother used to tell him when he was small (she is credited with the text), in a piece that comes close to a twelve-tone idiom and includes some satirical piano writing in the style of early Berg. Bernstein evokes the world of his father's Hasidic dancing in "Oif Mayn Khas'neh" ("At My Wedding"). The final number, "Nachspiel," represents an additional, unacknowledged tribute to his mother and to the piano. For this piece he adapted a song called "First Love" he had composed for her in March 1986 for her eighty-eighth birthday, removing lyrics that had related her to the eighty-eight keys of the piano and replacing them with wordless humming from the singers.

Bernstein's life after he left the Philharmonic had afforded him more time to compose, and there is a catalogue of late compositions to prove it. Equally important, it gave him the freedom to continue to grow as a conductor with a variety of great orchestras and to revisit much of the repertoire he had previously performed and recorded, music he never tired of restudying and never lost the ability to see freshly. A look at what he rerecorded during the 1980s reveals the repertoire he cared most about, as well as how he viewed the strengths of various orchestras. It is clear that his relationship with the Vienna Philharmonic deeply inspired him, and, in the opinion of many critics, his recordings with them contained some his greatest achievements. Bernstein was naturally increasingly conscious of his mortality throughout the 1980s, and his performances and recordings were his attempts to put down once and for all how he viewed various key works.

Among the particular triumphs of these years were his second complete Mahler symphony cycle, divided between four orchestras (the Vienna Philharmonic, Royal Concertgebouw Orchestra, Berlin Philharmonic, and New York Philharmonic); the Mozart Requiem with the Bavarian Radio Symphony; various Mozart symphonies with the Vienna Philharmonic; the complete Beethoven symphonies and the *Missa solemnis* with the Vienna Philharmonic (of which the Seventh and Ninth are often singled out for special praise); the complete Brahms symphonies and Bruckner's Ninth Symphony with Vienna; the Sibelius Symphonies Nos. 1, 2, 5, and 7, and superb recordings of the Schumann symphonies, also with Vienna; and the Tchaikovsky Symphonies Nos. 4, 5, and 6 and *Romeo and Juliet* with the New York Philharmonic. He revisited some, but not all, of the American music of his early conducting career, mainly with the New York Philharmonic, most notably the Second Symphony and small orchestral works of Ives; Gershwin's *Rhapsody in Blue;* the Harris Third Symphony; many of Copland's large-scale works, including *Connotations* and the Third Symphony; and William Schuman's Third Symphony. These remain incomparable performances of American music. Of current music he conducted Ned Rorem's Violin Concerto and David Del Tredici's *Tattoo.* But of the music he had once termed "avant-garde" there was virtually nothing. One is entitled to regret that he did not conduct Berg's *Lulu* or more Webern and Schoenberg; Stravinsky's *The Rake's Progress* or *Threni* (a late work Bernstein particularly admired, which set the Hebrew letters at the beginning of every stanza for four-part choir); more current music by contemporaries Kirchner, Messiaen, Ligeti, Takemitsu, Schnittke, or Kagel.

As Bernstein approached his seventieth birthday, he became ever more focused on young people and on teaching, and he was constantly working with young orchestras, composers, musicians, and conductors. Having founded the Schleswig-Holstein Orchestral Academy in 1987, he looked forward to joining Michael Tilson Thomas in Japan in 1990 for the inaugural season at the Pacific Music Festival in Sapporo (modeled on Tanglewood), which they were creating together. He planned on conducting both the London Symphony and the Pacific Music Festival Orchestra there. He hoped for time to compose one last major work but no longer seemed to speak of abandoning his other activities to do so. He also knew that he couldn't wrap up his accomplishments in a tidy package the way someone who had stayed at home composing for decades might have been able to. In 1988, he told a newspaper reporter, "I can't assess myself or decide whether I have achieved everything, or a portion, or a fraction. I feel as though I have led many, many lifetimes . . . and achieved more than I had any right to expect. . . . Certain risks have to fail. What's amazing is that so many have worked. . . . I don't know anybody who has been as lucky as I have."[3] Those around him worried about his health. "Always asthmatic and prone to emphysema, he remains a heavy smoker," wrote John Rockwell in 1988. "At times he is afflicted with a hacking cough that makes his friends wince." The truth was that the aerobic exercise of conducting usually alleviated the asthma and bronchitis that afflicted him when he was composing.

At Tanglewood his seventieth birthday was celebrated on an unprecedented scale. Sandwiched in between performances by two dozen musical luminaries from all over the world, a "musical bouquet" of eight variations on "New York, New York" composed by Berio, Kirchner, Jacob Druckman, Foss, John Corigliano, John Williams, Takemitsu, and William Schuman was offered. Kirchner's variation began with references to both Schoenberg and Stravinsky. After a dazzling quotation from the finale of Stravinsky's 1945 *Symphony in Three Movements*, a passage with upward whoops in the French horns and brilliant orchestral flurries, the instrumental canon from "New York, New York" was heard in the highest winds at twice its original speed, at which tempo it evoked the opening of *Petrushka*, suggesting Bernstein's provenance (Stravinsky via Copland) even more than the man himself. The fanfare-like rising "New York, New York" fourths in the horns that followed this passed by almost subliminally. How this was intended is anybody's guess, but Kirchner had a complicated sense of humor and probably regarded Bernstein's life with his characteristically complex emotions, as well as with admiration. After the concert Bernstein joked with Kirchner: "I know you; you're going to take the first two minutes and you are going to use it to write your own piece."[4] Kirchner later did just that, using the orchestral fragment as the opening of his *Music for Orchestra II* (dedicated "to Leonard Bernstein and to Igor and Arnold"), in which he achieved a visceral, sensual, colorful idiom that was unusually brash for him. Indeed, one could almost say that he met Bernstein in the middle of the same road, arriving there from the opposite direction, that of Schoenberg and Berg.[5]

The four-day birthday celebrations moved and exhausted Bernstein and also left him, as often in those years, wondering how he would be remembered. Perhaps this degree of acclaim surpassed what would have been reassuring.

Bernstein continued to use the visibility of his position to fight for political causes he believed in. The presidential campaign between George H. W. Bush and Michael Dukakis in the summer of 1988 was a dispiriting one for progressives. Bush had draped his party and his campaign in pro-American symbolism, making a fetish of the flag, the Pledge of Allegiance, and prayer in school, and intimidating his Democratic rival with an advertising campaign that portrayed him as weak on crime and in foreign policy. As Democratic candidates had frequently done, Dukakis backed away from articulating his more complex views on the campaign trail and didn't dare use the word "liberal," which Bush's rhetoric had somehow given an anti-American connotation. A week before the election, Bernstein published an op-ed commentary in the *New York Times* titled "I'm a Liberal and Proud of It," in which he described dreaming of a Dukakis who would stand up for the noble tradition of American liberalism:

> I want to redefine that word liberal, not run from it, nor cower defensively at its insulting abuse, but proudly to clarify it. The word derives from the Latin "liber," meaning free. . . .
>
> Who fought to free the slaves? Liberals. Who succeeded in abolishing the poll tax? Liberals. Who fought for women's rights, civil rights, free public education? Liberals. Who stood guard and still stands guard against sweatshops, child labor, racism, bigotry? Lovers of freedom and enemies of tyranny: Liberals.[6]

In April 1989 Bernstein was again in Israel and presented *Jubilee Games* in its final form, adding a fourth movement, a theme and variations (based on a duet originally written for recorder and cello), to what by then had already become a three-movement piece. The new structure begins with the raucous and exciting improvisational first movement (Free-Style Events), followed with the theme and variations, then Diaspora Dances, and concludes with the final prayer (Benediction). While the first movement emphasizes wildness and massed choirs, the second movement is a study in refined chamber music played by pairs of soloists: after the theme in the strings, the pairs are flute and French horn; trumpet and double bass; clarinet and trombone; tom-toms and mallet instruments; two violins; flute/piccolo and bass clarinet; and oboe and bassoon. These are followed by a coda of an almost Webernian spareness.

A spirit of acceptance hovers over *Jubilee Games*, now better known as the Concerto for Orchestra. One might almost call it the spirit of Nadia Boulanger, who believed that in many cases composers would do better to concentrate on celebrating music and their musicality, rather than to seek "greatness."

To emphasize this point, she would often quote words from Ecclesiastes: "Eat your bread and be satisfied." With the Benediction now at the end of the work, in the same position as the Hebrew prayer that closed *Jeremiah* forty-five years earlier, the opening trumpet melody sounds like an echo of the shofar calls in the first movement, and the open-string entrance of the strings harks back to their improvisatory tuning up. The piece is another work in which atonality and tonality coexist peacefully. Indeed, its use of dissonance is celebratory. It introduces a more personal note in the concluding prayer, but it also conveys a beneficent communal message.

In November 1989 Bernstein was expected at the White House to receive the National Medal of Arts, along with eleven other honorees, but within days of the occasion he withdrew himself from the proceedings in protest. His complaint was against the current climate of artistic intimidation spearheaded by Senator Jesse Helms of North Carolina, which had caused the National Endowment for the Arts to rescind a grant for an exhibition in New York of provocative works dealing with the AIDS epidemic. Bernstein wrote a letter to President Bush saying that he could not risk being seen as an "official artist content to collect a medal in kind and gentle silence" in such an environment.

With Tom Cothran and many other friends now dead from AIDS, the health crisis was near the top of the list of causes Bernstein publicly fought for. Sometimes his outspokenness struck observers as attention-grabbing, but from his point of view he was simply taking seriously his responsibilities as a citizen and public figure. He was not a political scientist, and his political views might not add up to a systematic ideology, but they were of a piece with his view of music as a social art, expressive of our shared humanity, and as such a force for peaceful coexistence, tolerance, and, by implication, for social progress. He had learned about Zionism and community and civic responsibility at the Mishkan Tefila Temple in Roxbury. When he was a student at Harvard, his social and political awareness had been expanded by contact with Copland, Blitzstein, David Prall, Archibald MacLeish, and many others, and he had offered his support to left-wing causes and produced an early performance of the pro-union *The Cradle Will Rock*. He believed in worker's rights, civil rights, women's rights, and gay rights. He revered the Declaration of Independence and the idealism behind the American Constitution, and wanted to hold those in power accountable for the eventual realization of the equitable, race-blind society these documents promised. He was a skeptic about the uses and abuses of American power, including the use of government agencies to squelch domestic dissent, and scornful of the values exemplified by American consumerism. His ideal of government had been formed in the Roosevelt era, exemplified by the New Deal. He had been essentially a socialist in his youth, a left-leaning "progressive" at a time when liberals opposed progressives, and then a liberal when the term had come to describe progressives. He believed in a people's right to self-determination. He advocated nuclear disarmament. He believed in mediation, coexistence, and brotherhood. His belief in the resolution of conflict by peaceful means might seem to be contradicted by his staunch support of Israel, but this support was rooted in Israel's fragile beginnings, when its very existence was at stake. He had supported the Middle East peace process pursued by President Jimmy Carter.

When the Berlin Wall began to come down on November 9, 1989, Bernstein seized on the opportunity to celebrate the ideals of peace and free speech on an international scale. He assembled German musicians from both East and West, and from the United States, Britain, and France, for a performance of Beethoven's Ninth Symphony. Audacious as always, he changed a crucial word in Schiller's text: "Freude" (joy) became "Freiheit" (freedom). The first performance took place on December 23 at the Philharmonie Hall in West Berlin, and the second took place on Christmas Day at the Schauspielhaus in East Berlin. That day bells tolled throughout the city. The performance combined his humanistic message and sense of music's purpose with the music of the composer he loved the most. Jon Deak, who experienced the Beethoven from his position in the bass section of the orchestra, said it was something one would remember for a lifetime: "There was so much joy, and suffering, and forgiveness in the same performance."[7]

The December trip to Berlin was the culmination of many grueling months of activity, even by Bernstein's usual standards. In September he had been in Warsaw on the fiftieth anniversary of Hitler's invasion, conducting the *Leonore* Overture No. 3 and *Chichester Psalms.* Then came Vienna and several important Beethoven performances, including another string quartet (No. 16 in F Major, op. 135) arranged for string orchestra. Then it was back to New York to lead an all-Copland program at the Philharmonic, which ranged from his favorite "roller coaster," *El salón México,* to the eloquently prophetic twelve-tone *Connotations.* Now in his late eighties, Copland was too unwell in body and mind to be present. In *Newsday* Tim Page remarked that future generations would think of such a program in legendary terms. Then there was the London Symphony Orchestra performance of the final and most complete version of *Candide,* when the conductor and stellar cast were dogged by the influenza that was sweeping through the city at the time. In the recording one hears a durable, expert work of American music performed as it should be, by a great orchestra, chorus, and soloists. In the video of the concert performance one sees a haggard, white-haired maestro, clearly drained and in pain, conducting with extraordinary discipline and control.

In late February he completed another series of videos and recordings with the Vienna Philharmonic of Sibelius's First, Second, Fifth, and Seventh Symphonies. Although he had recorded his first complete cycle of the symphonies in the 1960s, his belief in the composer (which had been shared initially among conductors primarily only by Herbert von Karajan and Sir John Barbirolli) had only deepened over time. By 1990 the Finnish composer, who had once seemed so connected to the nineteenth century, seemed prescient to younger composers such as John Adams, who viewed his organically expansive, visionary structures and unusual rhythms as a formative influence. In these videos, Bernstein the glamorous icon has disappeared. We see an elderly musician, visibly exhausted by the time of the final video (Sibelius's First Symphony), making transcendent music with a great orchestra against the inexorable forward motion of his own declining health.

On February 27 Helen Coates died. She had stood by her unruly piano student for fifty years. Her archive of Bernstein letters and 130 scrapbooks, spanning fifty-five years (1933–87), have now become central sources of information about his life and career.

Even though he was declining, Bernstein still had more fire than most people have in their prime. In 1989 he was rehearsing the Tchaikovsky Fourth Symphony, a work he had conducted countless times, with the New York Philharmonic, an orchestra that had played it so often that "it was like a weed-encrusted parking lot," in the words of bassist Jon Deak. "He came in with the last movement, no less, which is in a way the most clichéd movement in the piece, like he was just coming from a revival meeting, and he said, 'I just stayed up all night and rethought the whole fourth movement. From beginning to end we're going to do everything differently, you'll see, you'll get it'—he could hardly contain himself. He had one year to live. He had done it how many times, and we had, too, but . . . by God, after the rehearsal, that movement had suddenly been invested with such freshness—I couldn't believe it."

"Bernstein always had a need to have somebody to communicate with," Deak continued. "During a rehearsal, it was the musicians. Here he's exhorting the cello section to play this passage with passion, and he needs to reach them, to turn them on, right down to the last player on the last stand. Then, of course, at the concert, he is doing the same thing with the audience. If they are not responding, numerous times he would turn around, and he would say, 'You didn't get that at all. You didn't cry. This is one of the deepest expressions of the human spirit. I want you to *feel* this,' and he would play the movement again, and, boy, they would sit up and listen.

"He was not ever content talking into a vacuum. Some people speak and speak, and the person they are speaking to is not that important. But even at a cocktail party, he would always make sure that the person was responding, and he didn't let anyone interrupt their exchange. He needed to see a result, that he was getting to somebody, that he was reaching somebody.

"When we were flying over the Atlantic to Berlin for that famous concert we played on both sides of the Wall in 1989, I ran up to his seat and I said, 'Lenny, look, it's Greenland! We're flying over Greenland.' And he looked down, and he said 'Yeah? So?' I said, 'One of the ambitions of my life is to walk across Greenland, across the ice cap' (which, of course is melting now, but wasn't then). He looked out and said, 'You want to walk across that? Why?' I said, 'Because it's there to be discovered. I want to discover this new territory.' And he said, 'But there's nobody to talk to down there.'"[8]

My friend Hank Chapin, who narrated Benjamin Britten's *The Young Person's Guide to the Orchestra* in the Young People's Concert of March 19, 1961, when he was twelve years old, particularly remembered the feeling of connection Bernstein established with him in the context of the performance. After the conductor had suggested that it would be wonderful to have a child do the narration, Hank was chosen because he could read music—he played the cello—and had natural poise and a nice, clear speaking voice. He remembers being picked up by his father from school a few days before the concert and being taken to Carnegie Hall just as the morning rehearsal was ending, and then going up the back stairs to the dressing room overlooking Fifty-Seventh Street. There, during the musicians' lunch break, he and his father sat with Bernstein, the producer, and a secretary, going over the text in the Britten score. "Okay, Hank," Bernstein said in his beautifully resonant, surprisingly deep voice. "So the words here are kind of stodgy. Let's rewrite them." The conductor proceeded to go through the score, updating the somewhat pedantic language of the original, while not changing the placement of the narrator's words. The secretary took it all down, so that the new text could be pasted later into Hank's score and into the television script. "My one memory," said Hank, "is that when we got to the cellos, Bernstein said, 'Hank, you're a cellist. What do you think about the cello?' And I said, 'Oh! I think the tone is rich and warm and wonderful,' and he said, 'Great. I like it. We'll put that in: rich, warm, and wonderful,' and that went right into the script. He treated me as an equal, as a musician and a collaborator during that hour. I felt real, whole, honored, and comfortable. Then at the performance it was the same. He was somehow doing a flawless job of conducting the piece—the music of which was so extraordinarily vivid to me while I was sitting there onstage—and also of relating to me."[9]

In April 1990 Bernstein was diagnosed with "a tumor near the top of his left lung," and while a needle biopsy revealed no cancerous cells, it was determined that he had mesothelioma, a malignancy of the "membrane surrounding the lung," which is normally the result of exposure to asbestos rather than of smoking. He went for regular radiation treatments for two weeks, but the news that he was seriously ill was kept secret from his mother, from most of his professional colleagues, and from the public. From this point on, he proceeded with his plans but must have wondered at what point he would simply have to stop. He went to Prague to conduct Beethoven's Ninth Symphony at the Spring Festival there, and his sister Shirley went with him. He met with Czechoslovakian president Václav Havel, attended a party in his honor, and even took walks along the Moldau River, all the while with tubes of oxygen at the ready and receiving acupuncture many times a day to alleviate the pain when he breathed. While there he wrote a poem in which he imagined a bargain with God, hoping to be allowed to write that one major work he hadn't yet managed.

Someone who left such an enormous record of himself in action clearly needed a great deal of attention and love; one might imagine him having had an abnormal dread of extinction. Yet in this valedictory poem he wrote, "Afraid / Died in my vocabulary / Long ago—except of hurting / Someone I love and *then* / Of not writing my Piece / Before my Not-To-Be." In Bernstein's case, the need for attention can't be disentangled from an equal or greater hunger to know others, to reach them, and to benefit them by spreading what he called "the joy of music." These needs were the sources of his musical and political reach and of the human connections he kept forging up to his final days, particularly with young musicians such as those at the Schleswig-Holstein Festival who performed the Shostakovich First Symphony, and with all of the anonymous people he never met, whom he reached with his work.

Back in New York he had surgery to drain fluid from his lung and suffered a painful allergic reaction to tetracycline injections. He was scheduled to go to Sapporo, Japan, in early July to inaugurate the Pacific Music Festival along with Michael Tilson Thomas. He made the trip and appeared at a press conference in which he said in a shaky voice that he wished to spend "most of the remaining energy and time the Lord grants me in education and in sharing as much as possible with younger people." He conducted two programs with the London Symphony but then was found collapsed on the floor in his hotel room and was flown home. He was suffering from "progressive emphysema complicated by a pleural tumor."

On August 19, 1990, two weeks before his seventy-second birthday, Bernstein was scheduled to conduct the Serge and Olga Koussevitzky Memorial Concert with the Boston Symphony Orchestra at the Music Shed in Tanglewood. It had been fifty years since he first stood before an orchestra in this very spot, and fifty years since the founding of Tanglewood. He had already signaled that he was not well enough to take the student orchestra on a European tour in celebration of both anniversaries, as planned. A week earlier he had led them in a noble account of Copland's Third Symphony. His old friend Shirley Gabis Perle had met him after the rehearsal. When she came toward him, her face must have registered how terrible he looked. As they walked to his dressing room, he turned to her and said, "Don't cry."

The day of the Boston Symphony program, the Sunday afternoon sky was dark and overcast, and it rained, in complete contrast to the "Bernstein weather" that had become a kind of standing joke at Tanglewood over the years. Somehow when Bernstein was there, no matter what the weather had been doing in previous days, the sun would always shine, as if nature itself was somehow susceptible to his charm and energy. This day was exceptionally dismal. Bernstein, unable to lead some of the rehearsals for the program, had delegated the conducting of his own *Arias and Barcarolles*, in the orchestration by Bright Sheng, to a young protégé, Carl St. Clair. Looking extraordinarily frail, his face a sickly gray, and dressed in his Tanglewood summer white jacket and black bow tie, Bernstein mounted the podium for the very last time to lead Britten's Sea Interludes from *Peter Grimes*, followed by a performance of Beethoven's Seventh Symphony. The performance of the Beethoven represented a sustained and agonizing act of will. He had a lifetime of experience behind him thinking about and shaping this symphony, and a lifetime of responding to his own inner rhythms and sense of the moment in performances. Tim Page remembers that on this occasion Bernstein could barely stand upright, let alone do what he himself used to call his "Lenny dance." Trained by Fritz Reiner, he now by necessity came close to Reiner's measured and restrained conducting style.

Bernstein's experience did not fail him. As someone who could express a rhythm with the lift of an eyebrow, he probably could have led the orchestra with pure mind if he had wanted to. His face and gestures still contained a multitude of information and an amazing degree of strength and tension. It must have taken superhuman effort to mold such a majestic reading of the work, one that, on the recording later issued by Deutsche Grammophon, sounds extraordinarily spiritualized. The tempos are expertly judged and are not, as one might expect, excessively slow. In the first movement one can almost sense, at first, the orchestra's concern and caution. The *Poco sostenuto* has never sounded so modern and deliberately spacious; it opens up vast, strange vistas of abstraction.

The solemnity and grandeur of the funereal second movement has an extraordinary, singing eloquence and inner rhythm. The third bursts out with youthful energy. Here Bernstein "nearly broke down" according to Page, conducting much of it "leaning against the back of the podium, gasping for breath."[10] Yet somehow there is a sound of triumph in the exhortations heard from the brass in the wonderfully held-back trio section. The final movement, taken at a moderate tempo, has an irresistible forward momentum; it conveys not joy but rather an ecstatic struggle. Despite all that this performance must have cost in terms of physical effort and pain, it is not pain one hears but Beethoven's sublime architecture.

After the concert Bernstein made the effort to go to Seranak, Koussevitzky's house at Tanglewood, to attend the party that always followed the concerts. When he walked in, he said to the pianist Leon Fleisher, "Who am I kidding? I can't do this."

An announcement of his retirement from conducting was prepared, to be released on October 9. It indicated that Bernstein would devote his time to composing, writing, and education, and said that his physician had advised him that performing was "too strenuous for his stamina to support." Bernstein changed the wording to "too strenuous for his present stamina to support."

Many friends and colleagues came to visit him during this period. Among them were conductor John Mauceri, who told him that work on restoring Blitzstein's *Regina* had finally been completed and that the opera would be mounted the next year at the Scottish Opera. Bernstein seemed happy to hear this, yet also sad "that the project had gone on without him, and that he would never hear the fruits of his own work." Arthur Laurents called on him and was horrified by his convulsive coughing and the degree of his pain. (Still relishing an opportunity for a frank chat, Bernstein asked Laurents about his sex life.)

Bernstein spent his last days in a wheelchair, a shocking, almost unimaginable sight to his brother Burton. On October 13 he played a trilingual word game with actor Michael Wager, listened to Aaron Stern read poems by Rumi, and joked that his eulogy should begin "Cut down in the prime of youth." He had a horrible night in which he woke up frequently, gasping for breath, and was violently sick. On the morning of October 14 he seemed to feel better. He spent much of the day with his son Alexander. His sister visited; he phoned his daughters; he watched Yo-Yo Ma and Jeffrey Kahane play the Rachmaninov Cello Sonata on television, humming along. Late in the afternoon Betty Comden called on him. She sat on the side of his bed and, as she later wrote in a reminiscence, "he lay there, his beautiful leonine head looking diminished and his lids heavy from illness." For some reason she found herself chatting about an old song from the Revuers' nightclub act of 1938, about "three movie psychopaths," but all she could remember were a few scattered lines from it. Bernstein "rattled off the whole thing without hesitation, verse and all."[11]

Death came at 6:15 p.m. as Kevin Cahill, his doctor, was giving him an injection and his friend Michael Wager was holding him. Humphrey Burton writes that his "body suddenly stiffened," and he asked incredulously, "What is this?" Almost as soon as he had spoken, his heart gave out.

Suddenly this whirlwind life was over. Musicians all over the world expressed a sense of shock. The flagpoles at Lincoln Center were wreathed in black, and the marquees of Broadway theaters were darkened for a minute. Flags were lowered to half-staff in countries around the world, including Germany, but, to quote Burton Bernstein, "for reasons best known to the Bush administration," not in the United States. In contrast to the lavish, public, super-celebrations of his final birthdays, the funeral service in the Dakota apartment building was intimate and personal. A large coffin occupied the place in the living room where the two pianos normally stood. The rabbi intoned words from the Lamentations of Jeremiah (and Bernstein's First Symphony): "Eicha yashva vadad ha'ir" (How desolate lay the city). Crowded into the room were collaborators who had known him for nearly his entire life—Adolph Green, Betty Comden, Stephen Sondheim, Arthur Laurents, Jerome Robbins, and Sid Ramin—and younger ones such as Stephen Wadsworth and Michael Tilson Thomas. Bernstein's final lover, Mark Adams Taylor, was there. There were his children, Jamie, Alexander, and Nina; his ninety-two-year-old mother, Jennie; his sister, Shirley; and his brother, Burton, who seemed to sum up what everyone was thinking with his opening words: "My brother, Lenny, who was always larger than life, turned out to be smaller than death. Amazingly—just like that—he is no more."[12]

Bernstein had spoken of the transience of life quite often, particularly as it is evoked by the phenomenon of music. In the 1955 *Omnibus* program "The Art of Conducting," he said, "In music we are trapped in time. Each note is gone as soon as it is sounded, and it can never be recontemplated or heard again in that particular instant of ripeness."

The police-escorted motorcade of twenty black stretch limousines bearing his body to Green-Wood Cemetery in Brooklyn became momentarily stalled in heavy traffic in front of a construction site just outside the East River Tunnels. Hasidic Jews, mothers with baby carriages, people of all ages and ethnic backgrounds stopped to watch silently. When the cortege started up again, the workmen removed their hardhats, and everyone suddenly waved, shouting "Goodbye, Lenny! Goodbye!"

Leonard Bernstein was buried at Green-Wood next to Felicia. In his coffin were placed a piece of amber, a lucky penny, a baton, a pocket score of Mahler's Fifth Symphony, and a copy of *Alice in Wonderland.* Buried with him, along with his learning and his many gifts, was a nearly unmatched degree of aliveness, of "present stamina." It is doubtful that a person of such dynamism and wide-ranging interests could ever have existed in one dimension only. It is difficult to picture him living a twilight existence, composing quietly, without being able to leap to the podium, play the piano, teach, talk, sermonize, complain, argue, rage, provoke, laugh, embrace, recite poetry, and tell stories. A hunger for experience in all of its aspects and a need to share were essential to his nature.[13] Buried with him, preserved, as if in amber, beneath the extraordinary hubbub of his life, was his still vivid sense of wonder at the sounds he had discovered long ago in the music he heard at temple and in Aunt Clara's piano, when the universe suddenly made sense to him.

# NOTES

Short titles are used for those works included in the bibliography.

## Introduction

1. Ledbetter, *Sennets & Tuckets*, 106.
2. Bernstein, *Findings*, 330.

## Chapter 1. Dust

1. Sam was born Yisroel Yosef ben Yehuda, but his name was changed to Shmuel Yosef before his circumcision, a ritual performed by his father. His grandfather, Bezalel, had been a blacksmith, the one male nonrabbi in the family tree and a man legendary for his prodigious physical strength.

2. More than a million Russian Jews had in fact made such a journey in the previous twenty-five years. The onset of the Russo-Japanese War in 1904 meant that even more young Jewish men of conscription age—which Shmuel was approaching—were being drafted into the army. (Jews had always made up a disproportion-

ate percentage of recruits into the czarist army.) Anti-Semitic pogroms were on the rise, and life on the farm had become increasingly arduous too.

3. By 1911 there were six children in the family. Half of the workers in the factories were, like Jennie, girls between the ages of fourteen and eighteen. Because of the advent of industrialized means of production at the end of the nineteenth century, factories such as those owned by the American Woolen Company in Lawrence, Massachusetts, had been able to replace skilled workers with unskilled and unionized immigrant workers from Italy, Syria, Portugal, and Russia who could be paid less than nine dollars a week. Conditions in the mills were not just uncomfortable; they were lethal. Thirty-five percent of the unskilled male workers in the factories did not live to be twenty-five years old.

4. Sam had heard about Jennie through a friend who happened to be her distant cousin, and he had tagged along with him on the trolley ride to Lawrence for a visit. The two young men both became infatuated with Jennie and started to visit often. At first she remained almost indifferent to both of them, though, if anything, she found her cousin the more appealing of the two.

5. Burton Bernstein, *Family Matters*, 58.

6. His name was Louis on his birth certificate, out of deference to the wishes of Jennie's parents, who wished that he be named for his maternal grandfather. But his parents called him "Leonard" from the beginning, and the name change was made official after he turned sixteen.

## Chapter 2. A Piano

1. The language of the sermon was English, not Yiddish, and men and women were seated alongside each other. The presiding rabbi, Herman Rubenovitz, who had come to America as a child from Lithuania, traveled to the great reform synagogues of Paris, Berlin, and Vienna to experience firsthand how to incorporate music into his services. Bernstein later recalled the cantor as "a great musician and a beautiful man." This and the other quo-

tations in this paragraph are from Sarna, "Leonard Bernstein," 35–39.

2. Ibid., 35–46.

3. Gruen, *Private World*, 39.

4. Peyser, *Bernstein*, 128.

5. "Smose snapas" became "used as a prefix to indicate RST, or Rybernian Standard Time." Burton Bernstein, *Family Matters*, 110.

6. Niren, "Influence of Solomon Braslavsky," 117–19.

7. Sid Ramin, interview with the author, September 12, 2012.

8. Humphrey Burton, *Leonard Bernstein*, 97.

9. Heinrich Gebhard and his wife did attend the concert, however, and were deeply impressed. The well-brought-up student wrote Gebhard a thank-you note two days later: "I received many compliments that evening, but they were merely laws of etiquette. But to have heard you say those wonderful things about my playing was far beyond my highest expectations." Leonard Bernstein to Heinrich Gebhard, May 16, 1934, Leonard Bernstein Collection, Library of Congress.

10. This letter is shown in the film biography *The Gift of Music*.

11. Leonard Bernstein, "Friends and Freud," essay in English notebook from Boston Latin School, October 22, 1934, Leonard Bernstein Collection, Library of Congress.

12. Sigmund Freud, *Three Essays on the Theory of Sexuality*, trans. and ed. James Strachey (New York: Basic Books, 1962), 11. The late psychologist Elisabeth Young-Bruehl wrote that, while most people choose one sex over the other in their conscious thinking and behavior, "they retain in their unconscious minds the road not taken." Freud also thought that whatever the evolution of a person's sexual choices and desires, whatever their "object-choice," the shaping of their psychological characteristics in terms of what were traditionally considered "male" and "female" traits developed independently from this behavior. Bernstein's compulsion to seduce both sexes was accompanied by an appeal that was itself bisexual.

## Chapter 3. Harvard

1. Humphrey Burton, *Leonard Bernstein*, 35.

2. Swan, *Leonard Bernstein*, 48.

3. Prall, *Aesthetic Judgment*, 141–43, 165.

4. "Since the Greeks themselves, who created the beauties we recognize, used strong colors extensively, an unprejudiced mind must be willing to admit at least the possibility that richness of sensuous content in general simply adds richness to the most formal structural beauty, instead of contaminating it." Ibid., 142.

5. Information and quotations courtesy of the film *Bernstein's Sharon Documentary*, created by Shira Brettman for the course "Before *West Side Story:* Leonard Bernstein's Boston," taught by Carol J. Oja and Kay Kaufman Shelemay at Harvard University in Spring 2006.

6. Bernstein and Shapero requested a recording of the third movement of Beethoven's String Quartet No. 15 in A Minor, op. 132, because it was mentioned in a book they had both read, Aldous Huxley's *Point Counter Point.* (This movement was labeled by Beethoven as "Heiliger Dankgesang eines Genesenen an die Gottheit, in der lydischen Tonart" [A convalescent's holy song of thanks to the Divinity, in the Lydian mode].) However, to quote Shapero, at first they found it "a big bore." Only after they had listened to it repeatedly did they come to appreciate it. Harold Shapero, interview with the author, July 29, 2012.

7. Mitropoulos gave him a steel aircheck 78 rpm recording of the performance, an impermanent document that could only be played a few times before being worn out. Years later he would loan him his score, showing exactly where the basses had doubled the cellos in his version. Bernstein quickly copied the doublings into his miniature score. (Apart from this, there were no changes to the original work.) Jack Gottlieb, liner notes for Bernstein's recording of opp. 131 and 135 with the Vienna Philharmonic, Deutsche Grammophon D 100867.

8. During his sophomore and junior years he also composed two solo works for Mildred Spiegel: "Music for the Dance I" and "Music for the Dance II," as well as a substantial piano duo to

play with her, "Music for Two Pianos." "Music for the Dance I" is signed "with all my heart—LB" after the double bar. "Music for the Dance II" is dedicated "To Mildred on her 22nd Birthday in friendliest affection." There remains some uncertainty about the history of the two solo works and even about the number of movements they originally contained. All three works appear to have been completed by June 12, 1938. A program for a concert given by Gebhard's piano students on that day lists Leonard as performing "Music for the Dance I" (1. Allegretto, 2. Vivacissimo) and "Music for the Dance II" (1. Moderato, 2. Allegro non troppo), and Leonard and Mildred Spiegel together performing "Music for Two Pianos." In the Boosey & Hawkes published score, "Music for the Dance II" contains three movements (1. Moderato, 2. Waltz Time, 3. Allegro non troppo), and a single-movement piece called "Non troppo presto" is described as possibly "Music for the Dance I."

9. The dramatic counselor at Camp Onota was Monitor R. Weil. When he arrived at the camp, Green was told that the eighteen-year-old music counselor was a "musical genius."

10. Aaron Copland and Vivian Perlis, *Copland: 1900 through 1942*, 2nd ed. (New York: St. Martin's, 1999), 338.

11. Leonard Bernstein to Aaron Copland, October 20, 1938, quoted by Vivian Perlis in Oja and Tick, *Aaron Copland*, 161.

12. Leonard Bernstein, "The Absorption of Race Elements into American Music" (thesis, Harvard University, 1939), 10.

13. Swan, *Leonard Bernstein*, 43.

14. *The Birds* performances took place on April 21 and 22, 1939.

15. Pollack, *Marc Blitzstein*, 185.

16. Perlis in Oja and Tick, *Aaron Copland*, 163–64.

17. After Bernstein found out that it was too late to apply for a fellowship to study conducting with Albert Stoessel at Juilliard, Copland put him in touch with Fritz Reiner at the Curtis Institute.

## Chapter 4. Curtis, Tanglewood, Boston, and New York

1. Mitropoulos's conducting demeanor was even more extravagant than Koussevitzky's, "with a whole repertoire of . . . leaps and crouches." Robinson, *Bernstein*, 107. In Arthur Berger's words,

Mitropoulos was "monk-like, almost shy, retiring. He gave money away to needy composers, lived very modestly . . . and seemed completely bereft of the capacity for public relations." Arthur Berger, *Reflections of an American Composer* (Berkeley: University of California Press, 2002), 218.

2. Vengerova was also the aunt and first piano teacher of conductor, music theorist, and writer Nicolas Slonimsky.

3. Rezits, *Beloved Tyranna,* 23. Musicians such as Thomas Scherman, Leonard Pennario, Gary Graffman, Lillian Kallir, and Jacob Lateiner, among many others, credited her with the development of a musical conscience and an understanding of how to practice. As a concert approached, her temper increased: "Insults raged; sarcasm stung; furniture was thrown" (Rezits, *Beloved Tyranna,* ii). But as a result, no concert trial could ever scare her students as much as the lessons already had.

4. Vengerova was a representative of the "Russian school" of piano playing, exemplified by Vladimir Horowitz. She was particularly good at teaching legato playing, both through technical means —for example, a suppleness of the wrists—and through learning to match the tone of each note's decay with the one that follows it.

5. Anyone who listens today to his recordings of Mozart, Beethoven, Mahler, Gershwin, et al., can hear the results.

6. Before the rise of the Nazis, Stöhr had enjoyed hundreds of performances of his compositions and had published many of them, along with a widely used harmony textbook.

7. Aaron Copland to Margaret Grant, March 17, 1940, Aaron Copland Collection, Library of Congress.

8. For some reason, Nancarrow refers to it as "Three Pieces." Humphrey Burton notes that a "Chorale" from this work was incorporated into the "Jeremiah" Symphony.

9. Raphael Hillyer, who became the dedicatee of Bernstein's Violin Sonata, was born Raphael Silverman and changed his name (and instrument) sometime after August 1940. He is listed as Raphael Silverman in concert programs both at Harvard (such as the program for *The Birds,* in which he played the violin) and from the Berkshire Music Center.

10. Bernstein's description of showing his music to Copland is included in the documentary *Leonard Bernstein: Reaching for the Note.*

11. Leonard Bernstein to Aaron Copland, undated 1940 letter, cited in Humphrey Burton, *Leonard Bernstein,* 82.

12. Aaron Copland to Leonard Bernstein, March 23, 1938, in Crist and Shirley, *Selected Correspondence of Copland,* 124.

13. While the Ravel rings timbral changes on an unvarying theme and eventually harmonizes it, Copland begins with a bare strand of notes, which are then transposed to many different key areas and regrouped in different rhythmic characters and piano textures. Neither set of variations is based on a harmonic structure.

14. In the opening of the first movement, the layers of counterpoint are related to each other through canonic imitation, augmentation, diminution, and other devices, drawing the listener into the counterpoint itself rather than into a recognition of the themes.

15. Shirley Gabis Perle, interview with the author, July 14, 2012.

16. The esplanade concert resulted from his winning a music quiz. Paul Myers writes that "conductor Harry Ellis Dickson was present [at the event] and described Bernstein as 'a natural.'" Myers, *Leonard Bernstein,* 33.

17. "Conch Town" is a nickname for Key West.

18. The first theme is centered on a minor mode A. The second theme on major mode G is first accompanied by harmonies in A and then, when repeated, by harmonies centered on G. The short development section deals with motives mainly derived from the bridge passage. Having traveled to G, F-sharp, F, D, and C in the development, the recapitulation returns us to A, and brings back the climax of the first theme and then the music of the opening. The bridge passage is eliminated, and the second theme, now in A major, is played at a slower tempo, functioning as a coda to the movement.

19. Aaron Copland to Leonard Bernstein, March 25, 1943, cited in Humphrey Burton, *Leonard Bernstein,* 104–5.

20. The idiom of the Clarinet Sonata is much more tonally centered than that of the Violin Sonata, although with modal themes, quartal harmonies, and altered chords. The meters of the two movements are nicely varied. The first movement, Grazioso, is in cut common time, the second movement's Andantino is in 3/8, and its Vivace e leggiero section is in a pert, bouncy 5/8.

21. "Music: Wunderkind," *Time* magazine, February 4, 1957.

22. Secrest, *Leonard Bernstein*, 96.

23. Peyser, *Bernstein*, 102

## Chapter 5. Wonderful Times

1. Jennie Tourel was born with the surname Davidovich.

2. Marin Alsop, speaking in the radio documentary *Leonard Bernstein: An American Life*, part 7.

3. The set also includes an *Anniversary* in memory of Natalie Koussevitzky, composed on January 15, 1942, which replicates with some differences the last twenty-eight measures of the *Jeremiah* Symphony. Although the Hebrew lament at the heart of the symphony's third movement was composed in 1939, expansions and changes were made to it during the symphony's composition period in the spring of 1942, which followed Natalie's death. There is reason to believe that the material from this *Anniversary* was added to the Lamentation at that time. At m. 13 in the piano piece, a quiet passage in the low register, marked "somber," evokes the Russia of Tchaikovsky for a moment, whereas the equivalent moment in the symphonic finale echoes the theme of the lament. In the context of the symphony, the theme of this *Anniversary* sounds like a variant of what Jack Gottlieb calls the "Amidah" melody in the French horn at the start of the first movement.

4. Peyser, *Leonard Bernstein*, 129.

5. Robbins and his sister independently described their parents as cold and unaffectionate.

6. Robert Kotlowitz, "The North, South, East, and West Side Story of Jerome Robbins," *Show*, December 1964, 39.

7. Bernstein had come recommended by two composers Rob-

bins had visited, Vincent Persichetti and Morton Gould, and designer Oliver Smith had come along to make the introduction.

8. His only scheduled appearances at Carnegie Hall in the fall of 1943 were at the closed reading sessions of American compositions that Rodzinski held to evaluate newly submitted scores.

9. These performers were cellist Joseph Schuster and violist William Lincer.

10. Burton Bernstein, *Family Matters*, 145–46.

11. Jacques Margolies, interviewed in *Leonard Bernstein: Reaching for the Note.*

12. Jennie Bernstein to Leonard Bernstein, November 24, 1943, Leonard Bernstein Collection, Library of Congress.

13. *New York Herald Tribune*, December 17, 1943.

14. Peyser, *Leonard Bernstein*, 131.

15. Timothy Mangan and Irene Herrmann, eds., *Paul Bowles on Music* (Berkeley: University of California Press, 2003), 173–74.

16. Robbins sometimes even tried out ideas spontaneously with his dancers on the street, based on what he had just seen.

17. The solo, the third of the variations in which the sailors each show off in their competition for the two girls, clearly bears the imprint of Copland's *Danzón cubano* of 1942, as well as *El salón México.*

18. Comden and Green's later shows for theater and film included the classics *Bells Are Ringing*, *Singin' in the Rain* (for which they wrote the story and book), and *The Band Wagon.*

19. As Carol J. Oja points out in her authoritative essay, "Bernstein's Musicals: Reflections of Their Time," in Burton Bernstein and Haws, *Leonard Bernstein: American Original*, this was a period of remarkably fertile cross-pollination between "high" and "low" art. Disney's film *Fantasia*, using classical works conducted by Leopold Stokowski, had appeared in 1940; *Oklahoma!*, with choreography by Agnes de Mille, had opened the previous year; violinist Jascha Heifetz had recorded with singer Bing Crosby.

20. The little blues is a throwaway, cut off by Hildy, the cab driver, as "too depressing" after the words "I wish I were dead and buried." It starts with an upward minor ninth and snakes through

eleven of the twelve possible chromatic pitches in its first phrase. Its singer, Frances Cassard, was a young opera soprano who had sung for the troops in Italy and the Persian Gulf the previous spring and had been Tosca at the newly founded New York City Opera in the fall.

21. Both "Come Up to My Place" and a chase sequence used material from *The Birds*.

22. One would never guess that the music came first. The words feel welded to the ambiguity of the song's opening, which disguises its tonal center, could be in major or minor, and unfolds in unexpected phrase lengths of three, two, five, and two measures. Then they perfectly mesh with the melodic arc of its climax ("unless there's love the world's an empty place"), where the harmonic and metrical tensions of the song are resolved, coming to rest in a major key.

23. *Leonard Bernstein: Reaching for the Note.*

24. The "Miss Turnstiles" variations are: home-loving man (A major, 2/2); playboy (jazzy C major, blues scale, 4/4); army (C major, march); sailor (G major, loose-limbed ragtime piano solo over pizzicato accompaniment); more military music (A-flat major, 4/4); athlete (F major); and aesthete (balletic, 3/4, which begins with a humorously bitonal, "sensitive" violin solo in A major and then B-flat major, over a consistent B major accompaniment).

25. The scherzo can also be heard in "Gabey's Comin'," a song deleted from the musical that can be heard in the 1992 Michael Tilson Thomas recording of the show. In the dream ballet, when Gabey dances with Ivy, the "Gabey" motives mingle with music from the "Miss Turnstiles" ballet.

26. As composer David Schiff points out, the ballet evokes the slow movement of Gershwin's piano concerto, with its clarinet trio and bluesy trumpet. He also believes that, in *On the Town*, Bernstein "seems more comfortable with the extended dance numbers than with simple songs." Schiff, "Leonard Bernstein."

27. Schuller, *Gunther Schuller*, 157–58. Schuller continues, "It permitted him to do things with his hands that I have never seen with anyone else; it enabled him to get away with a variety of un-

orthodox manual movements, especially his (at times excessive) subdivision of beats that, to my knowledge, no other conductor could manage so successfully."

28. "The trouble of the Jews / In my dear guts does smolder / But sparkless is the fuse."

29. Humphrey Burton, *Leonard Bernstein*, 139.

30. Ibid., 90.

31. For example, he was fascinated by Paul and Jane Bowles and by Janice and Herschel Levit, an older couple he saw frequently in Philadelphia.

32. In *Jeux* the setting is a tennis match, and the protagonists are two women and one man.

33. Serge Koussevitzky to Leonard Bernstein, December 23, 1946; Bernstein to Koussevitzky, December 27, 1946, Leonard Bernstein Collection, Library of Congress.

34. On December 9 Jennie had written to Leonard, describing how lonesome they were for him: "What is it about you we miss you the minute you are out of sight."

35. Samuel Bernstein to Leonard Bernstein, December 26, 1946, Leonard Bernstein Collection, Library of Congress.

36. The end of the war, bringing to a rapid close the U.S. alliance with the Soviet Union, the increasing militancy of the Soviets, and the ascendancy of Truman to the presidency that followed upon the death of Roosevelt, had brought about a sea change in the American political climate. In 1947 the progressive side of the Democratic Party continued to be increasingly marginalized. Americans for Democratic Action, with Eleanor Roosevelt and Harold Ickes, two former New Deal progressives, at the helm, and the Truman Doctrine both favored a belligerent foreign policy and domestic "loyalty security probes" that were designed to distance Democrats from any taint of communist sympathies. On March 25, 1946, Bernstein had addressed a meeting of the Progressive Citizens of America, advocating a merger of all progressive groups into one.

37. Bernstein was also a natural choice to be the orchestra's music director and regular conductor. But it would have required

him to be there at least three months a year, and he was still awaiting word whether he would be named Koussevitzky's successor at the Boston Symphony. He had learned in February that he would not be made music director of the Rochester Philharmonic, a position for which he was under consideration.

38. Louis Biancolli, "Bernstein Forced to Lead Two Lives," *New York World-Telegram and Sun*, February 25, 1949.

## Chapter 6. Age of Anxiety

1. In April 1948, after their relationship had returned to its platonic state, Auden wrote to her: "I can't tell you, my dear, how I feel about all your goodness to me during the past winter—I don't deserve it and I never shall."

2. Among the links to his own experiences were the notion of solitary strangers joining in all-night conversations (as he had so often done as an undergraduate and continued to do throughout life); poetic travel through realms of the imagination; the lament in the taxi for "our lost dad"; the transitory ebullience of the festivities at Rosetta's house, which suggested his own excursions on Broadway; and the acknowledgment of faith that comes when one has let go of everything else. It is also conceivable that the grouping of three men and one woman reminded him of working with Comden, Green, and Robbins.

3. Indeed, the Dirge movement was largely composed in October and November in Israel, where he conducted the Israel Philharmonic during the final phase of the 1948 Arab-Israeli War.

4. Bernstein was trying to navigate through the new worlds he now inhabited, while remaining true to himself. He must have sometimes wondered whether his good fortune would last, if not even whether he deserved it. Auden's poem introduces the character of Emble with words that may have spoken to him:

> In certain cases—his was one—this general unease of youth is only aggravated by what would appear to alleviate it, a grace of person which grants them, without effort on their part, a succession of sexual triumphs. For then

> the longing for success, the doubt of ever being able to achieve the kinds of success which have to be earned, and the certainty of being able to have at this moment a kind which does not, play dangerously into each other's hands.
>
> So fully conscious of the attraction of his uniform to both sexes, he looked round him, slightly contemptuous when he caught an admiring glance, and slightly piqued when he did not.

5. Gottlieb discusses this in both his dissertation and his book *Working with Bernstein.* The "chain reaction" idea directly relates to the composer's fascination with anagrams and other word games. It could be compared to the game "Word Gold" (warm-worm-word-cord-cold-gold) or to a game of "Telephone" in which transformation happens one element at a time.

6. Bernstein consistently showed a remarkable ability to put together ideas that had origins in different previous compositions and to forge connections between them. Here he managed to move, by a chain of associations, from a passage in *The Birds* to one from his Violin Sonata. The symphonic version of this variation differs in a few respects from the one in the Violin Sonata. A pitch is altered in the fifth measure of the melody and is correspondingly changed in the inversion of the melody twenty-seven measures later. The last melodic phrase, the inversion, is an octave lower in the symphony and has a different accompaniment than it had in the sonata.

7. The fifth variation could be seen as illustrating the midlife rat race described by Auden as the fifth age: "The problems put you by opposing time, the fight with work, the feud of marriage." Advancing age might well be suggested by the wearily drooping piano figures of the sixth variation: "Our subject has changed / He looks far from well"; and the seventh variation simulates a return to childhood with a reprise of the music of the prologue, first by oboe and English horn and then, as it was originally, in the clarinets: "He grows backward . . . He lies down; he looks through the window/Ailing at autumn . . ."

8. For example, variation nine: "To the left go Rosetta and Emble, to the right Quant and Malin, these on foot, those by car."

Variation ten: "Our train is traversing at top speed / A pallid province of puddles and stumps."

9. The opening notes of the Dirge derive from the ending of the Seven Stages, continuing the "chain reaction" principle. The slow movement of Marc Blitzstein's Piano Concerto may have been an influence here.

10. In this middle section, the piano plays a lyrical theme related both to the Masque and to the theme from the Seven Ages, and the tension is maintained by cross-references to music from the Prologue as well, including the descending scale figure. The piano breaks free from the orchestra for a solo cadenza pitting the ten-note melody against the Masque theme, and this builds to the orchestral tutti.

11. A kind of up-tempo relative of the romantic tune in *Rhapsody in Blue* (analyzed in Bernstein's thesis), it features asymmetrical arrangements of eighth-note patterns within regular meters (for example, 3 + 3 + 2 and 3 + 2 + 3, rather than 2 + 2 + 2 + 2), and its middle section upends our perceptions of pulse further by its regular alternation of 2/4 and 3/8 time. (This "regular alternation" principle crops up in many later Bernstein works. Here it creates patterns of 7/8 time, one of his favorite meters.)

12. Furthermore, the motive's entrance over the dancelike music of the preceding movement, which functions here as the last link in a circular chain of associations, bringing the music back to the theme of the Prologue, recalls the way the Jeremiah melody entered boldly in the French horn during the Profanation movement of that symphony.

13. Gottlieb, *Working with Bernstein*, 282.

14. In 1965 he significantly revised the Epilogue, giving the piano a climactic and ruminative cadenza exploring the theme from the Prologue, alongside the one associated with "faith." This changed the character of its participation in the work's final measures, helping to unify what could be perceived as a rift between the two large sections of the symphony, with the first part being monolithic and stylistically consistent and the second breaking up into three contrasting episodes.

15. *New York Herald Tribune*, February 24, 1950, repr. in Thomson, *Music Reviewed*, 303–4. Thomson continues: "The piano writing is excellent; the figuration shines; the whole sounds out beautifully; but the expressive content seems to me (and I have read the score as well as heard it) banal, derivative in feeling. . . . As a concert piece it is lacking in the chief elements, or so it appears to me, that make for survival in the repertory."

16. Critics who reviewed *The Age of Anxiety* included Louis Biancolli, *New York World-Telegram and Sun*, February 20, 1950; Cyrus Durgin, *Boston Globe*, April 9, 1949; Olin Downes: *New York Times*, February 24, 1950; and Harold Schonberg, *New York Times*, February 1, 1968.

## Chapter 7. Serenade

1. Stravinsky paints a personal, dignified, rather Russian portrait of jazz, using its timbres and cubistically arranged facets and motives suggestive of improvisation. Always drawn to ritual, Stravinsky had been moved by New Orleans Dixieland funeral music, which can be heard as an influence behind the slow-moving "processional" passages in the second and third movements of this marvelous work.

2. Gottlieb points out a two-measure insert, before the "big-band outburst," that was added in 1963. Gottlieb, *Working for Bernstein*, 291–92.

3. Recent parallels might be found in works by John Harbison, Aaron Jay Kernis, and Louis Andriessen.

4. The ondes martenot is an electronic keyboard instrument that sounds something like a theremin. *Ondes* means "waves."

5. Bernstein had gotten to know Messiaen at Tanglewood when the latter was composer-in-residence there in 1949.

6. Olivier Messiaen to Leonard Bernstein, October 5, 1949, cited in Humphrey Burton, *Leonard Bernstein*, 194.

7. Naturally, the "Lonely Town" pas de deux is not included, since the song it refers to is gone.

8. Parts of "Tinkerbell Sick! Tink Lives!" reused music from the "Miss Turnstiles" ballet in *On the Town*. "Dream with Me" is a

harmonically sophisticated song for Wendy, with poignant words by Bernstein. Also absent were "Hook's Soliloquy," a complex extended number, six minutes long, that combines wry humor and musical substance in the manner of "Glitter and Be Gay."

9. The Mozart works were the overture to *Don Giovanni*, *Three German Dances*, K. 605, and the Piano Concerto No. 17 in G Major, K. 453, with Bernstein conducting from the piano. The Ives work was followed by Copland's *El salón México*.

10. Bernstein called him "our Washington, Jefferson, and Lincoln all rolled into one."

11. Gayle Sherwood Magee, *Charles Ives Reconsidered* (Urbana: University of Illinois Press, 2008), 175.

12. Ives had been to Carnegie Hall countless times in his youth, where, seated next to his father, he had listened to the Philharmonic, the Boston Symphony, and even to a recital by Ignacy Paderewski. He had said that if his Second Symphony were ever played there, he would go. Bernstein had offered to play the work for him privately in a special rehearsal of the work.

13. Tom C. Owens, ed., *Selected Correspondence of Charles Ives* (Berkeley: University of California Press, 2007), 357. In the *New York Times*, an enthusiastic Olin Downes marveled that the work could have been created at a time when Americans were "scarcely aware of the mature music of Debussy or Richard Strauss," and a decade before Stravinsky's *Firebird*. Nevertheless, he believed it to be still "an astonishing work today." *New York Times*, February 23, 1951. The piece also struck a sympathetic nerve with Virgil Thomson, who found that the work "speaks of American life with love and humor and deep faith. It is unquestionably an authentic work of art, both as structure and as communication." He added that it was "in a tradition of American music that is not afraid to speak from the heart." *New York Herald Tribune*, February 23, 1951.

14. The Second Symphony was followed by the Third, *A Symphony: New England Holidays*, *The Unanswered Question*, and many of the smaller orchestral pieces. (In 1969 Bernstein's protégé Seiji Ozawa presented Ives's Fourth Symphony with the Philharmonic.)

15. In his essay "Some 'Quarter-Tone' Impressions," Ives wrote,

"Why tonality as such should be thrown out for good, I can't see. Why it should be always present, I can't see. It depends, it seems to me, a good deal—as clothes depend on the thermometer—on what one is trying to do." Charles Ives, "Some 'Quarter-Tone' Impressions," *Franco-American Music Society Bulletin*, March 25, 1925.

16. Seldes, *Leonard Bernstein*, 51.

17. The letter to Shirley continues:

> Even the automatic straining toward general sexuality of the moment—which had always carried a big stick with me, was of no importance. I have been consistently aware of the great companionship of this girl—seen clearly and independent of the damnable tensions that discolored it, the fears melting into thin air. In fact, for the first time in my life, jealousy—a growing resentment of her current affair, and a certain knowledge that D. H. was horribly wrong for her. Over all this, a real knowledge that she and I were made for each other, then as now: that we have everything to give each other.
>
> . . . My day-dreams are of her flying to Israel, and our being married in Jerusalem. (Leonard Bernstein to Shirley Bernstein, April 26, 1950, Leonard Bernstein Collection, Library of Congress)

18. Ibid. In the context of this heartfelt letter, it is hard not to see significance in everything, even in the sentence, "My interest in Peter Pan has grown strangely neutral." Bernstein was trying to "grow up," make a commitment, and in the process please both his father and his father surrogate, Serge Koussevitzky.

19. Ibid.

20. Humphrey Burton recounts Bernstein's conversations with former Curtis student Phyllis Moss on this subject. See Burton, *Leonard Bernstein*, 68.

21. Quoted in ibid., 205.

22. Pollack, *Marc Blitzstein*, 185.

23. Olivia Skinner, "Felicia Montealegre Narrates a Story," *St. Louis Post-Dispatch*, October 23, 1961.

24. Martha Gellhorn, interviewed in *Leonard Bernstein: Reaching for the Note.*

25. Leonard Bernstein to Felicia Bernstein, October 9, 1951, Leonard Bernstein Collection, Library of Congress.

26. Felicia Bernstein to Leonard Bernstein, n.d., Leonard Bernstein Collection, Library of Congress.

27. Jay S. Harrison, "Professor Leonard Bernstein Prepares Some Unusual Lessons," *New York Herald Tribune*, May 11, 1952. *Trouble in Tahiti* lasts forty-five minutes, not "thirty minutes or so."

28. Schuyler Chapin described Felicia as "the one person whose theatrical judgment [he] trusted." Chapin, *Leonard Bernstein*, 148.

29. The title, however, came from the Hollywood version of *On the Town*'s "New York, New York," in which a line in the lyrics was changed from "It's a helluva town" to "It's a wonderful town."

30. For a comparison, listen to Duchin's rendition of "Shine On, Harvest Moon." Helen Smith describes Duchin as "a successful society bandleader" who was "well known through his band's radio broadcasts from New York's Central Park Casino." Smith, *There's a Place for Us*, 79.

31. It is illuminating that Bernstein considered the old-fashioned jazz style of the work evocative of the 1930s. Two thematic quotes can still be heard in the "Conquering New York" dance sequence, and a third motive from the piece—a galumphing start-and-stop oompah accompaniment used in both the Prelude and Riffs movements—became the vamp illustrating awkward embarrassment in "Conversation Piece."

32. Bernstein and Hellman had previously discussed a collaboration based on the life of Eva Perón. In May 1952 Hellman had faced down HUAC with an extraordinary letter in which she said she would not take the Fifth Amendment, as long as she was restricted to only speaking about herself. But, if speaking about her own activities required that she then do harm to others, she said that she would be forced to take the Fifth Amendment and say nothing at all, since "to hurt innocent people whom I knew many years ago in order to save myself is, to me, inhuman and indecent

and dishonorable. I cannot and will not cut my conscience to fit this year's fashions."

33. Some of what Pangloss teaches resembles twenty-first-century arguments for "intelligent design": "Observe how noses were made to support spectacles," he says; "therefore we have spectacles."

34. Hans Keller, "On the Waterfront," *The Score and I.M.A. Magazine*, June 1955, 81–84.

35. Among those in their circle also listed in the report were Copland, Blitzstein, Dorothy Parker, Arthur Laurents, and Judy Holliday.

36. Eryximachus and Aristophanes speak in reverse order in Plato's original.

37. Bernstein later used the same structure in his overture to *Candide*.

38. As Jack Gottlieb has pointed out regarding the link between Agathon and Socrates, Bernstein's chain reaction principle of linkages between movements is at work here, as so often in his larger-scale pieces.

39. An examination of the original *Anniversary* shows just how subtly and cleverly the original is modified and extended to suit the current purpose, a skill honed in the theater but native to some composers and not to others. A particularly deft sleight of hand is the parenthetical transposition of the *Anniversary*'s tune up a half step from E-flat to E, so that the violin solo can easily play it with double stops. The coda's last page of sixteenth notes recalls the scurrying music of Eryximachus, ironed out.

40. Each human being was "a rounded whole with back and sides forming a circle." Each had "four hands and the same number of legs," two faces, turned in opposite directions on one head, "four ears, two sets of genitals, and everything else was as you would imagine it from what I have said so far." Aristophanes explains that the sun was the parent of the male gender, the earth of the female, and the moon, itself the combination of earth and sun, the parent of the combined gender.

41. Reproduction occurred simply "on the earth, as in the

case of cicadas." (Apparently, Plato actually meant grasshoppers.) Eventually they started to die from hunger, and didn't want to do anything apart from their other half. "They threw their arms around each other, weaving themselves together, wanting to form a single living thing."

42. Marc Blitzstein to Leonard Bernstein, August 31, 1954, cited in Pollack, *Marc Blitzstein*, 186.

43. Virgil Thomson, *New York Herald Tribune*, February 11, 1966.

## Chapter 8. Broadway and Carnegie Hall

1. There was one African American blues singer in the program, the excellent Lou Elliott, and no doubt television or music union rules mandated that Bernstein use performers who worked for CBS.

2. Goodman had heard about the work and paid for a rehearsal to try it out.

3. He also presents the conductor as an "eternal student," who must know history and must understand the cultural context of each piece he leads and its relationship to other works of the composer. He explains how conductors study scores, internalize every detail of what the notation conveys, and then make innumerable decisions about what the notation cannot convey. He adds that conductors must hear two things at once—what is being played and what is about to be played; they must breathe with the music; their preparatory beat is an inhalation, the musical phrase an exhalation. In the end, the roots of great conducting are internal and cannot be taught.

4. Thomson used the phrase in a review in the *New York Herald Tribune*, October 9, 1947, cited in Humphrey Burton, *Leonard Bernstein*, 169.

5. Cott, *Back to a Shadow in the Night*, 212.

6. *New York Philharmonic: Bernstein Live*, CD booklet, 79.

7. Olga Curtis, "Bernstein Fosters Harmony at Home," *Milwaukee Sentinel*, December 7, 1957.

8. The theme of "Candide's Lament," for example, which was ultimately sung to the words "Cunegonde, is it true?" origi-

nated as a piano piece composed for friend Cesarina Riso in 1953. It eventually became no. 1 of *Four Sabras*, "Ilana the Dreamer."

9. He adds that Voltaire's satire "throws light on all the dark places" and lampoons matters germane to American society, including "phony moralism, inquisitorial attacks on the individual, brave-new-world optimism."

10. For example, the overture's opening fanfare, which is modeled on the "Ob-jec-tion!" motive in "The Best of All Possible Worlds," outlines a leap up to a sustained seventh above, which resolves by whole step to an octave; the seventh is harmonized by a perfect fourth, thereby creating a fourth chord with the note that preceded it (F–B-flat–E-flat). The tune of "The Best of All Possible Worlds" is an expansion of this: it begins with a fourth chord ("Paragraph two") and in the second phrase has a sustained note resolving a whole step above. "Candide's Lament" begins with the octave going down to the seventh, and then, in the second phrase, the ascending octave resolves upward by whole step in a rising shape that instantly recalls the opening of the overture.

11. The row is used primarily in three versions, which are then reordered so that each pair of notes is reversed, as if in parody of twelve-tone game playing. The vocal line of the middle section is derived from the row's inversion.

12. The tonal plan of the overture plays on traditional tonic and dominant relationships (E-flat and B-flat) but adds some tonal wild cards (D major and A-flat major).

13. Voltaire's concision is unmatched. He distills an analysis of slavery into a few lines that are still pertinent. In a scene taking place in the Dutch colony of Surinam, a black slave explains to Candide why he has lost his hand working in the sugar mill and then his leg for trying to run away from it: "It is the custom. . . . It is the price we pay for the sugar you eat in Europe." In reaction to this story, Candide questions what he has been taught by Pangloss and uses the word "optimism" for the only time in the book, defining it as "the mania for insisting that all is well when all is not well." See Voltaire, *Candide*, 52. A critique of American inequities could be easily read into the slave's account of how Dutch pastors

converted him to their religion by saying that "we are all children of Adam, blacks and whites alike." If this is so, he says to Candide, "you must admit that no one could treat his relatives worse than this." Hellman did not include the Surinam scene in her book for *Candide*, which boiled down Voltaire's whirlwind thirteen-nation tour to six.

14. Hellman, *Collected Plays*, 711.

15. Guthrie, *Life in the Theatre*, 241.

16. He also deeply admired Hellman's original book, which he called a "black" take on Voltaire, completely different in tone from Bernstein's effervescent music.

17. There are many performing versions of the work, including one made by Mozart, who composed additional wind parts for it. Sir Thomas Beecham even added glockenspiel and cymbals to his version.

18. In Bernstein's version, Part I ends with the "Hallelujah" chorus in blazing D major, and Part II begins in stark contrast with the severe chorus in G minor, "Behold the Lamb of God." The dramatic and religious meaning of the two sections flows in an uninterrupted way, culminating movingly with the final chorus, "Worthy Is the Lamb." Particularly affecting in the recording are the heartfelt arias of soprano Adele Addison and countertenor Russell Oberlin, which achieve a rare intimacy. A highpoint is the aria "He was despised."

19. Craig Zadan, *Sondheim & Co.* (New York: Macmillan, 1974), 16.

20. Bernstein's lyric instincts were always more flowery than Sondheim's. Sondheim wanted to cut his own line, "Today, the world was just an address" from the song "Tonight," because he doubted that a teenage boy would say such a thing, but he ended up retaining it because Bernstein liked it so much.

21. Simeone, *Leonard Bernstein*, 40–42.

22. Lawrence, *Dance with Demons*, 248.

23. Stephen Sondheim, interviewed in *Leonard Bernstein: An American Life*.

24. Carol Lawrence, interviewed in *Leonard Bernstein: Reaching for the Note*.

25. Lehrman, *Marc Blitzstein,* 83 and 556.

26. The "Taunting Scene" is a fast variation of the song's verse, "Puerto Rico / You lovely island." Both originated in the *Conch Town* sketch. A single page in the Bernstein archives at the Library of Congress contains music for "Build My House" from *Peter Pan* and "It Must Be So" from *Candide,* along with these two ideas. Simeone, *Leonard Bernstein,* 73.

27. In her perspicacious analysis, Helen Smith shows, among many other things, that the fugue subject (which contains the first three notes of "Somewhere") is essentially twelve-tone, and that it is put through a strict fugal exposition, with subject and countersubject entrances at pitches outlining a diminished seventh chord. The episode that follows explores the countersubject in a fugue with itself, against accented harmonies outlining the original subject. The unison rhythm of the fugue's climax is identical to that of "Something's Coming."

28. Mel Gussow, "West Side Story: The Beginnings of Something Great," *New York Times,* October 21, 1990.

29. Sid Ramin, interview with the author, September 12, 2012.

30. It was apparently Kostal who proposed extending repetitive figures in the composer's accompaniment to "Tonight" into a consistent beguine (slow rumba) rhythm. (Bernstein said he had a bias against beguines, but then found a way of implementing the idea he liked.) In orchestrating "Something's Coming," Ramin and Kostal suggested a countermelody doubled in octaves by cello and violins on the words "Around the corner, or whistling down the river." After giving it some thought, Bernstein agreed, went to the piano, and improvised a chromatically descending line that enriched the atmosphere of romantic anticipation in the song. Simeone, *Leonard Bernstein,* 91.

31. Helen Smith notes that the dream ballet is in seven parts, like the Seven Ages section of the Second Symphony, and that, as in the earlier work, they are joined by melodic or rhythmic links.

32. Just as Bernstein himself had always dreamed of using the musical theater idiom to produce a work of operatic depth, Robbins was trying in *West Side Story* "to be as serious about our work

as we would be if we were doing a major art work." "I didn't like the idea that we had to separate ourselves into two halves" (i.e., into the "entertainer" vs. the "serious artist"). Jerome Robbins, interviewed in *Leonard Bernstein: Reaching for the Note.*

33. An ostinato of seven eighth notes in the bass cuts across the regular pulse of 2/4 time for twenty-six measure at the point where "a Shark trips a Jet." The passage that follows introduces a new eighth-note ostinato that is identical to one used in *Le sacre du printemps,* while the Jet's motive above it echoes the *Petrushka* trumpet motif.

34. We may never know the extent to which Bernstein consciously designed it that way. The fact is that the contents of the show kept changing during rehearsal and incorporated music from *Candide* and from earlier works. (A few of its songs, such as "I Feel Pretty," would in fact have fit comfortably into *Candide.*) It could not possibly have been predesigned in the way Berg's *Wozzeck* and *Lulu* were.

35. The melody here corresponds to the pitches of "hand and we're halfway there" in the phrase "Hold my hand and we're halfway there" from "Somewhere."

36. Leonard Bernstein to Felicia Bernstein, August 3, 1957, Leonard Bernstein Collection, Library of Congress.

37. Simeone, *Leonard Bernstein,* 115.

38. In Philadelphia Henry T. Murdoch devoted particular attention to the lyrics and predicted a bright future for Sondheim. He also may have been the first to note the score's musical unity. Ibid., 120.

39. Sid Ramin, interviewed in *Leonard Bernstein: Reaching for the Note.*

40. Simeone, *Leonard Bernstein,* 129.

41. Harold Clurman, review of *West Side Story, Nation,* October 27, 1957; repr. in Marjorie Loggia and Glenn Young, eds., *The Collected Works of Harold Clurman* (New York: Applause Books, 1994), 335–36.

42. The Lisbon scene in *Candide* contains a striking reminder that the two works were composed side by side: when an altered,

dissonant version of the fanfare is played before the auto-da-fé, it contains the three-note cell of *West Side Story*, presented in the same rhythm as the Jets' call, and might make some listeners feel transported for a moment to the streets of New York City.

## Chapter 9. What Does Music Mean?

1. For example, on November 29, 1965, just back from his sabbatical, Bernstein, now forty-seven and a more sober, gray-haired conductor than the conductor of "What Does Music Mean?," approached the subject of intervals as "musical atoms," a scientific reference perfectly gauged to thirteen-year-olds. (Jamie Bernstein had turned thirteen in September.) Appropriately, he also incorporated a few measures from the Beatles song "Help!" into the discussion. (The movie *Help!* had been released the previous summer.) The insight that "an atom of music is not a note of music, as you might think, but at least two notes," and that it is this "relationship between notes" that bond to form "molecules" of music, which then merge together to form an entire work, such as the *Blue Danube*, is wonderful. It also sheds light on his view of the nature of music, a view that not all composers would share: "with that one lonely note—isolated—nothing is happening. It's just floating in space. But once you have two notes, you suddenly feel a relationship between them, like an electrical tension, that is already the beginning of musical meaning." Like a good science teacher, he took the trouble to clarify why the term "interval" is not only used as a "measurement of time" but also of distance between rates of vibration, and to explain that it is only our Western system of tuning that divides the octave up into twelve half steps.

2. The phrase "Music Appreciation Racket" was coined by Virgil Thomson.

3. Thomson, *Selected Letters*, 395.

## Chapter 10. At the Center

1. The nineteenth-century American composers represented were Edward MacDowell, Henry Gilbert, George Chadwick, and

Arthur Foote. Bernstein made sure that issues of national identity were likewise on the table from guest conductors, each of whom was asked to offer programs highlighting music of a particular nationality (English, Italian, French, German, and Austrian).

2. Pasternak's letter is read by Schuyler Chapin in *Leonard Bernstein: An American Life*. Even on the recording of the Shostakovich Fifth Symphony made in Boston in October shortly after the orchestra's return, a powerful unanimity of intent, a sense of occasion, remain palpable. The solemn ending of the beautifully paced first movement, which starts with an eloquent trio for oboe, clarinet, and bassoon, moves to two ripe chords in the French horns, then winds down with hushed solos from flute, violin, and celesta over a nearly static string accompaniment, is a dreamlike highlight. The Mahleresque grotesquerie of the Allegretto contains flavorful *giocoso* wind playing, and a superbly hesitant waltz played by concertmaster Corigliano. Shostakovich quotes Mahler specifically in the threnodic Largo, according to Richard Taruskin, who notes two quotations from *Das Lied von der Erde*, including from "Der Abschied" (The farewell), and comments that when the "farewell" melody is heard on the cellos (at fig. 90) only the Bernstein recording "does justice" to the "barks of pain" in the double basses. See Richard Taruskin, "Public Lies and Unspeakable Truth: Interpreting Shostakovich's Fifth Symphony," in *Shostakovich Studies*, vol. 1, ed. David Fanning (Cambridge: Cambridge University Press, 1995), 42. The performance of the enigmatic final movement, about which much ink has been spilled over the years, combines triumphalism and irresolution to just the right degree.

3. Dimitri Mitropoulos offered Mahler's Fifth Symphony on January 1, 2, and 3; the First on January 7, 8, 9, and 10; the Adagio from the Tenth Symphony on January 14, 15, 16, and 17; and the Ninth Symphony on January 21, 22, 23, and 24. Bruno Walter led *Das Lied von der Erde* on April 15, 16, 21, and 24. Besides Bernstein, Mitropoulos, and Walter, other conductors who had performed Mahler at the Philharmonic in the past were Willem Mengelberg, Walter Damrosch, Leopold Stokowski, and Artur Rodzinski.

4. Kolodin's review is quoted in Burton Bernstein and Haws, *Leonard Bernstein*, 177; Taubman's review appeared in the *New York Times*, September 23, 1947.

5. The majority of the European critics of the time would have agreed with the view expressed in May 1951 by a Hannover music critic, who said that "most of today's listeners have moved away from most of his symphonies, which, far from being timeless, were closely bound up with their age." Fischer, *Gustav Mahler*, 700.

6. Ibid., 254–57. From the late 1950s on, when Bernstein's own devotion to Mahler had become fully ingrained, and his concern about the demise of tonality was a personal leitmotif, the two living composers he probably most identified with, Shostakovich and Benjamin Britten, were also in Mahler's thrall.

7. *Leonard Bernstein: Reaching for the Note.*

8. Marni Nixon was renowned for her performances of contemporary music, but she also performed as an uncredited singer in several Hollywood movie musicals. She was the singing voice for Natalie Wood's Maria in the film of *West Side Story*.

9. Confessing that he was old-fashioned and preferred music with a recognizable melody, Luening's brother wrote, "You are searching for the sounds of the future and putting them in your compositions."

10. For evidence of this, see the Boulez's presentation regarding his *Sur incises*, included on *Pierre Boulez: "Éclat" / "Sur incises,"* directed by Frank Scheffer and Andy Sommer (Paris: Idéale Audience International, 2006), DVD.

11. He continued, "This is the same atomization that we tend to find in certain abstract painting, in the poems of E. E. Cummings, in the novels of Joyce, and of course in the physical sciences themselves." Bernstein's choice of authors was apt. Joyce's novels deeply influenced Boulez's musical thinking, and he set Cummings's poetry to music in his work *Cummings ist der Dichter.*

12. Karlheinz Stockhausen to Leonard Bernstein, August 11, 1946, Leonard Bernstein Collection, Library of Congress.

13. Bernstein also conducted Berg's Violin Concerto with Isaac Stern in December 1959.

14. The interview on Kennedy continues: "I think the thing that impressed me the most about him, and increasingly as time went on, was the reverence he had for thought itself or for the functions of the human mind in whatever form, whether as pure thinking—philosophical thinking, that is—or political thinking or creative functions of any sort, including art and literature, even things he understood very little about, and I think music was one of them." Leonard Bernstein, interview with Nelson Aldrich, July, 21, 1965, John F. Kennedy Presidential Library, Oral History Program.

15. Burton Bernstein, interview with the author, March 25, 2012.

16. Although Columbia Records canceled its plan to record the Brahms performance, the broadcast, including Bernstein's comments, can fortunately now be heard on CD. Bernstein considered Gould's second Goldberg Variations recording to be "a religious experience" and was shocked and saddened by Gould's early death at the age of fifty.

17. Like Bernstein, Haydn had not been born into the aristocracy, but he came to embody aristocratic traits through intelligence, learning, and a sense of style. Eventually Bernstein would lead the orchestra in all six Paris symphonies (Nos. 82–87); Symphony No. 88; all twelve London symphonies (nos. 93–104); the oratorio *The Creation;* and four Masses: the *Missa in angustiis* ("Nelson Mass"); the *Missa in tempore belli* (which he also memorably conducted at an antiwar concert in Washington on the occasion of Nixon's inauguration); the *Harmoniemesse;* and the *Theresienmesse*. The performance of the "Nelson Mass" is positively radiant, and the recording of *The Creation* glows similarly with a spirit of discovery and freshness.

18. H. C. Robbins Landon, review of Haydn, Symphonies Nos. 82 and 83, New York Philharmonic, Leonard Bernstein, cond., *High Fidelity*, November 1964.

19. Parts of the symphony were composed at the MacDowell Colony in Peterborough, New Hampshire. The composer turned a canon, written to a text consisting of the names of the artists staying at the colony, into the boys' choir canon, right before the

symphony's finale, illustrating the spreading of praise throughout the world.

20. The tone of the text is of a piece with the admonitions Bernstein sometimes voiced at press conferences or on political platforms. It was written under the shadow of what he later called in the Norton Lectures "the angel of planetary death."

21. More from Job 10:18–19: "Wherefore then hast thou brought me forth out of the womb? Oh that I had given up the ghost, and no eye had seen me! I should have been as though I had not been; I should have been carried from the womb to the grave."

22. In 1964 composer George Rochberg, in the wake of the sudden death of his teenage son, broke away from the serial approach and began pursuing a stylistic eclecticism epitomized by his Third String Quartet, which juxtaposed movements reminiscent of Beethoven and Mahler alongside those resembling Bartók and Schoenberg.

23. Gradenwitz, *Leonard Bernstein*, 159.

24. Likewise, the *Jeremiah* text was sung by a woman.

25. Bernstein, *Findings*, 218ff.

26. The all-Stravinsky evening was attended by Blitzstein and may have been the last concert he heard. Pollack, *Marc Blitzstein*, 464.

27. Roger Copeland, *Merce Cunningham: The Modernizing of Modern Dance* (New York: Routledge, 2004), 266.

28. Cage's music can resemble a Rorschach test. Pianist Margaret Leng Tan has written of his 1944 work *Four Walls* that its "silences and static repetitions . . . contribute to an atmosphere of growing entrapment," in which "each person brings to the piece what he wishes or, rather, what he is." Margaret Leng Tan, "Music of the Unquiet Mind," *New York Times*, September 1, 2012. For a conductor used to investing his entire being in another composer's will, conducting Cage must have posed a challenge.

29. Carolyn Brown, *Chance and Circumstance: Twenty Years with Cage and Cunningham* (New York: Alfred A. Knopf, 2007), 370.

30. Eric Salzman, *New York Herald Tribune*, January 24, 1964, cited in Pollack, *Marc Blitzstein*, 469.

## Chapter 11. Chichester, Vienna, Mount Scopus

1. Milton Babbitt, "Who Cares If You Listen?" *High Fidelity*, February 1958, 38–40, 126–27. His article was focused on the sad, undeniable truth that much serious music has "little, no, or negative commodity value," in Babbitt's words. It was given its title by the editors of *High Fidelity*, a choice that greatly distressed Babbitt himself. In a 1996 interview with Anthony Tommasini, he said, "It isn't 'Who cares if you listen?' It's that I care that you are *not* listening." Anthony Tommasini, "Finding Still More Life in a 'Dead' Idiom," *New York Times*, October 6, 1996.

2. When Hussey wrote again on December 22, 1964, he reiterated that "I hope you will feel entirely free to write your setting as you wish to. I hope you would not, at any rate on our behalf, feel any restrictions from the point of view of tradition or convention. . . . I am sure that it is a very good thing for something like our Three Cathedrals Festival to have a sharp and vigorous push into the middle of the 20th century, and if you feel inclined to write something that would do this I am sure nobody could do it better and we should be most happy and grateful." Laird, *Chichester Psalms*, 17–18, 22–25.

3. He composed the work quickly in the apartment in New York, with some work also accomplished in Fairfield.

4. The song was possibly intended for the first act, which takes place when an imminent ice age threatens human extinction. See Richard Walters, ed., *Bernstein Theater Songs: 49 Songs* (New York: Leonard Bernstein Music Publishing, 2010), xii. The consolation of natural cycles was already present in the chorus of the Comden and Green lyrics, which begin "Spring will come again. / Summer has to follow. / Birds will come again, / nesting in the hollow." Laird also mentions, as a further reference point, Britten's *A Ceremony of Carols*, a work for children's choir and harp by a composer surely on Bernstein's mind as he composed for Chichester Cathedral. A comparison of the original song with the psalm setting engenders respect for the care with which the composer adapts the melody to fit the Hebrew; simplifies and refines the ac-

companiment in writing for the two harps; and then expands the melody in canon for the full treble complement of the choir, adding an accompaniment in the strings, including a rising countermelody in the first violins.

5. The words of "Mix" began: "Mix! Make a mess of 'em. / Pay the Puerto Ricans back, / Make a mess of 'em. / If you let us take a crack, / There'll be less of 'em." Hearing Psalm 2, set to the melody intended for "Mix," one can't help recalling Bernstein's words from "What Does Music Mean?": "The picture that goes with music goes with it only because the composer says so."

6. In the course of expanding "Mix," Bernstein also cunningly emphasized an aspect of the tune that resembled the chorale motto of *Chichester Psalms.*

7. The harmonic hinge from the string introduction to the choral music, a B dominant seventh chord progressing to G major, sets the pattern for the all of the harmonic twists of the movement, which surround G major with surprising harmonies leading to it by common tones.

8. As Jack Gottlieb first pointed out, the motto's first three notes "correspond to the opening of Mahler's Eighth Symphony." Laird, *Chichester Psalms,* 60 and n. 11.

9. In New York the work was performed with a mixed choir (SATB) and in Chichester with an all-male chorus of boys and men, which was the standard English cathedral choir of the time and remains so in many cathedrals today.

10. The Webern performance can be heard in the 10-CD compilation *New York Philharmonic: The Historic Broadcasts, 1923 to 1987.*

11. Burton Bernstein and Haws, *Leonard Bernstein,* 146.

12. *London Times* review cited in Humphrey Burton, *Leonard Bernstein,* 350; Alan Rich, *New York Herald Tribune,* December 10, 1965.

13. Gruen, *Private World,* 166.

14. In June, after years of escalating tensions between Israel and its neighbors, and with efforts at peaceful resolution continually undermined by acts of terrorism, full-scale war had erupted

when Israel, under threat from three of its neighbors, had made a preemptive attack on Egypt. In a mere six days they had not only fended off the threat but had occupied portions of Egypt (the Gaza Strip and the Sinai Peninsula), Syria (the Golan Heights), and—of the greatest religious and historical significance—Jordan, the West Bank, and East Jerusalem.

15. He added, "Ever since 1945 the face of art has become cool, hip, put-on, campy. Everything except hopeful, noble."

16. The gesture recalled her dive into the Fairfield swimming pool when her husband completed his Third Symphony.

17. The passage from the Verdi Requiem they performed is for soprano solo and unaccompanied choir.

18. Alexander Bernstein, interviewed in *Leonard Bernstein: An American Life.*

19. Jacquelyn Kennedy to Leonard Bernstein, June 9, 1968, Leonard Bernstein Collection, Library of Congress.

20. Berio's *Sinfonia* was performed on October 10, 11, 12, and 14, 1968, alongside Stravinsky's *Agon* (which is itself quoted in *Sinfonia*) and Beethoven's Piano Concerto No. 4 in G Major, op. 58, with Eugene Istomin, both conducted by Bernstein.

21. Fischer-Dieskau, *Reverberations*, 179.

22. Babbitt's program notes for *Relata II* did not exactly meet the Philharmonic audience halfway: "The continuity and progression of *Relata II* perhaps can be most easily followed at first hearing in terms of the highly contrapuntal, polyphonic nature of the work, the extent to which coherence rests upon the structure of the individual lines, and the manifest interrelationships between and among these lines, whether these pitch lines be delineated by single instruments, by instrumental families, registrally, rhythmically, or dynamically. Naturally, each pitch element of these linear components, at every moment of the work, functions also as a constituent of, as a contributor to local harmonic units whose ordered interval structure as well as whose immediate succession derives, as do the lines themselves, from the compositional set."

23. Leighton Kerner, *Village Voice*, May 22, 1969.

## Chapter 12. Questions and Declarations

1. Felix Meyer and Anne C. Shreffler, *Elliott Carter: A Centennial Portrait in Letters and Documents* (Woodbridge, Suffolk: Boydell Press, 2008), 199.

2. During the 1968 Mexico City Olympics, for example, two American athletes who had won the gold and bronze medals in track and field, Tommie Smith and John Carlos, were expelled from the team and the games after giving the Black Power salute on the winning stand, and they subsequently faced public denunciation and even death threats.

3. "False Note on Black Panthers," *New York Times*, January 16, 1970.

4. The Berrigan brothers had first gained prominence in May 1968, when they forcibly entered the Selective Service office in Catonsville, Maryland, and set fire to six hundred draft files with homemade napalm in front of reporters they had called to the scene. The Berrigans considered it their religious duty to protest against a U.S. power "that supports right-wing death squads and regimes in Central America that napalm and encourage indiscriminate shooting and police brutality." Berrigan wrote, "Dear friends, how do we translate in our lives the bombing of helpless cities? How do we translate in our lives the millionth Vietnamese peasant perishing?" Daniel Berrigan, "Sermon from the Underground," August 2, 1970, quoted in Seldes, *Leonard Bernstein*, 121.

5. Daniel Berrigan, *America Is Hard to Find* (Garden City, NY: Doubleday, 1972), 150–51.

6. Humphrey Burton also points out that the brass band music was originally written for *The Skin of Our Teeth*. Humphrey Burton, *Leonard Bernstein*, 407.

7. Helen Smith also usefully places the music in relation to two works by Benjamin Britten: his 1962 *War Requiem*, which juxtaposed the Latin Requiem Mass with poems by World War I poet Wilfred Owen, and the church service scene in act 2, scene 1, of *Peter Grimes*, which Bernstein had conducted in its 1946 U.S. premiere, in which a matins service in a church is heard in ironic

counterpoint to a dialogue occurring outside. David Schiff draws an additional parallel to the theatrical work *Marat/Sade* (with music by Richard Peaslee), which Bernstein had seen in 1966.

8. Now that more than forty years have passed, and works such as Alfred Schnittke's Concerti Grossi and Requiem, Osvaldo Golijov's *Passion According to Saint Matthew*, John Adams's *I Was Looking Up at the Ceiling and Then I Saw the Sky*, and the music of John Zorn have made stylistic variety a commonplace, it is possible to begin to hear *Mass* more dispassionately. The notion of a powerful piece of such variety is certainly exciting, and just seeing characters from normal American life onstage (hippies, homeless, housewives) singing such interesting music is arresting in and of itself.

9. Mrs. Onassis attended the revival.

10. Sargeant continued, "Mr. Bernstein seems to have reached maturity as a composer and to have evolved a style that is very much his own." He observed the influence of Mahler, but only to note that Bernstein "merely uses certain of Mahler's methods, such as combining folk melodies with larger structures and placing instruments against each other in unexpected ways. It is, I think, quite a feat for a contemporary composer to evolve a style that is both a personal medium of expression and a wholly communicative one for the audience. . . . Extreme radicals will pronounce his score academic and traditional. But it is not academic, and if it is in any way traditional, that is entirely to its benefit." Winthrop Sargeant, "Musical Events: Missa cum Laude." *New Yorker*, July 8, 1972, 58.

11. Stephen Sondheim, interviewed in *Leonard Bernstein: An American Life*.

12. In the filmed version of *The Unanswered Question: Six Talks at Harvard*, Jamie Bernstein can be viewed in the onstage audience during some of the lectures.

13. In *Language and Mind* Chomsky wrote, "Suppose that we assign to the mind, as an innate property, the general theory of language that we have called 'universal grammar' . . . a skeletal structure for any language and a variety of conditions, formal and substantive, that any further elaboration of the grammar must

meet. . . . What faces the language learner, under these assumptions, is not the impossible task of inventing a highly abstract and intricately structured theory on the basis of degenerate data, but rather the much more manageable task of determining whether these data belong to one or another of a fairly restricted set of potential languages." Chomsky, *Language and Mind*, 77.

## Chapter 13. Dybbuk

1. In his early twenties Robbins had performed in Gluck Sandor's *El amor brujo*, which had a similar theme.

2. The play was first performed in this country in 1921 in New York, by the Yiddish Art Theatre. Stark Young, writing in the *New Republic*, later called it "the most complete work of art that I have seen on the stage since the performance of *The Cherry Orchard* by the Moscow Art Theatre three years ago." Stark Young, "The Dybbuk," *New Republic*, January 26, 1926, 187.

3. One of the score's loveliest passages later became the basis of an *Anniversary* for twelve-year-old Jessica Fleischmann, in *Thirteen Anniversaries*.

4. Richard F. Shepard, "Kaballah Numerology Inspires a Bernstein 'Dybbuk,'" *New York Times*, May 9, 1974.

5. The structure of the work resembles Stravinsky's in such episodic single-movement ballet scores as *Danses concertantes*, *Scènes de ballet*, and *Orpheus*.

6. Leonard Bernstein, quoted in "Possession," *New Yorker*, May 27, 1974, 23.

7. Arlene Croce, "Dancing: Body and Soul," *New Yorker*, June 3, 1974, 88.

8. He composed "A Julia de Burgos" between September 6 and 10, "Music I Heard with You" on September 8, "Zizi's Lament" on September 9, and "What Lips My Lips Have Kissed" also on September 9.

9. The original row suggests a blues scale, and all the forms derived from it that are used in the song gravitate toward the key of C minor. There is a hint of Berg in the few places where Bernstein adds a few extra notes not derived from the row. (The song

staked out rewarding compositional territory. One wishes he had produced an entire Ferlinghetti cycle in a similar vein.)

10. Dick White, "aged ten years," quoted in Secrest, *Leonard Bernstein*, 362; Angus Whyte, "one of the saddest," in *After-Dinner Tales* (Bloomington, IN: Xlibris, 2013), 56.

11. Humphrey Burton, *Leonard Bernstein*, 452.

## Chapter 14. In the Garden

1. Paul Bowles, "smarmy and false," quoted in Humphrey Burton, *Leonard Bernstein*, 440; "exactly the same," in Paul Bowles to Carol Ardman, May 2, 1977, in *In Touch: The Letters of Paul Bowles*, ed. Jeffrey Miller (New York: Farrar, Straus and Giroux, 1994), 477.

2. In 1986 Bernstein produced a second take on similar materials in another work, this one written for his daughter Nina, as the sixth of *Thirteen Anniversaries.*

3. As a suburban child taken regularly to the old Met by his parents, Wadsworth had seen *Don Giovanni*, *The Marriage of Figaro*, *Madama Butterfly*, *Il trovatore*, and *Der Rosenkavalier* at an impressionable age. The first musical he saw was *West Side Story*, and what most excited him about it was that it combined the operatic and the popular. At the time he met Bernstein, Wadsworth had been teaching acting to opera singers and directing opera and had written one libretto, but he was fired up to try again and pursue his "newborn, still blurry vision of a fresh germane language and style for American opera."

4. Stephen Wadsworth, in written exchanges with the author, and in the libretto booklet for the recording of Leonard Bernstein, *A Quiet Place*, Deutsche Grammophon 419761-2, 1987, 2 CDs.

5. While he had modeled the parents in *Trouble in Tahiti* on his own, it would be a mistake to conclude that Bernstein "is" Junior in the new opera or in the original one. Librettist Wadsworth created Junior in the image of members of his own immediate family. In any case, opera composers must identify with all their characters, since music assigns them the line readings—the dy-

namics, tempo, rhythm, accentuation, contour, melodic figures—that bring their personalities to life.

6. When Sam dissolves in tears, the music dissolves too, into a lyrical lullaby. Helen Smith identifies this music as "Saquina's Lullaby" from a projected 1980 show that never came to fruition, *Alarums and Flourishes*. Smith, *There's a Place for Us*, 265.

7. If one detects a hint of *West Side Story* in the opening harmonies of Dede's "Valse" it is because they, like the opening of the act, are based on a principal motive from *Trouble in Tahiti* and its final chord. The *Trouble in Tahiti* idea in turn happens to outline the same notes as a principal melody and harmony from *West Side Story*, one that is sung by the Jets to the words "You're never alone, / (you're never disconnected!) / You're home with your own / (when company's expected)."

8. Junior's music is rooted mainly in the verse of Dinah's garden aria (the pedal point A in the bass, the line in the tenor voice, the melody in minor); he doesn't sing the "There is a garden, / Come with me" melody. Dede sings many variants of it and generally takes more from the chorus. Her third-act aria melody relates to both verse and chorus. "Mommy, are you here?" derives from "I was standing in a garden," and the second phrase "Was it really us out here?" comes from the line "so handsome so serene" and the *Tahiti* chord.

9. I owe the description "internalized reminiscences" to musicologist Helen Smith.

10. In this context, the earlier work seems more like a play within a play, or an operetta based upon the past, than an actual flashback.

11. Botstein, "Tragedy of Leonard Bernstein."

12. Pierre Boulez has noted that there are "loose" and "strict" works of Bach—the Brandenburg Concertos, say, versus *The Art of the Fugue*, but that they exist on a single continuum with an infinite number of gradations. Bach uses dance forms in his most abstract, erudite works (such as the Goldberg Variations) and injects learned counterpoint into his lightest ones.

13. Meyer and Shreffler, *Elliott Carter*, 244.

## Chapter 15. Regrets, Celebrations, and Goodbyes

1. David Patrick Stearns, "The Maestro Turns 70: Bernstein Conducts Life of Contrasts," *USA Today*, August 23, 1988.

2. Comden, *Off Stage*, 144.

3. Stearns, "Maestro Turns 70."

4. Riggs, *Leon Kirchner*, 192.

5. An interesting letter from Bernstein to Leon Kirchner, written thirty-five years earlier, commented on performances given January 31 and February 1, 1952, by Mitropoulos and the New York Philharmonic of Kirchner's *Sinfonia in Two Parts.* Kirchner, then thirty-three, was just six months Bernstein's junior. The two had met in the early 1940s. A former student of Bloch and Schoenberg and, like his friend, a superb pianist and conductor as well as composer, Kirchner was also equally independent of two prominent approaches to composing—strict serialism and aleatoric music—that seemed, in both of their opinions, to deny composers the ability to draw from their intuitions and musical memory in the creative process. Consistent with his frankness to fellow composers, Bernstein wrote Kirchner that the *Sinfonia* "is a strange work, and touching," but that it "is so crowded with music within the short space of its duration that one feels it is of the wrong duration. . . . There is also some continuity problem. . . . But it drips with talent and the promise of communication, even if it doesn't succeed in communicating wholly and spontaneously everything it harbors as potential." He then wondered if this impression was the result of the performance or the fault of the score. Riggs, *Leon Kirchner*, 285–86.

6. Leonard Bernstein, "I'm a Liberal and Proud of It," *New York Times*, October 30, 1988.

7. Jon Deak, interviewed in *Leonard Bernstein: Reaching for the Note.*

8. Jon Deak, interview with the author, August 21, 2012.

9. Hank Chapin, interview with the author, October 20, 2012.

10. Tim Page, in booklet accompanying *Bernstein: The Final Concert*, Boston Symphony Orchestra, Deutsche Grammophon 431768-2, 1990, CD.

11. Comden, *Off Stage*, 139.

12. Burton Bernstein and Haws, *Leonard Bernstein*, 207. Burton Bernstein, a staff writer for the *New Yorker* for thirty-five years and the author of nine books, lives in Connecticut. Shirley Bernstein died of a blood disease in 1998 at the age of seventy-four. Their mother, Jennie Bernstein, died in 1992 at the age of ninety-four. Jamie Bernstein is a narrator, writer, and documentary filmmaker. Alexander Bernstein is president of Artful Learning Inc., a school transformation model, and vice president/treasurer of the Leonard Bernstein Office Inc. Nina Bernstein Simmons currently works as a culinary instructor for at-risk children, primarily in public housing.

13. The "need to share" phrase is from Nina Bernstein Simmons, interviewed in *Leonard Bernstein: Reaching for the Note:* "The need to share was the driving force of his life."

## A NOTE ON SOURCES

FORTUNATELY, THE MOST important sources available to those interested in the work of Leonard Bernstein—his music, recordings, films, and writings—are readily available to anyone who chooses to seek them out. In preparing to write this book I spent many happy hours studying the scores of Bernstein's music and listening to recordings of it, immersed myself in his recorded legacy as a conductor, and viewed much of the available audiovisual catalogue. I listened to the live broadcast recordings of Bernstein's performances to be found on the 10-CD box set *New York Philharmonic: Bernstein Live* and on another 10-CD compilation, *New York Philharmonic: The Historic Broadcasts, 1923 to 1987;* watched the twenty-five Young People's Concerts, six Norton lectures, the estimable film documentary made for PBS's *American Masters* series, *Leonard Bernstein: Reaching for the Note*, and countless Bernstein performances available on DVD; and listened to the eleven-hour National Public Radio audio documentary *Leonard Bernstein: An American Life.*

I have made extensive use of the following public online resources: the New York Philharmonic Archives, where one can study every concert program conducted by Bernstein with the orchestra; the Library of Congress's Leonard Bernstein Collection, which has digitized thousands of documents, including 15,500 pieces of correspondence and Bernstein's texts for his Young People's Concerts and Thursday evening previews; the *New York Times* archives; and the Leonard Bernstein website, which is an excellent source of biographical information and additional materials on the composer. I supplemented these sources with valuable glimpses into the Helen Coates scrapbooks made available to me through the courtesy of the Harvard Music Department. Through the Library of Congress, with the kind permission of the Leonard Bernstein Office, I was able to study many original musical manuscripts, original writings, and letters to and from Bernstein that are not publicly available. At the Paley Center for Media in New York I was able to view many television programs that have not been publicly released, including the televised 1962 opening of Philharmonic Hall at Lincoln Center, the 1955 interview with the Bernsteins on Edward R. Murrow's *Person to Person*, several Young People's Concerts not included in the commercially available compilation, and additional televised performances.

I was also particularly privileged to conduct lengthy interviews with two of the Bernstein children, Alexander Bernstein and Jamie Bernstein, and with Leonard Bernstein's brother, Burton Bernstein. (I had valuable exchanges with Nina Bernstein Simmons but did not meet with her in person.) I can hardly overstate my gratitude to each of them. These conversations were indispensable to me. The candor, insights, high spirits, and immediacy of these encounters with those who knew Bernstein best stayed with me as I tried to paint the portrait of him contained in my book. In addition I conducted significant interviews with Sid Ramin, Stephen Wadsworth, Jon Deak, Hank Chapin, Shirley Gabis Perle, and the late Harold Shapero and his wife Esther Shapero; their comments and firsthand accounts left significant traces in what I wrote. I had extended conversations about Bernstein with composers Daron

Hagen and Bruce Adolphe that taught me a great deal and helped me solidify my own thinking. I was also honored to speak with singer Adele Addison, whose memories and thoughts about her long performing association with Bernstein brought him to life for me. I benefited from a stimulating conversation with scholar and music professor Carol Oja of Harvard University, who also alerted me to an invaluable trove of research materials unearthed by the course she cotaught with Kay Kaufman Shelemay, "Before *West Side Story:* Leonard Bernstein's Boston" at Harvard in Spring 2006. I received valuable information and assistance from Bernstein authorities Helen Smith, Barry Seldes, Humphrey Burton, and Jonathan Sarna, all of whom were most gracious in sending me their thoughts and clarifications by e-mail, as well as from Glenn Gould biographer Kevin Bazzana.

Of the many biographies of Leonard Bernstein available, Humphrey Burton's *Leonard Bernstein* is, in my opinion, the most reliable and fair-minded. While I used it as an important source, I naturally have tried my utmost to confirm its facts on my own and to draw my own conclusions when it presented a viewpoint. In the cases where it alerted me to letters, newspaper articles, recordings, videos, or broadcasts, I sought out the originals. The biography by Paul Myers provided a useful outline of Bernstein's life, and those by Peyser and Secrest contained valuable interviews. Burton Bernstein's small masterpiece *Family Matters* was an indispensable source of information about Sam and Jennie Bernstein and about Leonard Bernstein's early life. I also drew information from Shirley Bernstein's touching and informative 1963 account of her brother's life, *Making Music: Leonard Bernstein.*

Of the more technical and scholarly texts on Bernstein's works, Jack Gottlieb's dissertation from 1964 deserves special mention as not only an excellent basic study but as perhaps the first effort to treat Bernstein's concert music seriously. I was also greatly indebted to Paul Laird's fine introductory overview in his *Leonard Bernstein: A Guide to Research* and to his study of background materials in *The Chichester Psalms of Leonard Bernstein*, as well as to Helen Smith's impressive and gracefully written *There's a Place for*

*Us: The Musical Theatre Works of Leonard Bernstein*, which alerted me to many technical details in the music. I am indebted to Nigel Simeone for his carefully researched book on *West Side Story*, and to Peter Gradenwitz for his book *Leonard Bernstein: The Infinite Variety of a Musician*. I grounded much of what I had to say about Bernstein's political views and experiences on Barry Seldes's excellent book *Leonard Bernstein: The Political Life of an American Musician*. (Bernstein's FBI file is, of course, another important publicly available source of information.)

Without the availability of these and many other resources I could never have even attempted, let alone completed, a "short life" of such a multifaceted and complex human being. My conclusions, however, are my own, and I alone am responsible for this book's interpretations, speculations, and insights, as well as for any errors I may have made. The musical observations are my own, unless otherwise credited.

# BIBLIOGRAPHY

## Books


Auden, W. H. *The Age of Anxiety: A Baroque Eclogue.* Edited by Alan Jacobs. Princeton, NJ: Princeton University Press, 2011.

———. *Collected Longer Poems.* New York: Random House, 1969.

Bazzana, Kevin. *Wondrous Strange: The Art and Life of Glenn Gould.* Oxford: Oxford University Press, 2004.

Bernstein, Burton. *Family Matters.* New York: Summit Books, 1982.

Bernstein, Burton, and Barbara Haws. *Leonard Bernstein: American Original.* New York: HarperCollins, 2008.

Bernstein, Leonard. *Findings.* New York: Doubleday, 1982.

———. *The Infinite Variety of Music.* New York: Hal Leonard, 2007.

———. *The Joy of Music.* Pompton Plains, NJ: Amadeus Press, 2004.

———. *The Unanswered Question: Six Talks at Harvard.* Cambridge, MA: Harvard University Press, 1976.

———. *Young People's Concerts.* Edited by Jack Gottlieb. Pompton Plains, NJ: Amadeus Press, 2006.

Bernstein, Shirley. *Making Music: Leonard Bernstein.* Chicago: Encyclopaedia Britannica Press, 1963.

Burton, Humphrey. *Leonard Bernstein.* New York: Doubleday, 1994.

Burton, William Westbrook. *Conversations about Bernstein.* New York: Oxford University Press, 1995.

Chapin, Schuyler. *Leonard Bernstein: Notes From a Friend.* New York: Walker, 1992.

Chomsky, Noam. *Language and Mind.* Cambridge: Cambridge University Press, 2006.

Comden, Betty. *Off Stage.* New York: Limelight Editions, 2004.

Comden, Betty, and Adolph Green. *The New York Musicals of Comden and Green.* New York: Applause Books, 1997.

Cott, Jonathan. *Back to a Shadow in the Night.* Milwaukee: Hal Leonard, 2002.

———. *Dinner with Lenny.* Oxford: Oxford University Press, 2013.

Crist, Elizabeth B., and Wayne Shirley. *The Selected Correspondence of Aaron Copland.* New Haven, CT: Yale University Press, 2006.

Epstein, Helen. *Music Talks: Conversations with Working Musicians.* New York: McGraw-Hill, 1987.

Fischer, Jens Malte. *Gustav Mahler.* New Haven, CT: Yale University Press, 2011.

Fischer-Dieskau, Dietrich. *Reverberations: The Memoirs of Dietrich Fischer-Dieskau.* Translated by Ruth Hein. New York: Fromm International, 1989.

Gottlieb, Jack. *Funny, It Doesn't Sound Jewish: How Yiddish Songs and Synagogue Melodies Influenced Tin Pan Alley, Broadway, and Hollywood.* Albany: State University of New York, 2004.

———, ed. *Leonard Bernstein: A Complete Catalogue of His Works.* New York: Amberson Enterprises / Boosey & Hawkes, 1978.

———. *Working with Bernstein: A Memoir.* New York: Amadeus Press, 2010.

Gradenwitz, Peter. *Leonard Bernstein: The Infinite Variety of a Musician.* Leamington Spa, UK: Berg Publishers, 1987.

Graffman, Gary. *I Really Should Be Practicing.* Garden City, NY: Doubleday, 1981.

Gruen, John. *The Private World of Leonard Bernstein.* New York: Viking Press, 1968.

Guthrie, Tyrone. *A Life in the Theatre.* New York: McGraw-Hill, 1959.

Hellman, Lillian. *The Collected Plays.* Boston: Little, Brown, 1957.

Horowitz, Mark Eden. *Sondheim on Music: Minor Details and Major Decisions.* Lanham, MD: Scarecrow Press, in association with the Library of Congress, 2010.

Laird, Paul. *The Chichester Psalms of Leonard Bernstein.* Hillsdale, NY: Pendragon Press, 2010.

———. *Leonard Bernstein: A Guide to Research.* New York: Routledge, 2002.

Laurents, Arthur. *Original Story: A Memoir of Broadway and Hollywood.* New York: Alfred A. Knopf, 2000.

Lawrence, Greg. *Dance with Demons: The Life of Jerome Robbins.* New York: Putnam, 2001.

Ledbetter, Steven, ed. *Sennets & Tuckets: A Bernstein Celebration.* Boston: Boston Symphony Orchestra, in association with David R. Godine, 1988.

Lehrman, Leonard. *Marc Blitzstein: A Bio-Bibliography.* Westport, CT: Praeger, 2005.

Locke, Ralph P. *Musical Exoticism: Images and Reflections.* Cambridge: Cambridge University Press, 2009.

Mendelson, Edward. *Later Auden.* New York: Farrar, Straus and Giroux, 1999.

Myer, Felix, and Anne C. Shreffler. *Elliott Carter: A Centennial Portrait in Letters and Documents.* Woodbridge, UK: Boydell Press, 2008.

Myers, Paul. *Leonard Bernstein.* London: Phaidon, 1998.

Oja, Carol, and Judith Tick, eds. *Aaron Copland and His World.* Princeton, NJ: Princeton University Press, 2005.

Peyser, Joan. *Bernstein: A Biography.* Rev. ed. New York: Billboard, 1998.

Plato. *The Symposium.* Translated by Christopher Gill. New York: Penguin, 1999.

Pollack, Howard. *Marc Blitzstein: His Life, His Work, His World.* Oxford: Oxford University Press, 2012.

Prall, David. *Aesthetic Judgment.* New York: Thomas Y. Crowell, 1929.

Revill, David. *The Roaring Silence: John Cage, a Life.* New York: Arcade, 1992.

Rezits, Joseph. *Beloved Tyranna: The Legend and Legacy of Isabelle Vengerova.* Bloomington, IN: David Daniel Music Publications, 1995.

Riggs, Robert. *Leon Kirchner: Composer, Performer, and Teacher.* Rochester, NY: University of Rochester Press, 2010.

Robinson, Paul. *Bernstein.* New York: Vanguard Press, 1982.

Schiller, David Michael. *Bloch, Schoenberg, and Bernstein: Assimilating Jewish Music.* Oxford: Oxford University Press, 2003.

Schuller, Gunther. *Gunther Schuller: A Life in Pursuit of Music and Beauty.* Rochester, NY: University of Rochester Press, 2011.

Secrest, Meryle. *Leonard Bernstein: A Life.* New York: Alfred A. Knopf, 1994.

Seldes, Barry. *Leonard Bernstein: The Political Life of an American Musician.* Berkeley: University of California Press, 2009.

Simeone, Nigel. *Leonard Bernstein: West Side Story.* Farnham, UK: Ashgate, 2009.

Smith, Helen. *There's a Place for Us: The Musical Theatre Works of Leonard Bernstein.* Farnham, UK: Ashgate, 2011.

Swan, Claudia, ed. *Leonard Bernstein: The Harvard Years, 1935–1939.* New York: Eos Orchestra, 1999.

Thomson, Virgil. *Music Reviewed, 1940–54.* New York: Vintage Books, 1967.

———. *Selected Letters of Virgil Thomson.* Edited by Tim Page and Vanessa Weeks Page. New York: Summit Books, 1988.

———. *The State of Music.* New York: Vintage Books, 1962.

Vaill, Amanda. *Somewhere: The Life of Jerome Robbins.* New York: Broadway Books, 2006.

Voltaire [François-Marie Arouet]. *Candide, or, Optimism.* Translated by Theo Cuffe. New York: Penguin Classics, 2005.

Wells, Elizabeth A. *West Side Story: Cultural Perspectives on an American Musical.* Lanham, MD: Scarecrow Press, 2011.

## Articles

Adams, Sarah, Carol J. Oja, and Kay Kaufman Shelemay. "Leonard Bernstein's Jewish Boston: An Introductory Note." *Journal of the Society for American Music* 3 (2009): 1–34.

Banagale, Ryan Raul. "'Each Man Kills the Thing He Loves': Bernstein's Formative Relationship with *Rhapsody in Blue.*" *Journal of the Society for American Music* 3 (2009): 47–66.

Bernstein, Leonard. "Speaking of Music." *Atlantic,* December 1957, 104–6.

Botstein, Leon. "The Tragedy of Leonard Bernstein." *Harper's Magazine,* May 1983, 38–40, 57–62.

Kaskowitz, Sheryl. "All in the Family: Brandeis University and Leonard Bernstein's 'Jewish Boston.'" *Journal of the Society for American Music* 3 (2009): 85–100.

Landon, H. C. Robbins. Review of Haydn, Symphonies Nos. 82 and 83, New York Philharmonic, Leonard Bernstein, cond. *High Fidelity,* November 1964.

Massey, Drew. "Leonard Bernstein and the Harvard Student Union: In Search of Political Origins." *Journal of the Society for American Music* 3 (2009): 67–84.

Sarna, Jonathan D. "Leonard Bernstein and the Boston Jewish Community of His Youth." *Journal of the Society for American Music* 3 (2009): 35–46.

Schiff, David. "Rehearing Bernstein." *Atlantic,* June 1993, 55–60.

———. "Leonard Bernstein." In *The New Grove Dictionary of Music and Musicians,* 2nd ed., edited by Stanley Sadie and John Tyrrell. New York: Grove's Dictionaries, 2001.

## Dissertations

Gottlieb, Jack. "The Music of Leonard Bernstein: A Study of Melodic Manipulation." PhD diss., University of Illinois, 1964.

Lehrman, Leonard. "Leonard Bernstein's *Serenade* after Plato's *Symposium:* An Analysis." PhD diss., Cornell University, 1977.

Niren, Ann Glazer. "The Influence of Solomon Braslavsky and Congregation Mishkan Tefila on Leonard Bernstein." PhD diss., University of Kentucky, 2013.

Pearlmutter, Alan Jay. "Leonard Bernstein's *Dybbuk:* An Analysis Including Historical, Religious, and Literary Perspectives of Hasidic Life and Lore." PhD diss., Peabody Institute of the Johns Hopkins University, 1985.

## Audiovisual (Partial List)

Beethoven. *Fidelio.* Chor und Orchester der Wiener Staatsoper, Leonard Bernstein, cond. Deutsche Grammophon 00440-073-4159, 1978.

Bernstein. *Candide.* London Symphony Orchestra, Leonard Bernstein, cond. Deutsche Grammophon B000ICLU3G, 1989.

———. *Chichester Psalms,* Symphony No. 1, Symphony No. 2. Israel Philharmonic Orchestra, Leonard Bernstein, cond. Kultur D1335, 1977.

———. *"Mass" at the Vatican City.* Coro e Orchestra Sinfonica del Conservatorio di Santa Cecilia, Boris Brott, cond., Enrico Castiglione, dir. Kultur D2823, 2000.

———. *Trouble in Tahiti.* Tom Cairns, dir. Kultur D0838, 2001.

*Bernstein Conducts Bernstein: Divertimento, Serenade,* Symphony No. 2 (*The Age of Anxiety*). Wiener Philharmoniker and London Symphony Orchestra, with Gidon Kremer and Krystian Zimerman, Leonard Bernstein, cond. Deutsche Grammophon/Unitel Classica 00440-073-4514, 1985, 1986.

*Bernstein in Rehearsal and Performance:* Shostakovich. Symphony No. 1. Schleswig-Holstein Music Festival Orchestra, Leonard Bernstein, cond. Medici Arts/Unitel Classica 2072158, 1988.

*Four Ways to Say Farewell.* Vienna Philharmonic, Leonard Bernstein, cond. Tony Palmer and Humphrey Burton, prods. Unitel/Kultur 1445, 1971.

Gershwin. *An American in Paris.* Ives. Symphony No. 2; *The Unanswered Question.* New York Philharmonic and Symphonieorchester des Bayerischen Rundfunks, Leonard Bernstein, piano and cond. Humphrey Burton, prod. Unitel/Deutsche Grammophon 00440-073-4513, 1976, 1987.

*The Gift of Music: An Intimate Portrait of Leonard Bernstein*. Deutsche Grammophon/Unitel Classica 00440-073-4336, 2007.

*Leonard Bernstein: An American Life*. National Public Radio documentary. Larry Abrams and Steve Rowland, prods. CultureWorks, 2005.

*Leonard Bernstein: Omnibus—The Historic TV Broadcasts*. Beethoven's Fifth Symphony; "The World of Jazz"; "The Art of Conducting"; "What Makes Opera Grand?"; "American Musical Comedy"; "Introduction to Modern Music"; "The Music of Johann Sebastian Bach." E1 Entertainment E1E-DV-6731, 2010.

*Leonard Bernstein: Reaching for the Note*. American Masters series, Thirteen/WNET Educational Broadcasting Corporation. WinStar Home Entertainment WHE73019, 1998.

*Leonard Bernstein's Young People's Concerts with the New York Philharmonic*. 25 programs, 9 DVDs. Kultur B0002S6410, 2004.

*The Little Drummer Boy: An Essay on Gustav Mahler*. Israel Philharmonic Orchestra, London Symphony Orchestra, and Wiener Philharmoniker, Leonard Bernstein, cond. Deutsche Grammophon/Unitel Classica 00440-073-4350, 1985.

*The Love of Three Orchestras*. New York Philharmonic, Vienna Philharmonic, and Israel Philharmonic Orchestra, Leonard Bernstein, cond. Humphrey Burton, prod. VHS. Kultur 1443, 1986.

*The Making of West Side Story*. Christopher Swan, dir. Deutsche Grammophon/Unitel 00440-073-4054, 2005.

*New York Philharmonic: Bernstein Live*. 10 CDs. New York Philharmonic Special Editions NYP 2003, 2000.

*New York Philharmonic: The Historic Broadcasts, 1923 to 1987*. 10 CDs. New York Philharmonic Special Editions NYP 9702–9711, 2002.

Sibelius. Symphonies Nos. 1, 2, 5, 7. Wiener Philharmoniker, Leonard Bernstein, cond. 2 DVDs. Unitel Classica 702208, 2010.

*The Unanswered Question: Six Talks at Harvard by Leonard Bernstein*. Kultur B00005TPL8, 1976.

## ACKNOWLEDGMENTS

I WANT TO extend my deepest thanks to all those I interviewed in the course of preparing this book, most especially to Burton Bernstein, Alexander Bernstein, Jamie Bernstein, Nina Bernstein Simmons, the late Harold Shapero, Esther Shapero, Stephen Wadsworth, Shirley Gabis Perle, Sid Ramin, Adele Addison, Hank Chapin, and Jon Deak. I am indebted to composers Bruce Adolphe and Daron Hagen, who shared their valuable insights with me in long conversations we had about Bernstein, and to the Reverend Edward T. Hougen, at whose home I first heard Bernstein's *Mass* in 1972, and whose comment that Bernstein's music "doesn't ignore the struggles and strife of life, but also moves toward something transcendent" has stayed with me. I am deeply grateful to Professor Carol Oja of Harvard University for our discussions, her encouragement, and her generous practical assistance.

For their expertise and helpfulness in matters large and small, I would like to thank the following writers and scholars: Zachary M.

Baker, Kevin Bazzana, Robert Craft, Mark Horowitz, Leonard Lehrman, Ann Glazer Niren, Helen Smith, Humphrey Burton, Eileen Scully, Barry Seldes, Annabel Davis-Goff, Jonathan Sarna, Charles Joseph, Ralph Locke, and Alan Pearlmutter. I am also indebted to Leonard Lehrman for his close early reading of my manuscript and his many informed recommendations and corrections. I owe to Helen Smith additional thanks for her careful reading of my final manuscript and her invaluable suggestions. I am grateful to Carl St. Clair, Andrea Schultz, and Thomas Bogdan for their helpfulness in the course of my work on this book, and to Shira Brettman for permission to quote from her delightful film about Bernstein's youthful productions in Sharon, Massachusetts.

My thanks go to the many librarians who helped me in my research: Oceana Wilson, Kathy Williams, Vanessa Haverkoch, Laura Payne, Jared DellaRocca, and Joe Tucker of Bennington College Library; the staff of the Williams College Library; Liza Vick, music reference and research librarian at the Loeb Music Library at Harvard University; Mark Horowitz, senior music specialist, Library of Congress, Music Division, and to other staff of the Library of Congress. Thanks also to Jane Klein, manager of research services at the Paley Center for Media in New York, and to her staff. I also gratefully acknowledge the helpfulness of Marie Carter of the Leonard Bernstein Office in New York City, who granted me permission to examine and to quote from documents, letters, and scores not publicly available at the Library of Congress.

Thank you to Yoshiko Sato, Noa Sato Shawn, Annie Shawn, and Harold Shawn for their patience and forbearance while I worked on this project. Other family members and friends who have provided support and encouragement for which I am very grateful include Wallace Shawn, Deborah Eisenberg, Tom Hayes, Debby Mills, Betsy Blachly Chapin, Alison Nowak, Lisa Kirchner, Elizabeth Wright, Maxine Neuman, Linda C. Smith, Frederick Seidel, Ida Faiella, Dr. Marjorie LaRowe, Neil Moss, Linda Hillyer, Jonathan Hillyer, Margaret Hougen, Cullen Murphy, Celeste Schepp, Judith Serkin, and Robert and Nan Lowary of Taraden Bed and Breakfast in North Bennington, Vermont.

I owe particular debts of gratitude to my superb editor, Ileene Smith; to Steven Zipperstein, series editor; to my meticulous copy editor, Duke Johns; and to John Palmer of the Jewish Lives series at Yale University Press. I send my warm and abiding thanks to my literary representative, Lynn Nesbit.

I also want to extend a special thank you to my expert and patient assistant, Gabriele Caras, who was an invaluable support to me in my work.

Finally, I want to thank Isabel Roche, Dean of Bennington College, for granting me an early sabbatical in the fall of 2012 so that I could devote myself fully to work on this book. This gift of extra time when I most needed it was wonderfully generous and an indispensable help.

# INDEX

Jewish Lives is a major series of interpretive biography designed to illuminate the imprint of Jewish figures upon literature, religion, philosophy, politics, cultural and economic life, and the arts and sciences. Subjects are paired with authors to elicit lively, deeply informed books that explore the range and depth of Jewish experience from antiquity through the present.

Jewish Lives is a partnership of Yale University Press and the Leon D. Black Foundation.

Ileene Smith is editorial director. Anita Shapira and Steven J. Zipperstein are series editors.

PUBLISHED TITLES INCLUDE:

*David Ben-Gurion*, by Anita Shapira
*Bernard Berenson: A Life in the Picture Trade*, by Rachel Cohen
*Sarah: The Life of Sarah Bernhardt*, by Robert Gottlieb
*Leonard Bernstein: An American Musician*, by Allen Shawn
*David: The Divided Heart*, by David Wolpe
*Moshe Dayan: Israel's Controversial Hero*, by Mordechai Bar-On
*Becoming Freud: The Making of a Psychoanalyst*, by Adam Phillips
*Emma Goldman: Revolution as a Way of Life*, by Vivian Gornick
*Hank Greenberg: The Hero Who Didn't Want to Be One*, by Mark Kurlansky
*Lillian Hellman: An Imperious Life*, by Dorothy Gallagher
*Jabotinsky: A Life*, by Hillel Halkin
*Jacob: Unexpected Patriarch*, by Yair Zakovitch
*Franz Kafka: The Poet of Shame and Guilt*, by Saul Friedländer
*Rav Kook: Mystic in a Time of Revolution*, by Yehudah Mirsky
*Primo Levi: The Matter of a Life*, by Berel Lang
*Moses Mendelssohn: Sage of Modernity*, by Shmuel Feiner
*Walter Rathenau: Weimar's Fallen Statesman*, by Shulamit Volkov
*Solomon: The Lure of Wisdom*, by Steven Weitzman
*Leon Trotsky: A Revolutionary's Life*, by Joshua Rubenstein

FORTHCOMING TITLES INCLUDE:

*Rabbi Akiva*, by Barry Holtz

*Irving Berlin*, by James Kaplan
*Hayim Nahman Bialik*, by Avner Holtzman
*Léon Blum*, by Pierre Birnbaum
*Louis Brandeis*, by Jeffrey Rosen
*Martin Buber*, by Paul Mendes-Flohr
*Benjamin Disraeli*, by David Cesarani
*Bob Dylan*, by Ron Rosenbaum
*Albert Einstein*, by Steven Gimbel
*George Gershwin*, by Gary Giddins
*Allen Ginsberg*, by Edward Hirsch
*Peggy Guggenheim*, by Francine Prose
*Ben Hecht*, by Adina Hoffman
*Heinrich Heine*, by Fritz Stern
*Theodor Herzl*, by Derek Penslar
*Jesus*, by Jack Miles
*Groucho Marx*, by Lee Siegel
*J. Robert Oppenheimer*, by David Rieff
*Marcel Proust*, by Benjamin Taylor
*Jerome Robbins*, by Wendy Lesser
*Julius Rosenwald*, by Hasia Diner
*Mark Rothko*, by Annie Cohen-Solal
*Jonas Salk*, by David Margolick
*Steven Spielberg*, by Molly Haskell
*The Warner Brothers*, by David Thomson
*Ludwig Wittgenstein*, by Anthony Gottlieb